THE
LOW-FAT
GOOD FOOD
COOKBOOK

BOOKS BY MARTIN KATAHN, PH.D.

The Rotation Diet Cookbook (with Terri Katahn)
The T-Factor Diet
The T-Factor Fat Gram Counter (with Jamie Pope-Cordle)
One Meal at a Time
The Low-Fat Supermarket Shopper's Guide (with Jamie Pope-Cordle)
The Low-Fat Fast Food Guide (with Jamie Pope-Cordle)
The 200 Calorie Solution
Beyond Diet
The Rotation Diet

THE
LOW-FAT
GOOD FOOD
COOKBOOK

MARTIN KATAHN, PH.D.
and TERRI KATAHN

Illustrations by Heather L. Warren

W·W·Norton & Company·New York·London

Printed in the United States of America

First Edition

The text of this book is composed in Caledonia, with the display set in Perpetor.
Composition by ComCom Typesetting Services, Inc. Manufacturing by Courier
Companies, Inc.

Library of Congress Cataloging-in-Publication Data
Katahn, Martin.
The low-fat good food cookbook / Martin Katahn and Terri Katahn.
p.   cm.
Includes index.
1. Low-fat diet—Recipes.   I. Katahn, Terri.   II. Title.
RM237.7.K368   1994
641.5′638—dc20   94-6548

ISBN 0-393-31149-X

W.W. Norton & Company, Inc., 500 Fifth Avenue, New York, N.Y. 10110
W.W. Norton & Company Ltd., 10 Coptic Street, London WC1A 1PU

1 2 3 4 5 6 7 8 9 0

To Enid Katahn,
wife and mother to this team,
with much love.

Contents

Acknowledgments

We want to thank, once again, the scores of friends, participants in the Vanderbilt Weight Management Program, and professional chefs and bakers who have contributed to our collection of recipes over the years. We have thanked you individually in our earlier books, and you may recognize some of your work here. We take full responsibility for the changes we have made to adapt your basic recipes to a lower-fat method of cooking. We tried hard not to hurt them, and our taste buds say we have succeeded.

A number of recipes that appear in this book were developed by master chefs in several of Nashville's finest restaurants. We included them in earlier books to illustrate how fine cooks concoct low-fat foods for their customers who wish to order such foods when eating out. These restaurants include Arthur's, Peking Garden, Kobe Steak House, Julian's, and Villa Romano, all located in our hometown of Nashville, Tennessee. Although Julian's and the Villa Romano are no longer in existence, we continue to include several of the wonderful recipes from all of these five restaurants, with great feelings of regret and nostalgia for the two that are no longer with us.

A number of our bread, muffin, and breakfast food recipes were created especially for us by the Kellogg Company, so we give them credit by mentioning the brand of cereal in the recipe. You may, of course, use your favorite brand of cereal in place of our brand.

As always, special thanks to our literary agents, Arthur and

Richard Pine, who agreed to represent the first author in 1981 when he asked them for help after he had had his first book, *The 200 Calorie Solution,* rejected by all six publishers to whom he had submitted it on his own. Thanks for your faith in me, and, of course, for linking me with Starling Lawrence, my editor at W. W. Norton and Co. Star, who, in addition to becoming a good friend, has provided me with invaluable editorial advice on what now amounts to a total of ten books in thirteen years. What a team!

And finally a word of thanks to Debra Makay, whose careful copy-editing and suggestions helped us make our recipes as clear and easy to follow as possible.

Preface: Why Write a Cookbook?

I published *The T-Factor Diet* in the spring of 1989. In it I explained that if my readers had a weight problem, the primary reason from a nutritional standpoint was almost always too much fat in the diet. Then, in 1991, I published *One Meal at a Time,* in which I pointed out that the primary nutritional culprit in heart disease and several forms of cancer was, once again, too much fat in the diet.

In both these books I tried to show people who wanted to lose weight and live a happier, longer, and healthier life *how to do it.* Today, as of this writing, over three million copies of these books are in print. I have received literally thousands of telephone calls and letters thanking me for giving advice that these persons could truly live with for the rest of their lives, advice which has helped them to achieve permanent weight management and a permanent lowering of risk factors for nutritionally related illnesses. I will quote a few sentences from a few of these letters to show you what you can expect if you follow my advice, which is simply to cut the fat in your diet, get active if you are a sedentary person, and lose weight if you need to.

This summer will be 3 years of the new me, and I love it. I went from size 16 (getting tighter) to size 5. I walk daily 3 to 5 miles for exercise along with counting those fat grams—which is easy. My whole life has changed and I feel great. My self-esteem is at its highest, I love being me, and I love your diet.

[M.P., Hampton, VA]*

Just a note to let you know how great I think your T-Factor diet is! I've been doing this now for 1½ years and am delighted to say that I've lost 120 pounds.

[S.S., Coral Springs, FL]

Last year I purchased the best diet book I have had in my life—THE T-FACTOR. Within 6 months I lost 60 pounds. Fantastic, right?

[M.C., St. Catherines, Ontario, Canada]

Happy New Year!! Your letter meant *so* much to me and I appreciate it more than you could ever know. All goes well with me. I have now lost 60 pounds. Isn't that an accomplishment to be proud of? I am indeed very proud and I give all the credit to the knowledge I gained from your book. Thank you, thank you! [And then, three months later:] At my last physical my blood pressure was 123 over 60—before that it was 180 over 90. My blood sugar was 90—before that it was 180 fasting and I took insulin twice daily. Now I take nothing! All other blood tests were normal. My doctor says I don't have to come back for six months!

[E.S., Corpus Christi, TX]

While writing *The T-Factor Diet* and *One Meal at a Time,* I was hard at work making changes in my favorite recipes, some of which Terri and I had published in *The Rotation Diet Cookbook.* My goal was to see how I could modify the fat content of these recipes and still end up with dishes that were just as delicious and satisfying as the original higher-fat versions. While I have decided to keep almost all the original titles

---

*I have decided to use only initials to preserve the privacy of the people who have been kind enough to write or call me.

which appeared in the earlier books, most of the recipes that appear here are different in that they are considerably lower in fat. They use the leaner cuts of meat that are now available and some of the very satisfying low-fat versions of high-fat foods that have been recently developed and which were not available in such tasty forms seven or eight years ago.

Although the approach we take in *The Low-Fat Good Food Cookbook* is designed to help everyone who wants to lose weight to achieve permanent success, it is also designed to provide all the other health benefits associated with sound nutrition. By being low in overall fat and salt content, and high in vitamins, minerals, and dietary fiber, our approach follows the most up-to-date guidelines for preventing heart disease and cancer.

If your primary goal is weight loss and permanent weight management, I feel compelled to make a point once again that I have made in all of my books: If you are an overweight person and want to weigh even five pounds less for the rest of your life, you must DO SOMETHING DIFFERENT from what you have been doing—for the rest of your life. You cannot return to your present life-style after losing even five pounds without regaining that weight and ending up right back on square one! Follow-up research on dieters who relapse after losing weight on a combination of diet and exercise clearly shows that they simply revert to a high-fat diet and to their previous sedentary ways.

So let's begin by thinking **not** in terms of "permanent weight loss" but about the "permanent changes in diet and activity level" that will make permanent weight loss possible. We outline the necessary permanent changes from a nutritional standpoint, based on *The T-Factor Diet,* in our chapter on how to use this cookbook to lose weight the T-Factor way. And, because physical activity is so important—to our general health and well-being as well as weight management—we also have included a chapter on physical activity. Since a sedentary person hardly ever can reach and maintain desirable weight and remain sedentary, we want to show you how to make physical activity a most enjoyable part of your daily life.

When it comes to reducing the risk of heart disease and cancer, however, cutting the fat from a high-fat diet is probably even more important than physical activity. Thus *The Low-Fat Good Food Cookbook* focuses on our main purpose—how to make low-fat cooking good eating!

The basic principles that Terri and I used in modifying our favorite recipes are:

1. Keep fat to a minimum but still come up with tasty dishes. What you don't like you won't continue to eat, so we do not go to extremes that only a masochist or martyr would want to live with. If you follow our suggestions, you should have no difficulty in arriving at a diet that averages around 25 percent of calories from fat. (If you want to lose weight, in the special chapter on weight loss we outline the basic principles of *The T-Factor Diet* and the recommended quantities of fat intake in terms of grams.)

2. Reduce the amount of sugar. Rather than use any artificial sweetener, which has at best questionable effectiveness in helping people lose weight and then maintain their losses over the long run, we prefer to use moderate amounts of sugar as a sweetener (or honey or molasses, when appropriate). We find that sugar and these other sweeteners taste better and are more satisfying.

3. Demonstrate the wise use of herbs and spices in adding to the attractiveness of your dishes, while avoiding an exotic or complicated approach to cooking that no one but a full-time cook would have the time to pursue. We focus on the use of spices and herbs, the latter used in their most easily found form, which is often dried rather than fresh. Of course, if fresh is available, all the better.

As for salt, we include minimal amounts because salt helps to bring out the flavor of other ingredients. You can prove this to yourself by mixing up a blend of herbs, tasting the mixture, then adding just a pinch of salt. Suddenly, there is an explosion of flavor.

In general, our recipes include about half the salt that salt-adapted taste buds might expect, so you may find yourself taking a little time getting used to the new blend of flavors. Do take the time, because, as you reduce salt in your diet, your sensitivity to its flavor will probably increase. You'll want less as you get used to using less!

In our opinion, the weight of scientific evidence suggests that healthy persons who do not have a familial tendency to hypertension can use salt in moderation, without danger to their health. However, if you are on a salt-restricted diet, be sure to check with your physician about the use of salt in our recipes before including the recommended amount.

4. Finally, we wanted dishes that are, for the most part, relatively simple and quick to prepare. Although we were fortunate to obtain the enthusiastic cooperation of several professional chefs and bakers in the development of our recipes, we ourselves are not professionals. Like most others who work full time or otherwise lead busy lives, we rarely wish to put a great deal of time into preparing meals at the end of a long day. If you learn to organize your approach to cooking as we suggest, you will find that most dishes that we have included in this book take less than 20 or 25 minutes to prepare (not including final cooking time). A few of the more elaborate may take an hour, although some of the preparation can be done in advance so that the time required for the final steps just before meal time is reduced.

Think of this book as a course in healthy food preparation as well as a cookbook. Try our way of low-fat cooking, then adapt any of your own favorite recipes and design your own healthy meal plans.

Martin Katahn, Ph.D.
Nashville, Tennessee
January 1994

THE
LOW-FAT
GOOD FOOD
COOKBOOK

Nutrition Notes and Guidelines Plus Hints for Creating Successful Low-Fat Recipes

NOTES AND GUIDELINES

We include information on total fat, calorie content, cholesterol, dietary fiber, and sodium with each recipe. Thus you will find it easy to calculate daily totals should you wish to design a special diet to limit fat grams or total calories, or determine whether your diet falls within guidelines for cholesterol, fat, sodium, and dietary fiber recommended by the major health organizations.

To reduce nutritional risk factors for heart disease and several forms of cancer, most health authorities now agree that while 30 percent of calories from fat might be a good first step, 25 percent would be an even healthier target as your average, daily goal. They also suggest about 60 percent of calories from carbohydrate and about 15 percent from protein. Research from the Vanderbilt Weight Management Program shows that when individuals who desire to lose weight use *The T-Factor Diet* and think in terms of total fat grams per day, rather than in terms of calories or percentages, they end up when they reach maintenance with a diet containing between 20 and 25 percent of calories from fat, and they find the fat-gram approach much easier and more effective than counting calories and calculating percentages.

For weight loss, *The T-Factor Diet* recommends 20 to 40 grams of fat per day for women, and 30 to 60 grams of fat per day for men. For weight maintenance, women may choose to eat as much as 50 grams of fat, on the average, per day, while it is not necessary, for health purposes, to increase beyond 60 grams of fat per day for men. Any extra calories needed for weight maintenance are more healthfully obtained by increasing your intake of fruits, vegetables, and grains, rather than fatty foods. (Additional advice on how to use *The Low-Fat Good Food Cookbook* for losing weight begins on page 383.)

Cholesterol intake should average 300 milligrams a day, or less, especially if you have a history of heart disease in the family.

Dietary fiber should fall between 20 and 35 grams per day, with many authorities suggesting that you gradually increase to the upper level of this range, provided that amount of fiber does not make you uncomfortable. We, too, think this is a good idea since consumption of foods relatively high in dietary fiber has extra value for weight control. This is because of their bulk, which tends to fill you up before you have eaten too much, as well as the tendency of fiber to bind with and prevent the absorption of a small amount of the fat in your diet.

The National Research Council Committee on Diet and Health suggests an upper limit of 2400 milligrams of sodium per day, and while people who are not salt sensitive and who have no history of hypertension in their families may possibly exceed this to a certain extent without danger to their health, we would rather err on the safe side. One teaspoon of salt contains about 2200 milligrams of sodium, so we tend to use very little in our recipes, and add a bit to taste at the table.

A "no" in our nutrient analyses indicates less than 0.5 gram of fat or fiber, and less than 0.5 milligram of cholesterol or sodium. We round off in other cases (0.5 to 1.49 will be listed as 1, 1.5 to 2.49 will be listed as 2, etc.). Recipes that contain tiny bits of fiber (for example, from small amounts of vegetables or nuts) will thus say "no" fiber even though up to 0.49 gram is present, and the same will be true of fat up to 0.49 gram. The decision to round off was arbitrary and was made to avoid confusing decimal values that would contain a small amount of error anyway due to the way nutritional analyses are performed in the laboratory.

We used low-sodium bouillon for our nutritional analyses when stock or bouillon is called for in our recipes, since many people do not care to make their own stock and low-sodium bouillon is available commercially. It's easy to make, though, and you will do better using our recipe for Chicken Stock (pages 64–65) than with commercial bouillons. It's a perfect base or stock. Regular bouillon (not low sodium) is typically about 50 percent salt. However, we used tamari sauce in our recipes and in our nutritional analyses rather than a low-sodium soy sauce because of its fuller flavor. We balance these ingredients by using a little additional salt in the case of a low-sodium bouillon, or no salt in the case of tamari sauce, aiming for the lowest sodium content that is still satisfying to our taste. Experiment to find the right balance for yourself, remembering that you can use just a little in the recipe itself, to bring out the flavor of the other ingredients, and then add a bit of salt at the table. Research shows that when people keep salt in their cooking at a minimum and then add it at the table, they tend to consume *70 percent less sodium* than when they use larger amounts in their recipes.

Many of our recipes give alternatives for certain ingredients, for example, "butter or margarine." *Our analyses are always based on the first ingredient listed.* In the case of "butter or margarine," we have returned to the general use of butter rather than margarine in most recipes, because, frankly, nothing tastes as good as butter. And from a health standpoint, recent research shows that the hydrogenation of fats in the margarine may make it equally as dangerous as any more saturated fat. Whatever your preferred fat—butter, margarine, or some particular oil—moderation is always the key.

Many of our recipes call for skim or low-fat milk. Our analyses are based on 1 percent milk when low-fat milk is called for, or the first ingredient if both are listed as choices. Per cup of milk, each percent of butterfat adds roughly 2 grams of fat and about 18 calories to the recipe.

Our nutritional analyses also *include* ingredients listed as "optional" because we think most people will want to include the added flavor and texture these ingredients bring to the recipes. Exceptions to this inclusion will be noted in the particular instances where they occur.

All preparation times listed are rough estimates, since everyone cooks at a different pace. The second or third time you prepare a recipe will not take as long as the first. Cooking times also vary slightly, since some ovens run hotter than others. We hope our advice on how to organize your kitchen, and to assemble all ingredients prior to starting meal preparation, will help move things along more quickly if you tend to be somewhat inefficient.

HINTS ON HOW TO CREATE SUCCESSFUL LOW-FAT RECIPES

While many of the recipes in this book were created originally as low-fat recipes and have no high-fat versions, others are low-fat modifications of traditional high-fat dishes, for example, Goulash, Easy Beef Stroganoff, Kahlua Chocolate Cheesecake, etc. If you have ever tried your own hand at modifying high-fat recipes and plunged in by substituting fat-free foods or other foods drastically reduced in fat for high-fat foods such as sour cream, cream cheese, and mayonnaise, you may have ended up with what was at best "an interesting experience." I have one friend who is finally able to laugh after the frosting on the birthday cake he was making liquified when he tried to use fat-free cream cheese in place of a higher-fat version.

Some substitutions work in traditional higher-fat recipes, and some don't. Before we began our own modifications, we had tasting sessions, with every variety of "light," "reduced-fat," "low-fat," and "fat-free" mayonnaise and dairy product that we could put our hands on laid out on our dining room table.

Here is what we found, and the decisions we made, in order to make sure our lower-fat versions tasted the way we think really good dishes (like goulash, stroganoff, and cheesecake) ought to taste. We do not want our recipes to be filed in your archives or in the trash can!

1. We found that nonfat yogurt works just as well as low-fat yogurt in all the recipes that previously called for the low-fat version. The low-fat versions generally have 2 to 3 grams of fat per cup, while nonfat has less than 0.5 gram. We ended up using the Dannon brand.

2. The only lowered-fat commercial mayonnaise that still tastes like "real" mayonnaise is the "light" variety. "Reduced-fat" and "fat-free" versions will not cut it most of the time. Taste them one after the other and see if you don't agree.

Regular "real" mayonnaise contains about 11 or 12 grams of fat per tablespoon, "light" contains about 5, "reduced-fat" contains about 3, and "fat-free" must contain less than 0.5 gram. We think that using light mayonnaise provides a compromise everyone can live with, and we ended up using Hellmann's Light (Best Foods brand in some parts of the country). Just try our Potato-Vegetable Salad (page 94), where we substituted nonfat yogurt for low-fat, and light mayonnaise for the regular variety, and you will see what we mean. This modification cut the fat by 60 percent—from 5 grams per ¾-cup serving to just 2.

3. Dishes that call for cheese and other high-fat dairy products often create real problems if you are trying to come anywhere close to the original versions. You just can't jump in willy-nilly and substitute nonfat yogurt and fat-free cottage cheese for cream cheese and sour cream in cakes and gravies. If the dish comes out at all it may taste lousy!

We compared sour creams of the "regular," "light," "reduced-fat," and "fat-free" varieties. Regular sour cream contains 6 grams of fat in a 2-tablespoon serving, light contains about 3, reduced-fat will be around 1, and fat-free is under 0.5 gram.

The reduced-fat and fat-free versions didn't even remind us of sour cream. The light had a true resemblance to the original and was made with all the natural ingredients of sour cream— no gums added or other artificial ingredients that must be used to maintain consistency in the reduced-fat and fat-free versions.

So we made the decision to stick with light, using Daisy brand, and once again it really works. Try, for example, our Goulash (page 123), where we substituted nonfat yogurt for the low-fat version, and light sour cream for the regular variety. We also used top round and sirloin tip roasts instead of a higher-fat cut of meat in our testing sessions and reduced the fat in this recipe by almost 50 percent.

With respect to cheese, food processors have made tremendous improvements in the last several years. But not all the new products can, in our opinion, pass muster if you are still after the great taste of good cheese.

We compared regular cottage cheese, 2 percent and 1 percent low-fat, and fat-free cottage cheeses (4, 2, 1, and less than 0.5 grams of fat per ½ cup, respectively). For eating plain, with fruit or different seasonings, and for a Cottage-Cheese Dressing (page 105), both 2 percent and 1 percent low-fat versions fared quite well. If you wish to use a fat-free variety, you'd better taste a few different ones first, since they vary greatly in taste and texture. By using 1 percent low-fat cottage cheese, Neufchâtel in place of regular cream cheese, and nonfat yogurt together with extra-lean beef in our Mock Lasagne (page 227), we cut over 50 percent of the fat compared with regular high-fat versions of this dish. Since different brands of cottage cheese taste quite different with the same fat content, we suggest you experiment until you find the one you like best.

It's a genuine challenge to devise a process for imitating fine sharp cheddar, Swiss, Jarlsberg, Monterey Jack, and other semi-soft to hard natural cheeses, but we think some processors have finally done it. However, forget the fat-free cheeses! It takes a true stretch of the imagination to think "cheese" when you taste these fat-free versions.

We are very fond of cheese, and after gorging ourselves on trays of lowered-fat cheeses in our taste tests, we found several "light" and "reduced-fat" cheddar, Jarlsberg, and Monterey Jack cheeses that fare well in almost all our recipes where such kinds of cheeses are used. We prefer the full-fat variety of some cheeses in certain recipes, and occasionally use it in moderation. However, we like Jarlsberg Lite (4 grams of fat per ounce), which is somewhat similar to Swiss (generally about 8 grams of fat per ounce), in almost all recipes where Swiss is called for. (There are reduced-fat Swiss cheeses available, but we did not find them to be quite as good as Jarlsberg Lite.) And where reduced-fat or light cheese is called for, we ended up preferring and using Kraft Healthy Favorites reduced-fat Monterey Jack (4 grams of fat versus 9 in the original variety) and Kraft Light Naturals sharp cheddar and Cracker Barrel Light shredded sharp cheddar (both 5 grams of fat versus 9 in the regular).

You can substitute Egg Beaters for eggs in many recipes (zero fat versus 4–5 grams per egg depending on size). We did, as noted in several recipes, and it worked just fine.

Finally—cheesecake!

One version of chocolate cheesecake that we used to make, years ago (when I weighed 70 pounds more than I do today), used a pound of cream cheese (about 160 grams of fat) and ¾ cup of heavy cream (66 grams of fat). Each piece of cake (¹⁄₁₂ of a springform pan) contained about 24 grams of fat and it certainly was delicious. We think our Kahlua Chocolate Cheesecake (pages 360–61), which uses a blend of cocoa and sugar in place of semisweet chocolate, a bit of butter, and Egg Beaters in place of whole eggs, is absolutely just as satisfying at only 9 grams of fat per serving. We replaced the cream cheese with a blend of low-fat cottage cheese and ricotta (about 20 grams of fat per pound of the blend instead of 160) and the heavy cream with light sour cream (about 12 grams of fat versus 66 grams). This is just one of the many recipes in which you can substitute Egg Beaters for whole eggs, which cuts another gram of fat per serving, and it worked just fine.

WHAT IF YOU WISH TO CUT YOUR FAT INTAKE STILL FURTHER?

Our goal was to reduce fat by about 50 percent wherever possible in our recipes, and then to try for a further reduction if that worked (as it did in our cheesecake, above).

As a first step, note that our recipes tend to start with about

half the fat usually found in similar "standard" recipes if butter, margarine, or vegetable oil is called for (compare similar
recipes in "regular" cookbooks, or, for a concrete example, the
standard recipe for bran muffins on the back of a cereal box).
Cutting by half the amount of fat added to a recipe is a good
first step in most recipes (you may need to compensate in
volume by increasing other liquids—a bit more milk, bouillon,
or another egg or Egg Beater equivalent—used in the recipe).
You may wish to experiment with even less fat added to your
recipes, and with even lower-fat substitutes for mayonnaise,
cheese, etc., than we used. We chose not to aim for fat-free
recipes or the extreme lowest range of fat that we personally
might live with, because it would be too extreme for most
people who are presently eating the typical American diet.

However, our decision to use the somewhat higher-fat versions of lowered-fat dairy products and mayonnaise in the
recipes in this book doesn't mean that you must stop at the
compromise we have chosen if your goal is a diet even lower
in fat. We have a friend who swears that his goulash with
fat-free sour cream is great (but we haven't sampled his recipe
yet). And it's possible to make an almost zero-fat chocolate
cheesecake using cocoa powder and nonfat yogurt cheese (yogurt from which the liquid has been almost completely
drained). It's pretty good—we make it and have even served
it to company with fresh-ground coffee and Kahlua on the side
for those who wanted it—but it doesn't have the thick consistency of a true cheesecake.

We hope this book will enable you to take that great big first
step toward a healthful low-fat diet, with delicious recipes you
can live with and enjoy the rest of your life. Once you get a
feeling for tasty low-fat cooking, you can take it from there,
and construct your own recipes to arrive at any level of fat
intake you wish.

Good luck and good health!

The Efficient Kitchen

The joy of cooking begins in an efficient kitchen that makes the preparation of food as pleasurable in the doing as in the eating. It's so much easier to prepare healthful meals for yourself and for your family when you work in an environment that's equipped to facilitate your efforts and that gives you the rewards that creative cooking so richly deserves.

Ask yourself this question:

How many times have you started to prepare a meal, whether it's after a long, late day at work when you're tired and hungry or it's a joyously anticipated holiday celebration when you have the whole day to cook, and found yourself getting tense and irritable?

Your change in mood may have occurred for several reasons, all of which are easily corrected if you take a little time to examine what happened.

Did you run out of counter space? Couldn't find the oregano? The knife was so dull you couldn't trim the meat without trimming your fingers? You twisted your back when you bent over and tried to crawl into the corner of a bottom cabinet to reach the roasting pan? You cut into a lemon and it squirted all over the toaster, which, for some reason, has for twenty years managed to stay smack at the rear of your work space and is still splattered with a sprinkle from yesterday's grapefruit?

Annoyances like these can quickly destroy the joy of cooking. We know it as well as anyone. *Every single one of these aggravations has happened to us!*

Finally, since we really love to cook, we learned to pay a little attention to the organization of our kitchens and the preparation process itself. There's no question about it: Inferior utensils, a poorly laid-out kitchen, inefficient storage, lack of essential ingredients, and poor cooking strategies can all make meal preparation an aggravating chore.

Here are some suggestions that have helped make meal preparation easier and a source of pleasure for us.

EQUIPMENT

Knives and Other Utensils

When it comes to knives, buy the very best you can afford! For years I was as susceptible to cheap promotions as anyone. For example, I only recently disposed of a set of impossible kitchen carving knives and steak knives that I received at our neighborhood service station for a dollar and ten gallons of gasoline during a promotion when our family first came to Nashville twenty-five years ago! We tried them once. They didn't have

enough body to cut a hamburger, and for ugliness they couldn't be beat, so they were stuck in the back of a drawer, taking up space needed for more important household goods.

There is a tremendous difference between fine knives and inferior knives. Haven't you always marveled at the ease with which your butcher trims a steak or roast, or skins a chicken? You can do the same if you treat yourself to Henckels or Wüsthof knives, which I use, or something of similar quality. Keep them sharp with a good steel, or with a ceramic sharpening stick, which we think is superior to either steel or stone. I like the Crock Stick, manufactured by Chicago Cutlery, although there are larger, more expensive ones available.

Our most used knives are:

10-inch chef's knife (for the heavy-duty jobs such as splitting
a winter squash or carving a big roast);

10-inch slicing knife (thinner blade more convenient for slicing turkey, for example);

6½-inch utility knife (better on carrots, potatoes, and larger
vegetables than a paring knife); and

4-inch paring knives (I like to have two since they are in
constant use).

It pays to keep your knives right next to the point of use in
a wooden knife block. With this setup, you won't have to leave
your work area or reach across sink or stove whenever you
need one.

Never put your knives in the dishwasher. This will ruin the
handles and dull the blades as well, since they knock up against
the other cutlery while washing.

I keep a large assortment of serving spoons, spatulas (mostly
wooden, a few plastic, all of which will not scratch our pots and
pans), and other implements stored upright in a canister, as a
"bouquet," on a counter near the stove. Terri keeps hers in a
large drawer right next to the stove. So small utensils such as
the can opener and corkscrew don't jam and jumble, they fit
in a deep drawer near the stove.

Pots and Pans

We have had a set of copper-bottom cookware in the family for
thirty-five years, and while I may still occasionally use one of
the saucepans, or the 6-quart covered stockpot when I cook
spaghetti, I feel that lightweight copper- or aluminum-clad
stainless cookware is just not suitable for either simple or seri-
ous cooking.

I prefer pots and pans made of an extra-thick, heavy-duty
aluminum alloy, such as the Leyse or Mirro brands, while Terri
has a set of pots and pans made of heavy-duty porcelain enamel
over steel. A heavy cast aluminum with a Silverstone, nonstick

interior also works well. My 10-inch and 12-inch Leyse skillets have received lots of use, and I keep a complete set of nonstick Silverstone in my motor home, since it is so much easier to clean when I am traveling.

Recently we were introduced to 7-ply stainless steel, which is excellent for waterless cooking; a 2-quart saucepan and 10-inch skillet are now the mainstays for food preparation in my household. A 5- or 7-ply stainless-steel bottom spreads the heat evenly, and, once the pan is hot, you can continue cooking on very low heat. I use these two pots for covered dishes, as the "whistle" vent on the cover, which lets steam escape, tells me when the interior is maintaining the right temperature. Even when panbroiling, food does not stick in the 7-ply skillet, as it will in a thinner stainless skillet. Let the pan get hot before you add any oil, and then add the meat, poultry, or other ingredients.

Most people will find that 2- and 4-quart covered saucepans and a 10-inch and 12-inch skillet are indispensable. We have never needed a stockpot larger than 6 quarts. As with your knives, buy the best you can afford, but keep function in mind, and your own preference for equipment. Don't buy things you won't use and don't keep things that you aren't using. Look in your cupboard right now—you may find pots you haven't used in years! I just got rid of two very heavy cast-iron skillets that many chefs swear by, but they didn't "feel right" or suit my style.

We use a variety of deep, porcelain-on-steel, covered roasting pans, ranging in interior size from 9½ × 14 inches to 11½ × 17 inches. Those extra inches really make a difference, since the smallest is right for roasting a chicken, while the largest takes care of a 22-pound turkey. A heavy-weight, porcelain-on-steel roasting pan can be used on top of the stove, since it will spread the heat quite evenly. My smallest roaster has a rack, which makes it excellent for steaming everything from fish to vegetables. And the largest one comes in handy for mixing great batches of stuffing when I prepare that 22-pound turkey for Thanksgiving. I also use a covered roasting pan to make stews (as well as roasts) in the oven, with a low heat setting.

Terri uses a plain carbon-steel wok for stir-frying, while I prefer a skillet, mainly because my electric-stove instructions warn against burning out the elements when using a stove-top wok. The skillet works fine, but the texture and flavor always seem to be better in the wok, as it heats faster and the "hot spot" makes for crisper vegetables in the stir-fry. You may want to try T-Fal's skillet wok—it's got a nonstick surface, a vented cover, is wok shaped, and is designed for stove tops.

Casseroles and Other Pots

Our favorite earthenware casseroles and baking dishes, as well as soup bowls and coffee mugs, are made by two of Nashville's fine potters, Burneta Clayton and Lenore Vanderkooi. Their work is available in many shops around the country, so if you're fortunate enough to see one of their pots, treat yourself!* I also find a 3½-quart glass casserole, recently introduced by Corning Glass, to be very useful, and for the biggies, I use a 5-quart stoneware casserole, one of those brown monstrosities that have been around for generations. Earthenware, glassware, and stoneware are also excellent for microwave cooking. We also have quite a large assortment of other baking dishes and, of course, muffin tins. (We are very fond of muffins, as you will note when you examine our recipes.)

Miscellaneous

We have a few other items in both our kitchens that do special jobs particularly well.

A **microwave oven** is particularly useful for cooking vegetables. Microwave cooking requires little water, while more nutrients are retained through microwave cooking than through any other cooking method. The microwave is also useful for

*You can also order cookware by mail from Burneta Clayton by writing to her at Clay Works, 4515 Harpeth Hills Drive, Nashville, TN 37215. Write to Lenore Vanderkooi at 1412 Graybar Lane, Nashville, TN 37215. Also look for handmade cookware from potters in your area.

reheating foods, melting cheese, baking a potato or two, and making scrambled eggs and omelettes. We do not rely on it for most of our food preparation, however. Most of our main courses—roasts, stews, casseroles, and poached and steamed foods—are best prepared on the stove top or in the convection oven.

We have both a **blender** and a **food processor.** The food processor does everything from grating Parmesan to slicing vegetables when we have great quantities to slice (we still prefer our fine knives and a manual approach for a few stalks of celery or an onion or two). It also works well for chopping something like a large quantity of Brazil nuts, or for making crumbs out of zwieback or graham crackers. But when it comes to *blending* or *pulverizing,* the blender does a better job than the food processor.

Big wooden salad bowls are essential. Salads don't look right and don't seem to taste as good in glass or metal. A modest-size walnut bowl, about 4 inches deep and 14 inches across the top, is fine for a family and for small dinner parties, but for a buffet, a festive way to serve a gigantic salad is in a truly generous bowl, 8 inches deep and 18 inches across at the summit!

Serving platters have been passed along in our family since our ancestors immigrated from Russia and Lithuania at the turn of this century. Among them are an English porcelain platter (the imprint of origin is now illegible) and a gold-leafed Standard whose finish is beautifully cracked. What a joy it is to display a 22-pound glistening red turkey made tandoori style on the outdoor grill, or a beef bourguignon, surrounded by an arrangement of colorful vegetables, new potatoes, and mushrooms, on one of these platters before serving dinner to family and friends! The platters have held such a wealth of goodness over the years that, each time we use them, we experience again the feelings of thanksgiving we have at being together · as a family and living in the United States of America.

For many years I always minced, and never pressed, fresh garlic. Of course, in many recipes, minced garlic is just fine. Finally, however, my wife Enid got tired of a surprise piece of garlic in her food and purchased an Ahner garlic press. It is now a mainstay in Terri's kitchen as well as ours. It handles cloves of all sizes, presses easily and completely, and, thank goodness, is easy to clean. You should have a fine garlic press since fresh garlic is a completely different experience from garlic powder. The powder will do in a pinch, as we demonstrate in some of our recipes, but fresh is best!

A piece of two-by-four is quite serviceable for pounding meat (I've done it) but it's not quite as good as an honest-to-goodness **meat pounder** when it comes to our wonderful veal recipes. It's worth the investment of four or five dollars, and you can use it for poultry and beef as well. A large **wooden cutting board,** well seasoned, and used for all pounding and cutting, is a must. I have a built-in oak board, 24 inches × 27 inches, next to the sink, and its convenience makes these jobs a joy. Some bakers prefer a marble slab for pastry-making, but we have never used one.

Other utensils that we find useful include a **pepper mill** (fresh-ground is far more flavorful than the canned ground pepper, which we never use); a **coffee grinder,** since fresh-ground coffee is also a completely different experience from pre-ground; and a **mortar and pestle,** which we use for grinding herbs, spices, and seeds when we mix recipes such as Herb Salt (pages 332–33). I have a mortar and pestle of attractive black marble, and Terri has a small lightweight wooden one that cost a dollar in a health-food store about ten years ago. If you don't wish to buy a mortar and pestle, you can use a bowl and a heavy spoon.

A NOTE ON BAKING AND ROASTING

We specifically indicate the instances in which baking or roasting requires a preheated oven. Although the probability is very low, earthenware or heat-resistant glass can crack when exposed to an extreme change in temperature. Therefore, we do not preheat our oven when we plan to use such cookware.

HERBS AND SPICES

Here is a guide to the use of herbs and spices that can add to your cooking and eating pleasure. I keep my herbs and spices handy in a wine-rack-style holder on the countertop at the rear of my work area, together with garlic and onion powder, and a few homemade blends that I use frequently. I keep others on three revolving shelves in the cupboard over the work area: one shelf for seeds of various kinds, another for liquid seasonings, and the third for infrequently used items. We have not tried all of the various foods with all of the suggested herbs and spices in the following list. But we think you will find one or two uses for all of them, as we do. You will find what we think are some particularly good suggestions in our recipes.

Allspice—meats, fish, gravies, relishes, tomato sauce

Anise—fruit

Basil—green beans, onions, peas, potatoes, summer squash, tomatoes, lamb, beef, shellfish, eggs, sauces

Bay Leaves—artichokes, beets, carrots, onions, white potatoes, tomatoes, meats, fish, soups and stews, sauces and gravies

Caraway Seed—asparagus, beets, cabbage, carrots, cauliflower, coleslaw, onions, potatoes, sauerkraut, turnips, beef, pork, noodles, cheese dishes

Cardamom—melon, sweet potatoes

Cayenne Pepper—sauces, curries

Celery Seed—cabbage, carrots, cauliflower, corn, lima beans, potatoes, tomatoes, turnips, salad dressings, beef, fish dishes, sauces, soups, stews, cheese

Chervil—carrots, peas, salads, summer squash, tomatoes, salad dressings, poultry, fish, eggs

Chili Powder—corn, eggplant, onions, beef, pork, chili con carne, stews, shellfish, sauces, egg dishes

Chives—carrots, corn, sauces, salads, soups

Cinnamon—stewed fruits, apple or pineapple dishes, sweet potatoes, winter squash, toast

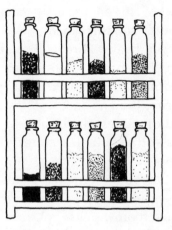

Cloves—baked beans, sweet potatoes, winter squash, pork and ham roasts

Cumin—cabbage, rice, sauerkraut, chili con carne, ground-beef dishes, cottage or cheddar cheese

Curry Powder—carrots, cauliflower, green beans, onions, tomatoes, pork and lamb, shellfish, fish, poultry, sauces for eggs and meats

Dill Seed—cabbage, carrots, cauliflower, peas, potatoes, spinach, tomato dishes, turnips, salads, lamb, cheese

Dillweed—vegetables, salads, poultry, soups

Ginger—applesauce, melon, baked beans, carrots, onions, sweet potatoes, poultry, summer and winter squash, beef, veal, ham, lamb, teriyaki sauce

Mace—carrots, potatoes, spinach, summer squash, beef, veal, fruits, sauces

Marjoram—asparagus, carrots, eggplant, greens, green beans, lima beans, peas, spinach, summer squash, lamb, pork, poultry, fish, stews, sauces

Mustard—asparagus, broccoli, brussels sprouts, cabbage, cauliflower, green beans, onions, peas, potatoes, summer squash, meats, poultry

Mustard Seed—salads, curries, pickles, ham, corned beef, relishes

Nutmeg—beets, brussels sprouts, carrots, cabbage, cauliflower, greens, green beans, onions, spinach, sweet potatoes, winter squash, sauces

Oregano—baked beans, broccoli, cabbage, cauliflower, green beans, lima beans, onions, peas, potatoes, spinach, tomatoes, turnips, beef, pork, veal, poultry, fish, pizza, chili con carne, Italian sauces, stews

Paprika—salad dressings, shellfish, fish, gravies, eggs

Parsley Flakes—all vegetables, soups, sauces, salads, stews, potatoes, eggs

Pepper—most vegetables, meats, salads

Poppy Seeds—salads, noodles

Rosemary—mushrooms, peas, potatoes, spinach, tomatoes, vegetable salads, beef, lamb, pork, veal, poultry, stews, cheese, eggs

Saffron—rice

Sage—eggplant, onions, peas, tomato dishes, salads, pork, veal, poultry, ham, cheese

Savory—baked beans, beets, cabbage, carrots, cauliflower, lima beans, potatoes, rice, squash, egg dishes, roasts, ground-meat dishes

Sesame Seed—asparagus, green beans, potatoes, tomatoes, spinach

Tarragon—asparagus, beets, cabbage, carrots, cauliflower, mushrooms, tomatoes, salads, macaroni-and-vegetable combinations, beef, poultry, pork

Thyme—artichokes, beets, carrots, eggplant, green beans, mushrooms, peas, tomatoes, pork, veal, poultry, cheese and fish dishes, stuffings

Turmeric—mustards and curries, chicken

ORGANIZING THE KITCHEN

We know a number of people who unpacked their dinnerware and kitchen utensils when they moved into their homes and put things away "temporarily," until they could find the time to "get organized." Twenty years later they are still scrambling all over the kitchen for things they use every day and reaching over things they haven't used in a year.

Here are some hints that can increase your efficiency and decrease some of the frustrations that can arise during food preparation.

1. Keep frequently used items as close as possible to their point of use (pots and pans by the stove, glasses near the sink, and so on).

2. Rearrange your kitchen so that cooking utensils, dishes, and other paraphernalia you use every day, or almost every day, are up front, at eye level in their storage areas and so you don't have to move anything else to reach them. Then, take the items you use perhaps once or twice a year and put them in the farthest, least convenient reaches of your storage areas. Everything left over, those items you might use once or twice a month, should be put in intermediate areas. (While reorganizing your kitchen, you might consider throwing out anything you haven't used for a year or more. Or, if you have an attic or basement that you don't mind cluttering, stick these little-used items there and throw them out next year if you haven't used them by then!)

3. Don't clutter work space on your countertops with kitchen equipment. Pick a space at least two feet wide and keep it completely clear for working. This spot is usually best placed either to the right or left of the sink. If at all possible, this should be a hardwood cutting-board surface of oak or maple. Then, clear another counter space to be used as a holding area for the cooking ingredients you assemble prior to cooking, and clear a third spot to be used, if necessary, as a holding area for partly finished dishes that are not yet ready to pop on the stove or into the microwave. If your countertops are deep enough, you can store canisters and frequently used small appliances in less used areas, but don't let them cramp your preparation space.

4. If your stove top is not large enough for hot pots when you take them off burners or out of the oven, prepare another area right next to the stove with a fully heat-resistant surface, such as a portable slab of stainless steel. If you are lucky enough to be able to design your own kitchen, build it in (along with that cutting board next to your sink).

5. Efficient kitchen work centers have sink, refrigerator, and stove all within a step or two of each other but on different walls, forming a triangle of space for you to work in.

6. Set up a logical system for storing canned goods and boxes of foods. Arrange spices in alphabetical order (some people find an alphabetical order good for canned goods, too). The best storage systems for spices have the jars laid on their sides, wine-storage style, with removable, replaceable labels on the tops so that you can add and delete spices when necessary. You can save a great deal of money buying spices in reasonable amounts from a store that sells spices in bulk. Keep the spices in your own jars.

7. Always assemble the ingredients you will need for cooking and lay them out, in order of use, in your holding area before starting to prepare your meal.

8. I have already mentioned that a convenient way to store serving spoons, spatulas, and other large items in constant use is as a "bouquet" in an open canister, vase, or jug near the stove. Silverware needs a drawer only about 2½

inches deep, while small utensils, such as can openers, corkscrews, jar openers, etc., can be kept in one deep drawer, about 4 inches deep, set aside for this purpose, using drawer organizers or cigar box bottoms to group them so they won't jumble and jam as you open the drawer.

9. Open wall space can be used to hang utensils, or hang them from the ceiling.

10. Label and date foods that you put in the freezer, and organize the freezer so that you know where things are. Some foods are best used within a few months, while others may last up to a year. For comprehensive advice on how long frozen foods last, check the classic cookbook *Joy of Cooking,* by Irma S. Rombauer and Marion R. Becker, published by Bobbs-Merrill.

11. A butcher-block-topped table on lockable casters, at counter height, can do double or even triple duty and is one of the most useful things you can have in your kitchen: The table is extra work space, it can be used to cart things from kitchen to eating area(s), and it can serve as a kitchen table for light meals. Attaching a 2-inch-thick maple top, 24 inches × 36 inches or 48 inches, to a trestle base will allow room for your knees and thighs underneath. Lightweight, easily movable stools can serve as seating for meals, food preparation, or dishwashing.

If you have the opportunity to redo your kitchen or your entire home, or if you have been telling yourself that it's time to "get organized" in just about any aspect of your life, we recommend looking into a book that we found helpful and entertaining—*Getting Organized: The Easy Way to Put Your Life in Order,* by Stephanie Winston, published by W. W. Norton. Some of our ideas are based on her suggestions.

Breakfast Foods

Many nutritionists consider breakfast the most important meal of the day. I think eating in the morning is important in a very special way for persons who are trying to manage their weight: When you skip breakfast, you tend to build up a "hidden hunger" that shows itself in overeating at night.

There is some research evidence that people who eat breakfast are more alert and better problem-solvers in the morning, and that eating a nutritious breakfast helps to avoid the afternoon blahs.

Although some people who wake early really don't feel comfortable if they eat before ten or eleven, or even noon, we think you should give breakfast a try. Experiment for two weeks with a variety of our breakfast suggestions and see if you feel and work better. If you tend to eat from the moment you get home from work until you hit the sack, that tendency to nibble all night might decrease once you start eating breakfast. You must, however, give the experiment a full two weeks to take effect, since it can take your system that long to readjust if you have been skipping breakfast for a long time. There are many hormones and enzymes that mobilize our bodies for the day and that aid in digesting food. They may be slightly out of rhythm, and it can take a while to retrain them. If you find yourself uncomfortable at the end of two weeks, well, go back to what you were doing! It must be right for you.

I like cereal with fruit and milk, or bread and low-fat cottage cheese seasoned with different herbs or spices, along with a piece of fruit, as my two "standard" breakfasts. Terri prefers yogurt and fresh fruit. Both of us like a good cup of fresh-ground coffee, followed by a second cup! In order to keep our caffeine intake at reasonable levels, we often mix decaffeinated with regular coffee; I usually drink only a half cup at a time. We rarely have eggs, and I cannot remember the last time I had bacon or sausage, although it might have been about a year and a half ago on a camping trip. (Yes, I must admit it: There is something wonderful about the smell and the taste of bacon or sausage and pancakes on the grill out there in the woods, and I don't intend to forgo that pleasure permanently!) But these foods are too high in fat and cholesterol to be part of my daily diet.

We include here some "special" breakfast foods for special occasions: pancake recipes with interesting blends of different flours and cereals; French toast; yogurt and fruit; and unusual ways to make eggs.

If you like plain fried or scrambled eggs for breakfast, you can prepare them with very little added fat by using a nonstick vegetable cooking spray or a nonstick-surface pan. Then, too, a plain boiled egg can be delectable if you know how to boil it properly. As you will see below, there really is a trick to it!

Boiled Egg

PREPARATION TIME: 5 MINUTES   COOKING TIME: 15 MINUTES

Place the egg in a saucepan with enough water to cover. Bring to a boil. Then cover immediately, *remove from the heat,* and let stand 15 minutes for a hard-boiled egg with a light, almost fluffy texture, and no sulfurous green ring. (The green ring results from the interaction of continuous high heat with the sulfur in the egg.) Soft-boiled eggs should stand about 4 to 5 minutes when prepared this way.

Per egg: **5 g. fat,** 78 calories, 212 mg. cholesterol, no dietary fiber, 62 mg. sodium

Basic Pancake Mix

PREPARATION TIME: 15 MINUTES   COOKING TIME: 20 TO 30 MINUTES

For your own, homemade, nutritious pancake mix, you can mix together the dry ingredients listed below, and store the mix in an airtight container. Add the wet ingredients when you're ready to cook.

The mix:

4 cups whole-wheat flour
3 cups all-purpose flour
1½ cups low-fat soy flour
2 cups wheat germ

1 teaspoon salt
1 cup instant nonfat dry milk
⅓ cup baking powder

The pancakes:

1½ cups mix
2 eggs, beaten well
1 cup skim milk or water

1 tablespoon oil
Nonstick vegetable cooking
  spray (optional)

1. Combine the mix with the eggs, milk or water, and oil. The batter will be slightly lumpy.
2. Heat a Teflon pan, or other pan sprayed with cooking spray, over medium heat. Pour about ¼ cup of batter per pancake into the pan. When the cakes are bubbly on top and brown on the bottom, flip them and brown the other side.

Makes 12 pancakes. 6 servings.

Per serving, 2 pancakes: **5 g. fat,** 149 calories, 71 mg. cholesterol, 2 g. dietary fiber, 98 mg. sodium

Mexican Eggs

PREPARATION TIME: 5 TO 10 MINUTES   COOKING TIME: 5 MINUTES

Try serving this with warm Whole-Wheat Tortillas (pp. 314–15), and/or Spanish Rice (p. 285). A tablespoon of Avocado Dip (p. 53) goes well with it, too.

Nonstick vegetable cooking
  spray
1 or 2 mild green chiles
  (canned, drained), chopped
  fine

1 small onion, chopped
1 large tomato, chopped
4 eggs, beaten
Dash of salt (optional)

1. Spray the skillet with vegetable spray. Add the chopped vegetables, cover, and cook over low heat until tender, stirring occasionally.
2. Push the vegetables to one side of the pan. Add the eggs, and scramble them. When the eggs are almost cooked, mix the vegetables in with them. Add a dash of salt, if desired.

4 servings.

Per serving: **5 g. fat,** 100 calories, 212 mg. cholesterol, 1 g. dietary fiber, 69 mg. sodium

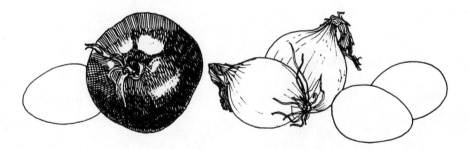

Raisin-Bran Pancakes

PREPARATION TIME: 10 MINUTES   COOKING TIME: 25 TO 30 MINUTES

¾ cup all-purpose flour
2 tablespoons sugar
1 tablespoon baking powder
½ teaspoon salt
1 egg, slightly beaten
1¼ cups skim milk

1 cup All-Bran or Bran Buds
  cereal
2 tablespoons butter or
  margarine
½ cup raisins

1. In a bowl, mix together the flour, sugar, baking powder, and salt. Set aside.
2. In a large bowl, mix together the egg, milk, cereal, and 1 tablespoon of melted butter. Let stand 1 to 2 minutes, or until the liquid is absorbed. Stir in the raisins.
3. Add the flour mixture all at once to the cereal mixture, and stir until moistened. The batter will be lumpy.
4. Heat the remaining tablespoon of butter in a large frying pan over medium heat. Drop the batter in, using 2 table-spoons of batter per pancake. Cook until golden brown, turning once, about 3 minutes on each side.

Makes 18 pancakes. 9 servings.

Per serving, 2 pancakes: **5 g. fat,** 141 calories, 24 mg. cholesterol, 4 g. dietary fiber, 283 mg. sodium

Good-for-You Scones

PREPARATION TIME: 20 MINUTES   COOKING TIME: 20 MINUTES

2 cups whole-wheat flour
1 cup All-Bran or Bran Buds
  cereal
1 tablespoon baking powder
1 tablespoon sugar

½ teaspoon salt
3 tablespoons butter or
  margarine
1 egg
½ cup skim milk

1. In a large bowl, mix together the whole-wheat flour, cereal, baking powder, sugar, and salt. Cut in the butter until the mixture resembles coarse meal.
2. Beat together the egg and milk. Add to the flour mixture, and stir until well combined.
3. Knead on a lightly floured surface for 2 to 3 minutes, or until smooth. Roll out the dough ½ inch thick, and cut with a 2-inch biscuit or cookie cutter.
4. Place the scones in a heated, lightly greased (vegetable cooking spray) or Teflon-coated frying pan. Cook over low heat for 10 minutes, turn, and cook 10 minutes more.

Makes 14 scones. 14 servings.

Per serving: **3 g. fat,** 108 calories, 22 mg. cholesterol, 4 g. dietary fiber, 182 mg. sodium

Raisin-Rice Cereal

PREPARATION TIME: 1 TO 2 MINUTES   COOKING TIME: 10 MINUTES

1 cup cooked brown rice or   1 tablespoon raisins
   other whole grain   Dash cinnamon or nutmeg
½ cup skim or low-fat milk

1. Heat the rice in the milk in a saucepan over medium-low heat until warmed. Do not boil.
2. Add the raisins, and heat another minute or two. Pour into a bowl, and top with a dash of cinnamon or nutmeg.

1 serving.

Per serving: **2 g. fat,** 286 calories, 2 mg. cholesterol, 4 g. dietary fiber, 74 mg. sodium

Brancakes

PREPARATION TIME: 15 MINUTES   COOKING TIME: 20 TO 25 MINUTES

1 egg
2 cups skim milk
¾ cup All-Bran or Bran Buds
  cereal

1½ cups all-purpose flour
1 tablespoon baking powder
¼ teaspoon salt
2 tablespoons sugar

1. Beat the egg until foamy. Stir in the milk and the cereal. Let stand 5 minutes.
2. Stir together the flour, baking powder, salt, and sugar in a medium mixing bowl. Add the cereal mixture, stirring to combine, and let stand 5 minutes.
3. Drop the batter, using ¼ cup for each pancake, onto a lightly greased, preheated griddle. Cook, turning once, until golden brown on both sides.

Makes 12 pancakes. 12 servings.

Per serving: **1 g. fat,** 102 calories, 19 mg. cholesterol, 2 g. dietary fiber, 135 mg. sodium

French Toast

PREPARATION TIME: 5 MINUTES   COOKING TIME: 7 TO 10 MINUTES

This is good served with fresh fruit, applesauce, or of course a tablespoon or two of real maple syrup.

1 egg
1 tablespoon skim milk
¼ teaspoon cinnamon

2 slices whole-grain bread
Nonstick vegetable cooking
  spray

1. Beat the egg and the milk with the cinnamon. Dip the bread in the egg mixture, coating both sides.
2. Spray a skillet with nonstick cooking spray, and heat over medium heat. Fry the bread in the pan, turning once, until golden brown on both sides.

VARIATIONS: Omit the cinnamon, and substitute ¼ teaspoon of grated lemon or orange peel.

1 serving.

Per serving (without syrup or fruit): **8 g. fat,** 252 calories, 212 mg. cholesterol, 5 g. dietary fiber, 439 mg. sodium

Yogurt and Fresh Fruit

PREPARATION TIME: 2 TO 3 MINUTES

Plain nonfat yogurt mixed with fresh fruit is one of Terri's standard foods for breakfast or for lunch. You can take it with you to work in a plastic container, if there is a refrigerator available for storing it until lunchtime.

Store-bought varieties of yogurt containing fruit also contain large amounts of sugar. Mixing your own means your fruit is fresh, and you can control the amount of sugar. Terri never uses any sweetener besides dried fruit or an occasional bit of sweetened coconut—which actually tastes too sweet to her now.

Her favorite combinations include raisin-apple-almond, raisin- or date-orange-pecan, and raisin-orange-banana with a dash of coconut.

You can use canned fruit, as long as it is unsweetened and canned in its own juices. Canned pineapple with added coconut is very good.

You may like to experiment with spices. A dash of cinnamon,

nutmeg, allspice, cardamom, clove, or mace, or a combination of a couple of these, will heighten the sweetness without adding calories.

Some fruits, however, such as apples or bananas, do turn brown when exposed to air, so they are best eaten right away.

Here's the basic recipe:

1 cup plain nonfat yogurt
1 medium-sized piece of fruit, chopped, OR ½ cup sliced mixed fruit

1 tablespoon raisins, or other chopped dried fruit
1 tablespoon chopped nuts of choice

Combine all the ingredients in a serving bowl, and it's ready to eat.

1 serving.

Per serving: **5 g. fat,** 249 calories, 4 mg. cholesterol, 2 g. dietary fiber, 190 mg. sodium

Scrambled Eggs and Cheese

PREPARATION TIME: 3 TO 5 MINUTES   COOKING TIME: 5 MINUTES

By using an extra egg white you can extend the amount of egg, without using another whole egg. By using very little cooking fat and a low-fat cheese, you also save fat grams and calories. The difference? Eight grams of fat versus 18, and 140 calories versus 240!

1 medium egg
1 egg white
1 ounce low-fat cheese (part-skim mozzarella,

Jarlsberg Lite, etc.), grated
Nonstick vegetable cooking spray (optional)

1. Beat together the egg and the egg white. Pour into a nonstick pan, or a pan sprayed with nonstick vegetable cook-

ing spray, and cook over medium-low heat, stirring occasionally.

2. After a minute, add the cheese. Keep cooking and stirring occasionally until done.

1 serving (with Jarlsberg Lite).

Per serving: **8 g. fat,** 139 calories, 203 mg. cholesterol, no dietary fiber, 210 mg. sodium

Wednesday's "Sunday Breakfast"

PREPARATION TIME: 3 TO 5 MINUTES   COOKING TIME: 2 MINUTES

This recipe is named for the fact that it's a quick, easy way to throw together something special in the middle of the week. Nutritious low-fat diets frequently list cottage cheese and a slice or two of bread as part of the breakfast meal. Below is one of the many ways you can dress up cottage cheese without adding many calories or fat. Spread it on a slice of Italian Whole-Wheat Bread (pp. 306–7), or any other whole-grain bread.

¼ **cup 1% low-fat cottage cheese**
1 **small clove garlic, crushed**
1 **scallion, bulb only, minced**

¼ **teaspoon Traditional Italian Herb Blend (p. 333)**
1 **slice whole-grain bread**

1. Combine the cottage cheese, garlic, scallion, and Herb Blend, and spread on the bread.
2. Broil for a couple of minutes until hot, and serve.

1 serving.

Per serving: **2 g. fat,** 132 calories, 2 mg. cholesterol, 3 g. dietary fiber, 414 mg. sodium

Whole-Wheat Corn Cakes

PREPARATION TIME: 5 TO 6 MINUTES

COOKING TIME: 20 TO 25
MINUTES

⅓ cup yellow cornmeal
⅓ cup whole-wheat flour
⅓ cup all-purpose flour
2 teaspoons sugar
2 teaspoons baking powder
Dash of salt

1 egg
1 cup skim or low-fat milk
1 tablespoon vegetable oil
1 teaspoon honey
Nonstick vegetable cooking
  spray

1. Combine the dry ingredients in a medium-sized bowl.
2. In another bowl, beat the egg, then beat in the milk, oil, and honey.
3. Spray a griddle or skillet with cooking spray, and heat over medium heat. When hot, spoon batter into pan to make pancakes about 4 inches in diameter. Cook until they begin to bubble and are golden brown on the bottom. Turn them over and cook until done.

Makes 8 large pancakes. 4 servings.

Per serving, 2 pancakes: **6 g. fat,** 197 calories, 55 mg. cholesterol, 3 g. dietary fiber, 153 mg. sodium

Appetizers

I have a confession to make: It's been ages since my wife and I have served anything except fruit as an appetizer at our dinner parties. So, Terri and I had to start from scratch to create appetizers that we would be comfortable serving to our friends at our own dinner and cocktail parties.

For casual dinner parties, I enjoy serving a large bowl of fruit on the coffee table, with individual plates and knives for our guests to use for carving up their own apples, pears, or peaches as we talk in the den before dinner.

For large parties and other occasions when you need many different appetizers, consider using a monster-size Creative Fruit Salad (see page 88) as your centerpiece. Hollow out half a watermelon, if available, or use a large punch bowl filled with various fruits, such as melon balls, sliced apples, chunks of fresh pineapple or pears or both, strawberries or blueberries, grapes, and sections of a citrus fruit. Mix in a few ounces of lemon juice to preserve the color, and then add a bottle of white wine or champagne. If you don't care to use an alcoholic beverage as a mixer, use ginger ale. The beverage serves as a marinade for the fruit. Guests can use toothpicks to spear the fruit. If watermelon is not available, we use a 6-quart clear glass brandy snifter to hold our assortment.

You can feature your fruit bowl along with some of the other hors d'oeuvres from this chapter at cocktail parties, but we assure you, a creation of this kind will easily compete for attention with any appetizers that might surround it!

Some of the appetizers in this section are lowered-fat modifications of standard recipes (the Stuffed Mushrooms, pages 56–57), while others are quite unusual. The Clam Dip (page 56) illustrates how to use lower-fat dairy products in place of cream and cream cheese and create perfectly acceptable dips with half the fat and 40 percent fewer calories. The Incredibly Edible Artichoke Dip (page 60) is our version of an even more incredibly edible, incredibly fattening dip. The original uses only cheese and mayonnaise and contains more than double the calories of our formula.

There are recipes in other sections of this book that can easily be adapted for use as appetizers. Two that seem particularly appropriate are Spinach Pizza (see pages 248–49) and Summer's Bounty Pizza (see pages 250–51). If you try these pizzas as appetizers, serving size can be determined by cutting the pie into quarters, and then cutting each quarter into eighths; the caloric and nutritional values here would be about one-eighth of those listed under the main-course recipes.

One final word of caution. Many dips and appetizers are unavoidably high in fat, and we all know how hard it is to resist a bowl or plate of those goodies, *especially* when we are hungry! A sure way to ruin a good dinner is to encourage your guests to satisfy their appetite before they even get to the table. So try making individual servings of your appetizers, or perhaps pass them a couple of times and leave the plate in the kitchen. Remember that you can do yourself and your friends a favor by at least providing the alternative of fresh fruits.

We also cut calories when serving dips by using fresh, sliced vegetables or whole-grain crackers for dipping, instead of potato chips and other high-fat snacks.

"Where in hell is today's Melon Fruit Jubilee?" DRAWING BY BOOTH; © 1985 THE NEW YORKER MAGAZINE, INC.

Avocado Dip

PREPARATION TIME: 5 MINUTES

Though avocados are high in fat, they are nutritious, and can be eaten sparingly. Mixed with yogurt, the protein level is boosted. Go easy on the salt if you are watching your sodium intake.

Often the avocados in the supermarkets are not yet ripe. Simply leave them on the kitchen counter or a windowsill for a day or two until they feel slightly soft. You can speed the process by putting them in a brown paper bag.

Although it doesn't matter a great deal which avocado you use for this dip, the larger Florida (or West Indian) avocados are somewhat lower in fat than the California (or Mexican) avocados. Because of the difference in the size of the seed, the total usable flesh (and thus the total calories) is pretty much the same.

2 medium Florida avocados (about 1 cup, mashed) **1 cup plain nonfat yogurt**	**Garlic, cumin, salt, and fresh-ground black pepper to taste**

Peel and mash the avocados in a medium-sized bowl. Add the remaining ingredients and mix well with a fork, or, for a very smooth consistency, use a wire whisk or blend in a blender. Serve with cut-up fresh vegetables, whole-grain crackers, or Quick Tortilla Chips (pp. 314–15).

Makes about 2 cups. Serving size is 1 tablespoon.

Per serving: **1 g. fat,** 12 calories, no cholesterol, no dietary fiber, 31 mg. sodium (with ¼ teaspoon salt used in the complete recipe)

Cheese and Olive Party Toast

PREPARATION TIME: 8 TO 10 MINUTES   COOKING TIME: 2 MINUTES

¼ cup black olives, chopped
¼ cup scallion, chopped
¼ cup shredded Jarlsberg Lite cheese
1 tablespoon light mayonnaise
¼ teaspoon Indian Spice Blend (p. 332) or other curry powder

¼ teaspoon salt
¼ teaspoon fresh-ground black pepper
1 tablespoon grated Parmesan cheese
14 slices rye party-round bread

1. Combine all ingredients except bread, and mix well.
2. Spread a scant teaspoon of the mixture on each slice of bread. Broil for 2 minutes, until the cheese melts.

Makes 14 rounds. 14 servings.

Per serving: **1 g. fat,** 34 calories, 1 mg. cholesterol, 1 g. dietary fiber, 140 mg. sodium

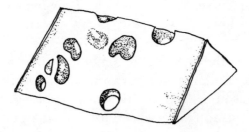

Eggplant Caviar

PREPARATION TIME: 1¼ HOURS   COOKING TIME: 35 TO 40 MINUTES

Eggplant is thought to have been cultivated first in India over four thousand years ago. Though popular in Middle Eastern countries, it made its way westward slowly, being regarded with some suspicion by Europeans, who thought it might be dangerous. John Gerard of England wrote in his *Herball* in 1597 that eggplant had "a mischievous quality." We are not sure precisely what he meant by that, but he admonished his readers to "forsake" the eggplant.

For those who don't mind making a little mischief, serve this tasty spread chilled, with whole-grain, low-salt crackers, wedges of pita bread, or Quick Tortilla Chips (p. 62).

1 large eggplant
½ cup scallions, chopped fine
1 small bell pepper (red, green, or yellow), minced
2 cloves garlic, minced or crushed
1 tablespoon olive oil
2 medium tomatoes, chopped

½ teaspoon fresh-ground black pepper
⅛ teaspoon cayenne pepper
½ teaspoon cumin
½ teaspoon salt
Dash of Tabasco (optional)
2 tablespoons lemon juice

1. Preheat oven to 400 degrees. Pierce the eggplant several times with a fork, and place on a foil-covered baking sheet. Bake for about 1 hour, turning the eggplant occasionally.
2. When the eggplant is done, the skin will be wrinkled and soft. Take it out of the oven and let it cool. Cut it in half, scoop out the pulp, and chop it finely. Place it in a colander in the sink to drain while you prepare the other ingredients.
3. Sauté the scallions, pepper, and garlic in the oil over medium heat until the onion is translucent. Add all the other ingredients except the lemon juice, stirring the eggplant in last.
4. Cover and let simmer on low heat for about 30 minutes, stirring occasionally. Then remove the cover, and let simmer until liquid is reduced.
5. Let cool, then stir in the lemon juice, and refrigerate.

Makes about 2½ cups. Serving size is 1 tablespoon.

Per serving: **no fat**, 10 calories, no cholesterol, 1 g. dietary fiber, 287 mg. sodium

Clam Dip

PREPARATION TIME: 6 TO 7 MINUTES

We are pretty generous with the garlic when we prepare this recipe, and suggest you serve it with a large variety of fresh vegetables. Compared with recipes that use cream cheese or other dairy products with higher fat contents, this recipe has as much as half the fat and 40 percent fewer calories.

4 ounces Neufchâtel cheese
¼ cup plain nonfat yogurt
1½ teaspoons white or red
  Worcestershire sauce

1 can (6½ ounces) minced
  clams
Garlic powder, salt, and
  fresh-ground black pepper to
  taste

1. Let the Neufchâtel cheese soften to room temperature, then blend it in a bowl with the yogurt and Worcestershire sauce.
2. Open the can of clams, drain and reserve the liquid, and add the clams to the dairy mixture. Add a small amount of the reserved clam liquid to make a light (but not soupy) dip.
3. Add the seasonings to taste, and chill until serving time. Serve with whole-grain crackers, celery sticks, or other fresh vegetables.

Makes about 1½ cups. Serving size is 1 tablespoon.

Per serving: **1 g. fat,** 22 calories, 7 mg. cholesterol, no dietary fiber, 38 mg sodium

Stuffed Mushrooms

PREPARATION TIME: 20 MINUTES   COOKING TIME: 15 MINUTES

Here is an example of how to combine a small amount of butter, for flavoring, with other fats (in this case, olive oil) and herbs. The combination of parsley, garlic, and onions is basic to many recipes and here provides for a mild, noticeably buttery stuffing. If you prefer a spicier appetizer, add to the stuffing recipe below freshly ground black pepper or your favorite herb blend to taste, or just ONE splash of Tabasco.

24 large mushrooms (about 8 to 10 ounces)
1 small clove garlic, crushed
¼ cup onions, finely minced
¼ teaspoon dried parsley
2 teaspoons olive oil

3 heaping tablespoons Whole-Wheat Bread Crumbs (p. 305)
1 tablespoon egg white
1 teaspoon butter, melted

1. Rinse the mushrooms and remove the stems. Dice six of the stems and reserve.
2. Sauté the garlic, onions, and parsley in the oil, stirring constantly until onions are translucent. Carefully drain any liquid from the pan.
3. Stir in the bread crumbs, egg white, and butter, and mix thoroughly.
4. Fill the mushrooms with this mixture. Place on a foil-covered baking pan, and bake at 350 degrees for 15 minutes.

6 servings. Serving size is 4 mushrooms.

Per serving: **3 g. fat,** 55 calories, 2 mg. cholesterol, 1 g. dietary fiber, 47 mg. sodium

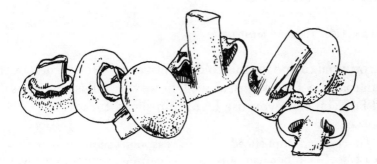

Mexican-Style Hot Sauce ✓

PREPARATION TIME: 10 MINUTES

This is a good salsa-type dip for fresh vegetables, Quick Tortilla Chips (p. 62), or for use in any Mexican recipe. It requires no cooking, and contains no oil. We like it spicy hot, but if you prefer a milder sauce, cut back on the Tabasco . . . or the crushed red pepper . . . or the jalapeños!

1 can (28 ounces) whole
   tomatoes
1 can (6 ounces) tomato paste
3 to 4 scallions, finely chopped
½ medium bell pepper, diced
4 jalapeño peppers, finely
   chopped, plus 3 tablespoons

juice from the can
½ ounce (¼ bottle) Tabasco
   sauce
1 tablespoon crushed red
   pepper
¾ cup water

1. Pour the can of whole tomatoes into a large bowl, along with their juice. Chop the tomatoes into small pieces.
2. Add all the other ingredients, blending well. Store in a *glass* container in the refrigerator.

Makes about 6 cups. Serving size is 1 tablespoon.

Per serving: **no fat,** 4 calories, no cholesterol, no dietary fiber, 2 mg. sodium

Roast Beef Roll-Ups

PREPARATION TIME: 15 MINUTES

The original recipe for this cold appetizer calls for corned beef. Lean roast beef works just as well, however, and is lower in salt and fat. You can even use lean, thin-sliced turkey.

2½ ounces lean, thin-sliced
   roast beef or other lean meat
3 ounces Neufchâtel cheese,
   softened to room
   temperature

2 teaspoons skim milk
¾ teaspoon tamari sauce or soy
   sauce
1 small clove garlic, crushed
1 small scallion, minced

1. Slice the roast beef into 26 pieces about 4 inches long and 2 inches wide.
2. In a small bowl, combine the remaining ingredients. Spread a teaspoon of the mixture across each piece of beef, roll up the beef, and secure it with a toothpick. Place on a serving platter, and serve.

26 servings.

Per serving: **1 g. fat,** 15 calories, 4 mg. cholesterol, no dietary fiber, 61 mg. sodium

Garbanzo Dip

PREPARATION TIME: 10 MINUTES

A low-fat alternative to traditional hummus. And, by the way, if you can find the unhulled sesame seeds, they are an excellent source of calcium. They are usually available in specialty food shops. See pages 235–36 for instructions on how to toast seeds without added fat.

1 can (15 ounces) garbanzo
  beans
1 teaspoon onion powder
2 to 3 cloves garlic, crushed
¼ teaspoon salt

½ cup plain nonfat yogurt
2 tablespoons toasted sesame
  seeds, ground with mortar
  and pestle

1. Drain the garbanzos, and pour the beans into a blender or food processor.
2. Add the onion powder, garlic, salt, and yogurt, and blend until smooth.
3. Pour the mixture into a serving bowl, and top with the sesame seeds. Chill until serving time.

Makes about 2 cups. Serving size is 1 tablespoon.

Per serving: **no fat,** 22 calories, no cholesterol, 1 g. dietary fiber, 20 mg. sodium

Incredibly Edible Artichoke Dip

PREPARATION TIME: 7 TO 8 MINUTES

For variety, this dip is also good with about ½ teaspoon of Traditional Italian Herb Blend (p. 333) in addition to the spices listed. Serve it with whole-grain crackers (Ak-Mak, a sesame cracker available in the imported foods section of supermarkets, is particularly good).

1 can (14 ounces) artichokes
¾ cup plain nonfat yogurt
1½ tablespoons light mayonnaise
½ cup grated Jarlsberg Lite or low-fat Swiss cheese
½ teaspoon garlic powder

1 tablespoon dried parsley OR 3 tablespoons fresh parsley, minced
2 tablespoons Parmesan cheese
Fresh-ground black pepper to taste
Paprika (optional)

1. Drain the artichokes in a colander and rinse to remove some of the salt. Whir them in a blender or food processor for a few seconds until coarsely chopped.
2. In a medium bowl, combine the chopped artichokes with all the other ingredients except the paprika. Pour into a serving bowl, and sprinkle with paprika. Chill until serving time.

Makes about 3 cups. Serving size is 1 tablespoon.

Per serving: **no fat,** 8 calories, 1 mg. cholesterol, no dietary fiber, 51 mg. sodium

Salmon Mousse

PREPARATION TIME: 10 MINUTES

Serve this as an appetizer on whole-grain crackers, or use it as a sandwich spread. It is also good on whole-grain English muffins and broiled for a couple of minutes. This is one of our new appetizers that is slightly higher in fat, but it is so delicious that it's worth showing off on occasion. The use of Neufchâtel cheese in place of cream cheese helps lower the saturated-fat content, and salmon is a good source of the "good" omega-III fatty acids that we discuss on page 191.

1 can (16 ounces) salmon,
  drained and flaked
8 ounces Neufchâtel cheese
3 tablespoons lemon juice
2 tablespoons diced red onion
1 tablespoon fresh parsley,
  minced

2 teaspoons pure horseradish
¼ cup chopped nuts (walnuts
  or pecans are good)
Black olive or teaspoon of nuts
  for garnish (optional)

1. In a blender or food processor, combine all ingredients except the nuts, and blend until smooth.
2. Stir in the ¼ cup of nuts, then pour the mousse into a serving bowl. Chill until serving time. Garnish with a black olive in the center, or decorate with the teaspoon of nuts, if desired, and serve.

Makes about 2 cups. Serving size is 1 tablespoon.

Per serving: **3 g. fat,** 43 calories, 11 mg. cholesterol, no dietary fiber, 86 mg. sodium

Quick Tortilla Chips

PREPARATION TIME: 5 MINUTES   COOKING TIME: 10 MINUTES

Keep your eye on these while they are baking, as they brown
quickly.

Nonstick vegetable cooking   **1 package corn tortillas (10**
  spray   **6-inch rounds)**

1. Spray a foil-covered baking sheet with nonstick cooking
   spray.
2. Stack the tortillas on top of each other and cut into eighths.
   Spread the tortilla pieces on the baking sheet, and spray
   lightly with cooking spray.
3. Bake at 350 degrees for about 10 minutes, or until just
   beginning to turn crispy and brown.

VARIATIONS: Sprinkle the chips with garlic powder,
Parmesan cheese, paprika, or other seasonings before
baking.

Makes 80 chips.

Per 5 chips: **no fat,** 42 calories, no cholesterol, 1 g. dietary fiber,
30 mg. sodium

Soups

As a main meal or a first course, soups are always in season: refreshing cold soups for the summer, invigorating hot soups for the winter.

We like to start most of our soups with our own homemade chicken or vegetable stock, and we have included some basic stock recipes (see Basic Soup Stocks, pages 64–67).

Another trick we like to use is to save the liquid from steaming or simmering vegetables for use in soups. Pour the liquid into a plastic freezer container, seal it, and freeze. Whenever you cook vegetables, simply add the leftover juices to the container. Then, when you want to use the stock for soups or for cooking grains or any other dish, run the container under warm water to loosen the sides, and pop the whole cube into a saucepan. Heat until you melt as much as you need for your recipe; if you don't need it all, put the rest of the cube back in the freezer for another time. We use most vegetable juices for this purpose, but we avoid stronger ones, such as asparagus, which tend to overpower the flavor of milder ingredients.

We realize that many people don't want to take the time to make their own stock and, in a pinch, we, too, will use instant bouillon granules or bouillon cubes. If you use instant, you should be aware that *the* primary ingredient in commercial preparations is *salt.* A single cube or teaspoon of granules, the measure ordinarily used to create one cup of bouillon, can contain 900 to 1500 milligrams of sodium. When we do use a commercial instant bouillon, we use a low-sodium brand or Wyler's at half strength or less.

Clear soups are generally lower in calories than cream soups, but we have found that substituting skim or low-fat milk in place of cream works very well.

Cornstarch, flour, and arrowroot are good thickeners. A roux is another thickener, made with flour and butter or margarine. It should be cooked over low heat long enough to turn golden brown, or you will have a floury flavor in your food. Arrowroot is good, but I have never used it and Terri rarely uses it because it doesn't reheat well, and she likes to make enough of a recipe for leftovers. You can also mix flour or cornstarch with a small amount of water or stock to make a thin paste and add this to soups or sauces. Soups with vegetables can be thickened by whirring a few of the vegetables in a blender or food processor until puréed and stirring the mixture back into the soup.

Making a meal out of a hearty soup is one of our standard winter dinners, along with a bountiful salad and a slice of whole-grain bread. Thus, we've included a couple of chili recipes, and other warm, filling soups in this section. Also check the Beef, Lamb, Poultry, Fish, and Veal sections for some wonderful stews.

Finally, soup appears to be an excellent aid in preventing overeating. Persons who frequently include soup with their meals find it easier to lose weight and maintain their losses.

BASIC SOUP STOCKS

Chicken Stock

PREPARATION TIME: 15 TO 20 MINUTES   COOKING TIME: 2 HOURS

This is the basic stock that we use for making soups of various kinds, rice, and boiled potatoes. It is excellent for soaking and cooking beans.

Save all chicken and turkey giblets (necks, hearts, gizzards, but *not* livers). Freeze these parts immediately, first trimming skin and any fat from the necks, and hold in your freezer until you have accumulated the parts of 4 to 6 birds.

You may substitute a beef soup bone or two for the giblets, but we prefer the lighter flavor and lower cholesterol of chicken stock.

You can also freeze the soup stock in plastic containers for later use as needed.

Giblets of 4 to 6 birds
1 large bay leaf
Salt and pepper to taste
1 teaspoon each: rosemary, sage, thyme, tarragon

1 large onion, coarsely chopped
2 large stalks celery, cut into 2-inch pieces (include leaves)
2 large carrots, cut into 2-inch pieces

1. Place the giblets in a deep soup kettle, with enough water to cover (about 8 to 10 cups). Bring to a boil and skim as necessary. When finally clear of fat scum, add the remaining ingredients. You may also throw in any other greens or wilted vegetables you have on hand in your refrigerator (except for asparagus, cabbage, broccoli, and cauliflower, which taste too strong).
2. Bring to a boil once again, then reduce heat and simmer for at least 2 hours.
3. Separate the giblets and vegetables from the water. Blend the vegetables in a blender or food processor until smooth, and return to the stock. Save the cooked giblets for low-calorie snacks.

Makes about 10 to 12 cups, depending on how many giblets and how many vegetables you add.

Per cup (10 cups): **1 g. fat,** 31 calories, 20 mg. cholesterol, 1·g. dietary fiber, 82 mg. sodium

Vegetable Stock

PREPARATION TIME: 10 MINUTES   COOKING TIME: 1 HOUR

Here's a basic recipe for a stock made from water and a variety of fresh vegetables. You can add other vegetables, such as parsnips, turnips, leeks, etc., if desired.

3 medium carrots, cut in
  chunks
2 stalks celery, cut in chunks
3 medium onions, cut in
  chunks
3 cloves garlic, minced

⅓ cup fresh parsley, minced
1 bay leaf
6 whole peppercorns
½ teaspoon tarragon and/or
  other dried herbs
6 cups water

1. Combine all ingredients in a large soup pot, and bring to a boil. Reduce heat to simmer, cover, and let cook for about 1 hour.
2. You may strain the vegetables out and use the clear broth, or put the stock in a blender and purée for a thicker stock, adding more water if necessary.

Makes about 8 cups.

Per cup: **no fat,** 24 calories, no cholesterol, 2 g. dietary fiber, 23 mg. sodium

Onion Stock

PREPARATION TIME: 15 MINUTES   COOKING TIME: 5 MINUTES

If you are out of vegetable or other stock, try making a quick onion broth for soups, as follows:

1 large onion, sliced
1 tablespoon vegetable oil

5 cups water

1. Sauté the sliced onions in the oil over medium heat until golden brown, stirring often.

2. Add the water, bring to a boil, then reduce heat and let simmer for about 5 minutes. You may strain the onions out, depending on the type of dish you are planning to combine with the stock. We usually prefer to leave the onions in, as they provide added fiber, vitamins, and minerals.

Makes about 5½ cups of stock.

Per ½ cup: **1 g. fat**, 15 calories, no cholesterol, no dietary fiber, 1 mg. sodium

SOUPS

Asparagus Soup

PREPARATION TIME: 25 MINUTES   COOKING TIME: 10 TO 15 MINUTES

You may substitute canned asparagus if necessary, but, as usual, fresh is best.

1 pound fresh asparagus	**½ to 1 teaspoon dry mustard**
2½ cups skim milk	**Fresh-ground black pepper to**
1½ teaspoons onion powder	**taste**
½ teaspoon salt	**Fresh parsley sprigs or chives**

1. Wash and trim asparagus spears, and steam until just tender.
2. Chop the asparagus into 1-inch pieces, and place in a blender or food processor. Add the milk, onion powder, salt, and mustard, and blend at high speed until smooth.
3. Pour the soup into a pot, and heat over medium heat. Do not boil.
4. Pour into serving bowls, grind some black pepper on top, and garnish with a couple of parsley sprigs.

6 servings. Serving size is about 1 cup.

Per serving: **1 g. fat**, 58 calories, 2 mg. cholesterol, 2 g. dietary fiber, 232 mg. sodium

"Before you go accepting a dinner invitation, remember their dollar stretcher gumbo with potato balls." DRAWING BY GEO. PRICE; © 1979 THE NEW YORKER MAGAZINE, INC.

Chunky Tomato Soup (Fat-Free)

PREPARATION TIME: 10 TO 15 MINUTES   COOKING TIME: 45 MINUTES

This is a spicy soup if you use the cumin. You may also prefer to reduce the amount of scallion, if you find it too strong.

1 cup scallion, minced
2 cloves garlic, crushed
¼ teaspoon cumin (optional)
Fresh-ground black pepper to taste

3 cans (28 ounces each) tomatoes, plus their juice
2 medium tomatoes, diced
2 tablespoons fresh parsley, minced

1. Sauté the scallion and garlic in a tablespoon of water in a large covered saucepan over medium heat, stirring occasionally. Add a little extra water if necessary to keep the ingredients from sticking.
2. Add the cumin and pepper, turn heat to low, and cover.
3. Drain the canned tomatoes and reserve the juice. In a blender or food processor, whir the canned tomatoes until smooth. Add tomatoes to the onion mixture, along with the reserved juice and the fresh tomatoes. Cover and let simmer over low heat for about 45 minutes.
4. Sprinkle with parsley and serve.

12 servings. Serving size is 1 cup.

Per serving: **no fat,** 48 calories, no cholesterol, 4 g. dietary fiber, 327 mg. sodium

Quick Clam Soup

PREPARATION TIME: 4 MINUTES   COOKING TIME: 10 MINUTES

2 cans (6½ ounces each) clams, with juice
2 cups low-sodium vegetable or chicken stock
1 bay leaf

½ teaspoon dried thyme
Salt and fresh-ground black pepper to taste
4 teaspoons chopped chives

1. Combine the clams with their juice, the stock, bay leaf, thyme, salt, and pepper in a saucepan, and heat through.
2. Pour into 4 serving bowls and top each with a teaspoon of chives.

4 servings. Serving size is 1 cup.

Per serving: **3 g. fat,** 96 calories, 46 mg. cholesterol, no dietary fiber, 607 mg. sodium

David's Chili

PREPARATION TIME: 35 MINUTES   COOKING TIME: 4½ HOURS

This is my son David's multi-bean chili. The beans-and-rice combination provides protein, boosted by the judicious use of a small amount of beef.

1 cup white beans
½ cup black beans
1½ quarts water
4 or 5 cloves garlic, minced or crushed
1 teaspoon salt
1 tablespoon olive oil
¼ cup uncooked brown rice
¼ cup lentils

1 cup water
2 medium onions, quartered
2 tablespoons chili powder
1 teaspoon crushed red pepper (optional)
½ pound extra-lean ground beef
1 can (10 ounces) tomato purée

1. Rinse the white and black beans. Place them in a 2½-quart saucepan with the 1½ quarts of water. Bring to a boil, then reduce heat to simmer.
2. Add the garlic, salt, and oil. Cover and simmer for about 2½ hours, stirring occasionally.
3. Add the rice and the lentils, along with the 1 cup of water. Bring to a boil again, then reduce the heat to simmer.
4. Add the onions, chili powder, and the red pepper if desired.
5. Cover and simmer for about 2 more hours, stirring occasionally, and adding extra water if necessary to keep the beans covered.
6. Meanwhile, brown the ground beef in a skillet. Drain off any excess fat, and stir in the tomato purée. Simmer for about 15 minutes.
7. When most of the water has cooked away from the beans, add the meat sauce, and mix well.

12 servings. Serving size is 1 cup.

Per serving: **4 g. fat,** 184 calories, 19 mg. cholesterol, 7 g. dietary fiber, 308 mg. sodium

French Onion Soup

PREPARATION TIME: 15 TO 20 MINUTES COOKING TIME: 30 MINUTES

One bowl of onion soup for dinner in a restaurant can tip the scales a couple of pounds higher in the morning. This is due to the large amount of salt usually found in these soups; the salt makes you retain water. Here's a recipe using no- or low-salt bouillon or homemade stock that eliminates some of the sodium without eliminating the soup. (The cognac helps make up for some of that lost salt flavor.)

2 medium onions, sliced in rounds
4 cups low-sodium beef stock
1 bay leaf
1 teaspoon dried basil
½ teaspoon dried thyme
½ teaspoon salt
½ teaspoon fresh-ground black pepper

Dash of cognac or dry sherry (optional)
4 slices Whole-Wheat French Bread (pp. 308–9)
4 slices low-fat Swiss cheese, ½ ounce each
2 tablespoons grated Parmesan or Romano cheese

1. Sauté the onions in a tablespoon of water until they are translucent, stirring occasionally. Add a little extra water if necessary to keep the onions from sticking.
2. Add the stock, seasonings, and the cognac if desired, and bring to a low boil. Reduce heat, and let simmer for 30 minutes.
3. Meanwhile, toast the bread on a foil-covered baking sheet under the broiler until crisp. Top each slice of bread with a slice of Swiss cheese, and broil for several minutes more, until cheese is melted. (Keep your eye on it!)
4. Place ½ tablespoon of grated Parmesan or Romano cheese in each of four soup bowls. Pour 1 cup of soup in each bowl, and float the bread slices on top.

4 servings. Serving size is 1½ cups.

Per serving: **5 g. fat**, 185 calories, 7 mg. cholesterol, 3 g. dietary fiber, 619 mg. sodium

Potato and Cheese Soup

PREPARATION TIME: 10 MINUTES   COOKING TIME: 45 MINUTES

Use low-fat Swiss or Jarlsberg Lite for this one.

2 cups low-sodium
  stock—vegetable, chicken,
  or beef
1½ cups water
1 bay leaf
½ teaspoon salt
Fresh-ground black pepper to
  taste
1 medium onion, diced
2 large potatoes, diced
2 stalks celery, diced

4 ounces fresh mushrooms,
  sliced
1 tablespoon butter or
  margarine
1 tablespoon skim milk
2 tablespoons whole-wheat
  flour
3 tablespoons fresh parsley,
  minced
4 ounces shredded low-fat
  cheese

1. Combine stock, water, bay leaf, salt, pepper, onions, potatoes, celery, and mushrooms in a large pot, and bring to a boil. Reduce heat, and let simmer covered for 30 minutes, or until potatoes are tender.
2. In a small saucepan, melt the butter or margarine over medium heat, add the skim milk, and stir in the flour. Stir constantly until golden brown, then add the mixture to the soup.
3. Raise the heat to medium high, and stir the soup until it bubbles and thickens. Sprinkle with parsley and cheese, and serve.

8 servings. Serving size is 1¼ cups.

Per serving: **3 g. fat**, 109 calories, 9 mg. cholesterol, 2 g. dietary fiber, 219 mg. sodium

Patti's Vegetable Soup

PREPARATION TIME: 30 MINUTES   COOKING TIME: 1 HOUR

1 tablespoon vegetable oil
4 medium white onions,
  peeled, halved, and sliced
3 leeks, trimmed, halved
  lengthwise, and sliced
4 medium carrots, sliced
2 small turnips, peeled,
  quartered, and sliced
4 stalks celery, sliced
5 large cloves garlic, minced
½ teaspoon dried thyme
¼ teaspoon dried tarragon

5 large potatoes, skins on,
  sliced
8 cups low-sodium chicken
  stock
1½ cups skim milk
¼ teaspoon nutmeg
Fresh-ground black pepper to
  taste
1 medium bunch endive
  lettuce, well rinsed, shredded
½ cup grated Parmesan cheese

1. Heat the oil in a large kettle over medium-high heat. Add the onions, leeks, carrots, turnips, celery, garlic, thyme, and tarragon, tossing to coat. Cover and cook vegetables, stirring occasionally, until they begin to soften, about 10 minutes.
2. Stir in the potatoes and the stock. Cover and bring to a boil, then simmer, partially covered, for 45 minutes, stirring occasionally.
3. With a slotted spoon, transfer half the vegetables to a food processor or blender, and purée until smooth. Return the purée to the kettle. If the soup seems thin, purée a few more vegetables.
4. Add the milk, the nutmeg, and a generous grinding of black pepper. Return the soup to a low boil. If soup seems too thick, add a little more stock.
5. Scatter the endive on the surface of the soup, cover, and simmer about 5 more minutes. Stir, and serve with 2 teaspoons of grated Parmesan sprinkled on top of each serving.

16 servings. Serving size is 1½ cups.

Per serving: **3 g. fat**, 149 calories, 3 mg. cholesterol, 3 g. dietary fiber, 271 mg. sodium

Barley Chicken Soup

PREPARATION TIME: 10 TO 15 MINUTES   COOKING TIME: 2½ HOURS

A complete meal in one pot. Omit the cayenne pepper and crushed red pepper if you don't like spicy food. You can also decrease or omit the salt if you are trying to cut down on your sodium intake.

6 chicken breasts, skinned
½ cup barley
2 quarts water
3 large carrots, cut in ¼-inch
   slices
1 large stalk celery, sliced
1 medium onion, diced

1 teaspoon salt
½ teaspoon thyme
¼ teaspoon cayenne pepper
   (optional)
⅛ teaspoon crushed red pepper
   (optional)

Combine all ingredients in a large soup kettle. Bring to a boil, then reduce heat and simmer for 2½ hours.

6 servings. Serving size is 2½ cups.

Per serving: **2 g. fat,** 212 calories, 68 mg. cholesterol, 5 g. dietary fiber, 466 mg. sodium

Cold Tomato Soup (Julian's)

PREPARATION TIME: 10 MINUTES   COOKING TIME: 45 MINUTES

This delicious soup was the first course of a full meal prepared by the chef at Julian's, in Nashville, that contained fewer than 600 calories for the whole meal. The main course was Grilled Duck Breast (p. 181), followed by the Crêpes with Fresh Strawberries (pp. 362–63) for dessert.

1 teaspoon unsalted butter
½ cup diced carrots
½ cup diced onions
1 clove garlic, minced
3 pounds fresh tomatoes

1 quart low-sodium chicken
   stock
1 tablespoon chopped fresh
   basil

1 tablespoon chopped fresh
  parsley

½ teaspoon black peppercorns
Pinch of thyme

1. Melt the butter in a large pot, add the carrots, onions, and garlic, and cook over low heat for 2 minutes. Add all the remaining ingredients, and bring to a boil. Simmer for 45 minutes.
2. Put the soup in a blender and purée. Cool, then chill in the refrigerator. Garnish with a leaf of fresh basil, if available, before serving.

8 servings. Serving size is 1 cup.

Per serving: **2 g. fat,** 91 calories, 2 mg. cholesterol, 6 g. dietary fiber, 60 mg. sodium

English Cucumber Soup

PREPARATION TIME: 10 TO 15 MINUTES   REFRIGERATION TIME: 4 HOURS

You may garnish this soup with a tablespoon per serving of either chopped hard-cooked egg, finely chopped scallions, chives, croutons (preferably whole grain), or avocado.

2 pounds cucumbers
3 cups low-sodium chicken
  stock
3 cups plain nonfat yogurt
3 tablespoons white wine
  vinegar

1 garlic clove
1 teaspoon salt
½ teaspoon white pepper (or
  black)

1. Wash but do not peel the cucumbers. Cut them into 1-inch chunks, and purée along with the remaining ingredients in a blender or food processor.
2. Refrigerate at least 4 hours.

8 servings. Serving size is 1¼ cups.

Per serving (without garnishes): **1 g. fat,** 64 calories, 1 mg. cholesterol, 1 g. dietary fiber, 343 mg. sodium

Gazpacho

PREPARATION TIME: 10 MINUTES   REFRIGERATION TIME: 24 HOURS

Serve this chilled soup in bowls with one of the following garnishes: chopped hard-boiled egg, finely chopped scallions, chives, croutons, or avocado (1 tablespoon per serving; the avocado will add more fat and calories than the other choices).

1 large tomato
½ small onion
½ medium cucumber
½ medium green pepper
1 celery stalk
2 teaspoons fresh parsley, finely chopped
2 cloves garlic, minced or crushed

2 cups tomato juice
3 tablespoons red wine vinegar
½ cup white wine
2 tablespoons dried basil
1 tablespoon lemon juice
1 teaspoon salt
½ teaspoon white pepper
1 teaspoon Worcestershire sauce
Dash of Tabasco sauce

Finely chop all vegetables. (A food processor is ideal for this.) Combine all remaining ingredients and refrigerate for 24 hours.

6 servings. Serving size is ¾ cup.

Per serving (without garnishes): **no fat,** 42 calories, no cholesterol, 2 g. dietary fiber, 658 mg. sodium

Minestrone

PREPARATION TIME: 25 MINUTES   COOKING TIME: 2 HOURS

You may use 2 teaspoons or more of Traditional Italian Herb Blend (p. 333) in place of the garlic, basil, salt, and pepper in this recipe. Another handy feature is that you don't have to soak the beans overnight before cooking, as there is plenty of cooking time in the recipe itself. Try it with our Italian Whole-Wheat Bread (pp. 306–9).

3 cups low-sodium chicken stock
3 cups water
½ cup uncooked navy beans
1 bay leaf
2 medium carrots, sliced
1 medium potato, diced
½ small head of cabbage, shredded
1 can (16 ounces) unsalted tomatoes
1 medium onion, diced
1 stalk celery, sliced

1 tablespoon olive oil
1 medium zucchini, cut into chunks
2 cloves garlic, minced or crushed
¾ teaspoon dried basil leaves
¼ teaspoon salt
¼ teaspoon fresh-ground black pepper
2 tablespoons fresh parsley, minced
½ cup whole-wheat macaroni, uncooked

1. In a 6-quart soup pot, combine the stock, water, navy beans, and bay leaf. Bring to a boil, then reduce heat and let simmer for 1 hour.
2. Add the carrots, potato, cabbage, and tomatoes, and let cook another 30 minutes.
3. Meanwhile, sauté the onions and celery in the oil over medium heat, until onions are translucent. Stir in the zucchini, garlic, and the other seasonings, including the parsley. Cover, and let sauté/steam until tender. Add this mixture to the beans, and let simmer together for about 15 to 20 minutes.
4. Add the macaroni, and cook until tender, about 10 minutes, adding more water if necessary.

10 servings. Serving size is 1½ cups.

Per serving: **2 g. fat**, 118 calories, no cholesterol, 5 g. dietary fiber, 103 mg. sodium

Split-Pea Soup with Vegetables

PREPARATION TIME: 15 MINUTES   COOKING TIME: 2 TO 2½ HOURS

Here is a basic recipe for meatless split-pea soup. Instead of the usual ham hock or other pork meat (and fat) that is customarily added to split-pea soup, we recommend adding to this recipe a couple of whole cloves, and/or about ¼ teaspoon of sage, and/or ¼ teaspoon of rosemary. We think these additional seasonings complement the taste of the peas best, though of course you can use any other herbs that you like.

This is delicious served with Breadsticks (p. 317).

1 pound dried split peas
Water or low-sodium vegetable
  stock
1½ cups celery, sliced into
  ½-inch pieces
1 cup carrots, sliced into
  ¼-inch pieces

3 medium red potatoes, cut
  into eighths
2 teaspoons salt
⅛ teaspoon fresh-ground black
  pepper

1. Rinse the peas and combine with 2½ quarts of water or stock. Bring to a boil, then reduce the heat and let simmer for 1 hour, stirring every 15 minutes.
2. Add 2 more cups of water, the celery, carrots, potatoes, salt, pepper, and other seasonings if desired. Return to a boil, then reduce heat again, and simmer another hour, stirring every 15 minutes. The soup is done when the peas are creamy, the vegetables are soft but hold their shape, and the soup is thick but not stiff. If necessary, add more water and simmer an additional 20 minutes.

8 servings as a main course. Serving size is 2 cups.

Per serving: **1 g. fat**, 256 calories, no cholesterol, 10 g. dietary fiber, 322 mg. sodium

Vichyssoise

PREPARATION TIME: 30 MINUTES   COOKING TIME: 30 MINUTES

Again, yogurt and low-fat milk come to the rescue. Vichyssoise is a traditional French delicacy, heavy on the heavy cream. Here's our low-fat version to be served hot or cold.

2 medium potatoes
1 pound leeks
1 tablespoon butter or margarine
2½ cups low-sodium chicken or vegetable stock

3 cups 1% milk
1 cup plain nonfat yogurt
Fresh-ground black pepper to taste
2 tablespoons chives

1. Scrub the potatoes and dice them finely. Wash and trim the leeks, and dice them finely.
2. Melt the butter in a large saucepan or pot over medium heat. Add the potatoes and leeks, and turn the heat to low. Cover and let sauté/steam for about 10 minutes, stirring often. You may wish to add a little bit of the stock to keep the vegetables from sticking.
3. Pour in the stock, and bring to a boil. Add the milk, and reduce the heat to medium low. When milk is heated through, cover and reduce the heat to low. Let simmer for about 30 minutes, then set aside to cool for another 30 minutes.
4. Pour the soup in a blender or food processor, and add the yogurt and pepper. Blend until smooth. Chill for several hours in the refrigerator, or serve hot, sprinkled with a teaspoon of chopped chives per serving.

6 servings. Serving size is 1¾ cups.

Per serving: **4 g. fat**, 198 calories, 11 mg. cholesterol, 3 g. dietary fiber, 161 mg. sodium

Navy Bean Soup

PREPARATION TIME: 15 MINUTES   COOKING TIME: 2 HOURS

Another hearty soup to warm you up in chilly weather.

2 cups navy beans
6 cups water
2 lean soup bones
½ cup chopped leeks or
   scallions
1 large clove garlic, crushed
¼ cup green pepper, diced
2 stalks celery, diced

1½ cups carrots, sliced
4 ounces mushrooms, sliced
1 teaspoon chili powder
1 teaspoon salt
½ teaspoon fresh-ground black
   pepper
¼ teaspoon cumin
1 bay leaf

1. Soak the beans overnight in the water.
2. The next day, add all the other ingredients, and bring to
   a boil. Reduce heat to simmer, cover, and let cook for 2
   hours, or until the beans are tender.

8 servings. Serving size is 1 ¼ cups.

Per serving: **1 g. fat,** 181 calories, no cholesterol, 12 g. dietary
fiber, 311 mg. sodium

Spinach Egg-Drop Soup

PREPARATION TIME: 10 MINUTES   COOKING TIME: 10 MINUTES

6 cups low-sodium chicken
   stock
1 package (10 ounces) frozen
   spinach
1 tablespoon sesame seeds,
   ground with mortar and
   pestle
1 tablespoon chives

2 eggs, lightly beaten
1 teaspoon Traditional Italian
   Herb Blend (p. 333)
Dash ginger
¼ teaspoon salt
¼ teaspoon fresh-ground black
   pepper

1. Bring the stock to a boil in a large kettle. Add the spinach
   and bring back to a boil.
2. Reduce heat, and let simmer until spinach is cooked.

3. Stir in the sesame seeds and chives, and bring to a boil again. Remove the pot from the heat, and slowly pour the beaten eggs in, stirring slightly. Add the seasonings, and serve.

8 servings. Serving size is 1 cup.

Per serving: **3 g. fat**, 63 calories, 53 mg. cholesterol, 1 g. dietary fiber, 200 mg. sodium

Meatless Chili ✓

PREPARATION TIME: 10 MINUTES   COOKING TIME: 2½ HOURS

You can boost the protein in this chili by topping each serving with an ounce of reduced-fat cheese.

2 cups dried pinto beans
Water
2 medium onions, quartered
2 large cloves garlic, minced
1 can (15 ounces) kidney beans,
   drained

1 can (6 ounces) tomato sauce
2 tablespoons chili powder
1 tablespoon ground cumin
1 teaspoon salt

1. Wash and sort the pinto beans. Cover them with water, and soak overnight.
2. The next day, pour off the water from the beans. Pour in fresh water, covering the beans with 2 inches of water. Bring to a boil. Add the onions and garlic. Reduce the heat, and simmer for 1 hour.
3. Add the drained kidney beans, tomato sauce, and seasonings. Simmer for another 1½ hours. Stir occasionally, adding a little more water as necessary to keep the beans covered. Let cook until the beans start to break down and form a gravy with the water. Adjust seasonings to taste.

6 servings as a main course. Serving size is 1½ cups.

Per serving: **1 g. fat**, 321 calories, no cholesterol, 20 g. dietary fiber, 541 mg. sodium

New England Clam Chowder

PREPARATION TIME: 15 MINUTES   COOKING TIME: 20 TO 25 MINUTES

This is a traditional favorite that substitutes skim milk for dairy products that contain more calories and have a higher fat content. The wine adds a flavorful flair and helps reduce the need for salt. For a thicker chowder, use the cornstarch.

2 cans (6½ ounces each) minced clams, with liquid
1 tablespoon cornstarch (optional)
1½ cups skim milk
½ cup white wine
1 small potato, diced

4 ounces fresh mushrooms, sliced
1 medium onion, diced
1 teaspoon oregano
½ teaspoon salt
¼ teaspoon fresh-ground black pepper

1. Pour the clams and their liquid into a large saucepan or kettle. If using the cornstarch, mix it with 1 cup of the milk in a small bowl or measuring cup. Reserve.
2. Add the other ½ cup of the milk to the clams, and begin heating over medium heat. Do not boil.
3. When the clam mixture is hot, stir in the cornstarch mixture, or the plain milk if you're not using cornstarch.
4. Add the remaining ingredients, stirring well. Cover and cook, stirring occasionally, over medium to medium-low heat until the potatoes are tender and the soup is hot, but never boiling.

4 servings. Serving size is 1¼ cups.

Per serving: **1 g. fat,** 162 calories, 32 mg. cholesterol, 1 g. dietary fiber, 455 mg. sodium

Manhattan Clam Chowder

PREPARATION TIME: 20 MINUTES   COOKING TIME: 20 MINUTES

1 tablespoon vegetable oil
1 medium onion, diced
½ medium bell pepper, diced
1 stalk celery, diced
1 large clove garlic, minced or
crushed
2 cans (16 ounces each)
tomatoes, undrained
2 cans (6½ ounces each)
minced clams, undrained

1 bay leaf
3 medium potatoes, diced,
skins on
4 cups water
½ teaspoon salt
½ teaspoon fresh-ground black
pepper
¼ teaspoon thyme

1. Heat the oil in a large soup pot over medium heat. Add the onion, bell pepper, celery, and garlic, and stir well. Cover and reduce the heat to medium low. Sauté until onions are translucent, stirring occasionally. Add a little water if necessary to prevent sticking.
2. Meanwhile, whir the tomatoes in a blender or food processor. When onions are ready, add to the onion mixture the tomatoes, the clams plus their liquid, and the remaining ingredients.
3. Bring to a boil. Reduce heat, cover, and simmer for about 20 minutes, or until potatoes are tender.

12 servings. Serving size is 1¼ cups.

Per serving: **2 g. fat,** 88 calories, 10 mg. cholesterol, 2 g. dietary fiber, 269 mg. sodium

Salads

In America, salads are traditionally eaten before the meal, while in Europe they are served after the main courses and before the dessert to clear the palate and aid the digestion.

Salads as full meals, or on the side as appetizers, can be among the most attractive dishes on your table. We enjoy seeing the contrasting colors of the various vegetables, grains, legumes, cheeses, or meats we toss into a salad, sprinkled with an array of herbs, and glistening with our favorite dressing.

Our recipes vary from the everyday dinner salad to the more exotic Middle Eastern tabbouli, which uses bulgur wheat as its base. We include a couple of Greek-style salads, one using lettuce and one with black-eyed peas. There are more; some originate from other countries, and some from our imaginations.

Nutritionists recommend that approximately half the vegetables you eat each day should be raw. Eating vegetables uncooked preserves both bulk and nutrient content. Using cut-up raw vegetables (carrots, celery, radishes, summer squash) with meals and as snacks is highly recommended for weight management. We hope the suggestions we give you will prompt you to increase your consumption of vegetables, both cooked and raw, and to create some of your own salads to make it interesting.

Artichoke-Spinach Salad

PREPARATION TIME: 12 TO 15 MINUTES

Jícama is a Mexican vegetable, similar to a turnip, which can be served raw or cooked. You can usually find it in the produce section of better-stocked supermarkets.

¾ pound fresh spinach
4 ounces jícama or radishes
½ medium red onion, sliced

1 can (14 ounces) artichokes,
drained

1. Wash carefully and trim the spinach, and tear the leaves into bite-sized pieces. Wash, trim, and slice the jícama.
2. Toss all ingredients in a salad bowl, and serve with your favorite low-fat dressing.

4 servings. Serving size is about 2 cups.

Per Serving: **1 g. fat,** 68 calories, no cholesterol, 7 g. dietary fiber, 116 mg. sodium

"You know? . . . I think I'd like a salad." *BEYOND THE FAR SIDE.*
© 1986 UNIVERSAL PRESS SYNDICATE. REPRINTED WITH
PERMISSION. ALL RIGHTS RESERVED.

Apple-Carrot Salad

PREPARATION TIME: 10 MINUTES

A delicious variation on the usual carrot-raisin salad.

2 medium apples, diced
1½ cups carrots, grated
⅓ cup raisins

¼ cup chopped walnuts
½ cup plain nonfat yogurt
1 tablespoon honey

1. Combine apples, carrots, raisins, and walnuts.
2. Blend the yogurt with the honey and pour over the other ingredients, mixing thoroughly.

8 servings. Serving size is about ½ cup.

Per serving: **2 g. fat,** 87 calories, no cholesterol, 2 g. dietary fiber, 26 mg. sodium

Garbanzo Salad

PREPARATION TIME: 10 MINUTES   REFRIGERATION TIME: 3 TO 4 HOURS

2 cups garbanzo beans
  (chickpeas), cooked
1 medium onion, diced
½ medium red bell pepper,
  diced
2 medium tomatoes, diced

1 tablespoon olive oil
½ teaspoon fresh-ground black
  pepper
¼ teaspoon salt
Herb and Onion Dressing
  (p. 103)

Combine all ingredients in a large bowl, and refrigerate for several hours before serving.

8 servings. Serving size is about ¾ cup.

Per serving: **3 g. fat,** 95 calories, no cholesterol, 3 g. dietary fiber, 73 mg. sodium

Chef's Salad

PREPARATION TIME: 8 TO 10 MINUTES

The fat content of this salad will range between 5 and 15 grams, with total calories between 250 and 350, depending on whether you include the egg, and how much dressing you use.

¼ head of your favorite lettuce, shredded
1 medium tomato, quartered
1 slice (ring) of green pepper
¼ cup red cabbage, shredded
¼ cup shaved carrots
Choice of fresh cut-up raw vegetables
1 ounce Jarlsberg Lite cheese, cut in narrow strips

1 ounce white meat of turkey or chicken, cut in strips
1 hard-boiled egg, quartered (optional)
Several large leaves of romaine lettuce
Herb Salt (pp. 332–33)
Fresh-ground black pepper
Your favorite low-cal dressing

Arrange your vegetables, cheese, and meat attractively on the romaine, and sprinkle with seasonings to taste. We use about 1 tablespoon of dressing.

1 serving. Serving size is about 2 cups.

Per serving (with egg): **9 g. fat,** 269 calories, 248 mg. cholesterol, 4 g. dietary fiber, 766 mg. sodium

Creative Fruit Salad

PREPARATION TIME: 5 MINUTES

This is called *Creative Fruit Salad* because you can create a different salad every time you make it, using whatever fruits, spices, or nuts you have on hand. Cut the fruit into chunks, and sprinkle with lemon juice to keep the fruit looking fresh and to add a bit of tang. Then, for every 2 cups of fresh fruit, add 1 tablespoon of any one of the following:

Grated coconut
Raisins or chopped dates

Chopped unsalted nuts of any kind

Then add a sprinkle of any of the following spices:

Cinnamon
Nutmeg
Allspice

Ginger
Anise
Cardamom

A main-course serving is 2 cups of any combination of fresh fruit, plus the tablespoon of nuts or raisins. The spices, of course, add few or no calories.

Average serving: 3 g. fat, 205 calories, no cholesterol, 7 g. dietary fiber, 8 mg. sodium (no fat without coconut or nuts)

Cucumber-Radish Salad

PREPARATION TIME: 12 MINUTES

½ large cucumber
12 radishes
¼ large red onion, thinly sliced
4 ounces Jarlsberg Lite or reduced-fat Swiss cheese, grated
¼ cup fresh parsley, minced

1 tablespoon red wine vinegar
1 tablespoon Dijon or spicy brown mustard
⅓ cup plain nonfat yogurt
1 tablespoon light mayonnaise
2 teaspoons dried basil
⅛ teaspoon celery seed

1. Scrub cucumber clean, removing waxy substance if necessary; it is preferable not to peel it. Slice the cucumber as

thinly as possible. Clean, trim, and slice the radishes as thinly as possible.

2. Combine the cucumbers, radishes, and onion in a bowl, along with the cheese.
3. Add the remaining ingredients, tossing lightly. Serve chilled.

4 servings. Serving size is about 1 cup.

Per serving: **3 g. fat,** 87 calories, 11 mg. cholesterol, 1 g. dietary fiber, 164 mg. sodium

Dinner Salad

PREPARATION TIME: 10 MINUTES

Since salads are usually a mainstay for most persons interested in managing their weight, people often ask what constitutes a "dinner salad." Actually, you can eat unlimited quantities of almost any vegetable, so you can feel free to create your own dinner salad, but generally we tell people a dinner salad is what you would normally get along with a meal in a typical restaurant—asking for your dressing on the side, of course.

The basic dinner salad is as follows.

Lettuce or greens
½ carrot, thinly sliced
1 stalk celery, thinly sliced, OR
    ¼ green pepper, diced
¼ cup shredded red cabbage
    OR 4 sliced mushrooms
2 thin slices sweet red onion

Arrange all ingredients in a bowl or on a plate. Add your favorite no- or low-fat dressing (see pp. 102, 108) and flavor with Herb Salt (pp. 332–33) or other seasonings if you like.

1 serving. Serving size is about 1½ cups.

Per serving (without dressing): **no fat,** 44 calories, no cholesterol, 4 g. dietary fiber, 46 mg. sodium

Greek Black-Eyed Pea Salad

PREPARATION TIME: 6 MINUTES   REFRIGERATION TIME: 6 TO 8 HOURS

3 cups black-eyed peas, cooked
½ cup bell pepper, diced (red or yellow is attractive)
½ cup scallions, diced
1 small clove garlic, crushed
½ teaspoon dried oregano

3 tablespoons olive oil
4 tablespoons red wine vinegar
1 teaspoon lemon juice
2 tablespoons fresh parsley, minced
¼ teaspoon salt

Combine all ingredients in a large bowl. Marinate 6 to 8 hours in the refrigerator, stirring occasionally.

8 servings. Serving size is about ½ cup.

Per serving: **5 g. fat,** 111 calories, no cholesterol, 5 g. dietary fiber, 71 mg. sodium

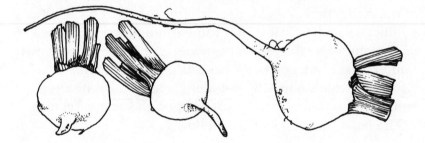

Peas, Beets, and Water Chestnuts

PREPARATION TIME: 5 MINUTES   REFRIGERATION TIME: 1 HOUR

1 can (8 ounces) baby peas, drained
1 can (8 ounces) beets, drained and diced
1 can (2½ ounces) water chestnuts, drained
2 tablespoons plain nonfat yogurt

2 tablespoons light mayonnaise
¼ tablespoon tarragon
⅛ teaspoon dillweed
¼ teaspoon (or less) salt
Fresh-ground black pepper to taste
Dash garlic powder

Combine all ingredients in a large bowl. Chill for 1 hour, and serve on lettuce leaves.

6 servings. Serving size is about ½ cup.

Per serving: **1 g. fat,** 59 calories, 1 mg. cholesterol, 2 g. dietary fiber, 305 mg. sodium

Fennel Salad with Pecans

PREPARATION TIME: 10 MINUTES

If you like licorice, you will love fennel. Raw fennel smells and tastes strongly of licorice when served alone. However, diced and added to a salad, it blends delectably, adding a touch of sweetness to a vinaigrette dressing (along with a healthy dose of potassium and vitamin A).

Look for firm fennel bulbs in the produce section of your supermarket. Test the bulbs with your thumb for firmness.

½ **head Boston or Bibb lettuce**
½ **head radicchio, escarole, or other lettuce**
½ **medium fennel bulb**
2 **tablespoons pecan pieces**
3 **tablespoons red wine vinegar**
2 **tablespoons vegetable oil**
1 **tablespoon water**

1 **teaspoon mustard seed, ground with mortar and pestle**
¼ **teaspoon dried tarragon**
¼ **teaspoon salt**
¼ **teaspoon fresh-ground black pepper**

1. Wash and dry the lettuce. Tear the leaves into bite-size pieces, and place in a large salad bowl.
2. Trim the tough outer leaves of the fennel. Wash and core the bulb. Dice, and add to the bowl. Add the pecans.
3. Combine the remaining ingredients in a jar. Cover and shake, then pour into the salad. Toss and serve.

4 servings. Serving size is about 1 ½ cups.

Per serving: **9 g. fat,** 105 calories, no cholesterol, 2 g. dietary fiber, 152 mg. sodium

Oriental Spinach-Sesame Salad

PREPARATION TIME: 12 MINUTES

This salad is good served chilled or at room temperature. It is at its best served the same day it is made. See pages 235–36 for instructions on how to toast seeds.

Water (about ¼ cup)
1½ pounds fresh spinach, washed thoroughly and trimmed
1 tablespoon honey

2 tablespoons tamari sauce or soy sauce
3 tablespoons toasted sesame seeds, ground with mortar and pestle

1. Bring the water to a boil in a saucepan, toss in the spinach, cover, and cook about 30 *seconds,* until wilted.
2. Drain the spinach (reserve the liquid for other recipes, such as a soup, if you like) and rinse it in a colander in cold water. Drain well, and transfer to a serving bowl.
3. In a small bowl, combine the honey, tamari sauce, and sesame seeds. Pour this dressing over the spinach, toss, and serve.

4 servings. Serving size is about 1 cup.

Per serving: **4 g. fat**, 97 calories, no cholesterol, 5 g. dietary fiber, 540 mg. sodium

Elegant Asparagus

PREPARATION TIME: 5 MINUTES

This recipe is delicious with fresh, very lightly steamed asparagus. However, the canned variety works well too. You can substitute green asparagus, of course, but the white is more elegant—and more expensive.

1 can (15 ounces) white (or green) asparagus
2 tablespoons vegetable oil
1 tablespoon red wine vinegar
1 large clove garlic, minced or crushed

¼ teaspoon salt
⅛ teaspoon fresh-ground black pepper
½ teaspoon Dijon mustard
¼ teaspoon thyme
¼ teaspoon dried parsley

1. Chill the asparagus.
2. Combine the remaining ingredients, cover, and chill.
3. To serve, place the asparagus on 4 salad plates. Spoon some dressing over each serving, dividing it up equally.

VARIATIONS: Try this with any of your favorite no- or low-fat dressings. Terri especially likes the Fennel Dressing (p. 103). You might also try sprinkling one-quarter of a diced, hard-boiled egg across each serving, and/or add a teaspoon of chopped nuts, such as walnuts, pecans, or almonds, or sunflower or sesame seeds.

4 servings. Serving size is about 1 cup.

Per serving: **7 g. fat,** 76 calories, no cholesterol, 1 g. dietary fiber, 512 mg. sodium

Vegetable Slaw

PREPARATION TIME: 10 MINUTES   REFRIGERATION TIME: 1/2 HOUR

The onion and garlic can be pulverized in a food processor with the lemon juice, mayonnaise, yogurt, and salt, if desired. A food processor is wonderful for grating vegetables!

½ small onion, grated
1 clove garlic, grated
Juice of 1 lemon (about 2 tablespoons)
4 tablespoons light mayonnaise
½ cup plain nonfat yogurt
½ to ¾ teaspoon salt
Fresh-ground black pepper to taste
1 small head cabbage, grated
1 large carrot, grated
1 medium bell pepper, grated

Combine all ingredients and mix well. Refrigerate for at least a half hour. Mix well before serving.

6 servings. Serving size is about 1½ cups.

Per serving: **3 g. fat,** 86 calories, 3 mg. cholesterol, 3 g. dietary fiber, 277 mg. sodium

Potato-Vegetable Salad

PREPARATION TIME: 20 TO 25 MINUTES   REFRIGERATION TIME: 1 HOUR

Simply the best potato salad we have ever tasted! Thanks to my wife, Enid, for coming up with this low-fat, low-calorie version of an all-time American favorite.

6 medium potatoes, boiled and
    cubed
3 hard-boiled eggs, diced
½ small onion, grated
2 medium carrots, diced
1 medium bell pepper, diced
2 stalks celery, sliced thin
1 cup plain nonfat yogurt

¼ cup light mayonnaise
¼ teaspoon garlic powder
Fresh-ground black pepper to
    taste
1 teaspoon tarragon
1 tablespoon Dijon mustard
1 teaspoon salt

Combine all ingredients, chill for at least an hour, and serve.

12 servings. Serving size is about ¾ cup.

Per serving: **2 g. fat,** 111 calories, 48 mg. cholesterol, 2 g. dietary fiber, 249 mg. sodium

Greek Salad

PREPARATION TIME: 8 MINUTES

4 ounces feta cheese
20 cherry tomatoes OR 2
    medium tomatoes, sliced
1 large bell pepper, thinly
    sliced
1 medium onion, thinly sliced
1 teaspoon dried oregano

1 clove garlic, minced or
    crushed
Lettuce
Fennel Dressing (p. 103)
16 Greek olives (or use regular
    black olives)

1. One hour before preparation time, cut the feta cheese into chunks and soak in cold water for 1 hour to reduce salt content.

2. Cut the cherry tomatoes in half, or slice the regular tomatoes into wedges. Combine the tomato, pepper, onion, oregano, and garlic. Drain the feta cheese, pat dry with paper towels, and toss with the vegetables.
3. Divide into 8 servings, place on lettuce leaves, and garnish with 1 tablespoon of Fennel Dressing and 2 olives per serving.

8 servings. Serving size is about ¾ cup on two large lettuce leaves.

Per serving: **4 g. fat,** 68 calories, 13 mg. cholesterol, 1 g. dietary fiber, 207 mg. sodium

Marinated Broccoli and Cauliflower

PREPARATION TIME: 15 TO 20 MINUTES   REFRIGERATION TIME: 2 HOURS

2 tablespoons olive oil
2 tablespoons red wine vinegar
1 cup water
2 cloves garlic, crushed
½ teaspoon fresh-ground black pepper
1 bay leaf
1 teaspoon dried basil
¼ teaspoon salt

½ medium cauliflower, cut into flowerets
3 medium stalks broccoli, cut into flowerets
1 medium red onion, chopped
½ teaspoon oregano
Fresh parsley
8 cherry tomatoes

1. Combine all the ingredients except the oregano, parsley, and tomatoes in a large saucepan. Bring to a slight boil, reduce heat, and simmer, covered, until broccoli and cauliflower are cooked *al dente*—just barely tender; about 5 to 7 minutes.
2. Chill 2 hours, then garnish each serving with a sprinkle of oregano, parsley sprigs, and 2 tomatoes.

4 servings. Serving size is about 1½ cups.

Per serving: **7 g. fat,** 106 calories, no cholesterol, 4 g. dietary fiber, 168 mg. sodium

Japanese-Style Crab Salad

PREPARATION TIME: 12 MINUTES

Slicing cucumbers *very* thin is easy with a special low-cost gadget made only for that purpose. Inquire at your local cookware shop for such a slicer. As for the "light soy sauce" and the rice-wine vinegar, they can be found in Oriental markets and in many supermarkets. They have a unique, delicate flavor, but if you wish to substitute, you may: Use tamari sauce or regular or low-sodium soy sauce for the soy sauce, and white vinegar for the rice-wine vinegar.

2 medium cucumbers, unpeeled, sliced thin
1 package (6 ounces) frozen crab, thawed, OR 1 can (6½ ounces) crab

1 teaspoon peanut oil
1 tablespoon sesame seeds
3 tablespoons light soy sauce or tamari sauce
2 tablespoons rice-wine vinegar

1. Drain the sliced cucumbers well; also drain the crab.
2. Heat a small skillet over medium-low heat, and brush with the oil. Add the sesame seeds and toast, stirring constantly, until lightly browned, then grind with mortar and pestle.
3. Lightly toss all ingredients together in a bowl and serve.

6 servings. Serving size is about ½ cup.

Per serving: **2 g. fat**, 64 calories, 28 mg. cholesterol, 1 g. dietary fiber, 509 mg. sodium

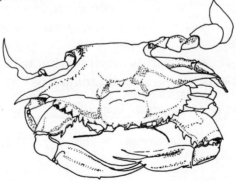

Red Bean and Pasta Salad

PREPARATION TIME: 10 MINUTES   COOKING TIME: 1 HOUR

All you have to do is look at the restaurant salad bars to know that pasta salads are "in." The problem with most pasta salads, when it comes to weight control, is not the pasta, but the dressings that are used. If you use our Italian Dressing or the oil and vinegar dressing, in the amount we suggest, you will be adding very few fat calories to this salad. If you find that the flavor is too mild, use additional seasoning (such as Herb Salt, or a commercial no- or low-salt seasoning) at the table, or add another splash of vinegar.

½ pound dried red beans
½ pound pasta
1 package (10½ ounces) frozen peas, defrosted in time for mixing
6 tablespoons Italian Dressing (p. 108) or Basic Low-Fat Dressing (p. 102)

1 tablespoon lemon juice
1 teaspoon Traditional Italian Herb Blend (p. 333)
Dash of salt
Fresh-ground black pepper to taste
Fresh parsley for garnish

1. Soak beans overnight, cook for about 1 hour or until just tender, and drain.
2. Cook pasta, drain, and cool in cold water.
3. Mix beans, pasta, and peas with dressing in large bowl, and add lemon juice, Herb Blend, salt, and pepper.
4. Serve garnished with parsley.

12 servings. Serving size is about ½ cup.

Per serving: **1 g. fat**, 163 calories, no cholesterol, 7 g. dietary fiber, 124 mg. sodium

Tabbouli

PREPARATION TIME: 10 MINUTES

There are almost as many versions of this traditional Middle Eastern recipe as there are cooks. Some people like to add tomato, fresh mint leaves, or other ingredients. This is how Terri usually makes it.

The salad:
2 cups bulgur wheat
Water
¾ cup shredded or finely chopped carrots
¾ cup shredded or finely chopped cucumber
½ cup minced fresh parsley

The dressing:
¼ cup safflower oil
¼ cup red wine vinegar
¼ cup tamari or soy sauce
2 tablespoons lemon juice
3 or 4 garlic cloves, crushed

1. Soak the bulgur wheat in a bowl in enough water to cover for 3 to 4 hours. The wheat will soak up the water and become puffy and chewable.
2. In the meantime, combine all dressing ingredients and set aside. Chop the vegetables as directed.
3. When the bulgur is ready, add the vegetables, mixing well, then add the dressing. Toss and serve.

6 servings as a main course. Serving size is about 1¼ cups.

Per serving: **10 g. fat**, 265 calories, no cholesterol, 10 g. dietary fiber, 557 mg. sodium

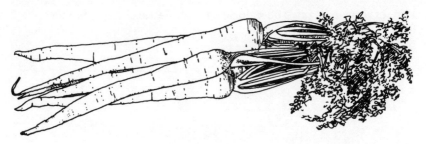

Vegetable-Cheese Salad with Herb Dressing

PREPARATION TIME: 15 TO 20 MINUTES   REFRIGERATION TIME:
                                        ½ HOUR

Combine two or more of your favorite low-fat or part-skim cheeses, such as cheddar, Swiss, or mozzarella. Try this with Patti's Vegetable Soup (p. 73). She did!

3 cups low-fat cheese, cut in
   julienne strips
1 medium cucumber, diced
1 medium tomato, diced
1 medium bell pepper, diced
1 scallion, minced
⅓ cup fresh parsley, chopped
Juice of 1 medium lime
Juice of 1 medium lemon

2 tablespoons light mayonnaise
½ cup plain nonfat yogurt
1 teaspoon Dijon mustard
½ teaspoon horseradish
½ teaspoon dillweed
½ teaspoon tarragon
½ teaspoon marjoram
½ teaspoon dried basil
1 teaspoon paprika

1. Combine cheese, vegetables, and parsley in a large bowl.
2. In another bowl, blend together the remaining ingredients to make the dressing.
3. Pour the dressing over the cheese and vegetables, chill for about a half hour, and serve.

8 servings as a main course. Serving size is about 1 cup.

Per serving: **8 g. fat,** 141 calories, 26 mg. cholesterol, 1 g. dietary fiber, 241 mg. sodium

Dressings

A good dressing is a blessing. Here's why.

As we said in our introduction to salads, most nutritionists agree that a good percentage of our vegetables, **perhaps even 50 percent,** should be eaten raw. Although many vegetables taste very good raw and without adornment, most of us prefer salad vegetables with some kind of dressing. Plain lemon juice or plain vinegar can take you only so far!

So, we place a major emphasis in this cookbook on salad dressings. Ours are generally relatively low in fat, but not all. Being fans of bleu cheese dressing, we struck a compromise in order to include one here. We have experimented with the use of yogurt, together with higher-calorie ingredients, such as mayonnaise, looking for blends that considerably reduce the fat calories below those contained in mayonnaise alone.

We feel that olive oil is the best oil for salads. Fortunately, olive oil may be pretty good for you in reasonable amounts. Olive oil, as well as peanut oil, is primarily monounsaturated, and oils of this kind may have a cholesterol-reducing effect. We blend olive oil with vinegars of various kinds and water, and add herbs and spices, of course. For the most part, we aim for a low-fat dressing, which averages around 4 grams of fat and 30–40 calories per tablespoon.

We use wine vinegar most often in our salads, but if you can find some of the fruit vinegars, especially the strawberry and raspberry flavors, give them a try. They are not as popular as they were a few years ago, but some salads, such as a spinach salad, are especially good with fruit vinegars, as are the more delicate varieties of lettuce, such as Bibb and Boston.

You can make your own herb vinegars at home by heating vinegar and bottling it with a wide assortment of herbs. However, our No-Fat Salad Dressing (page 108) illustrates an easy herb vinegar that requires no heating, bottling, or straining.

Mustard-Seed Dressing

PREPARATION TIME: 5 MINUTES

In ancient times, people apparently ate mustard seeds whole, especially as a condiment to meats, without any grinding, combining, cooking, or diluting whatsoever. We sometimes add whole mustard seeds to this dressing; they provide a pleasant burst of flavor that is not as strong as you might think. However, for the less adventurous, we suggest grinding them first, which distributes the flavor throughout the dressing.

¼ cup olive oil	½ teaspoon oregano
¼ cup red wine vinegar	½ teaspoon basil
¼ cup water	¼ teaspoon dillweed
2 large cloves garlic, crushed	Salt and fresh-ground black
1 teaspoon whole mustard seeds	pepper to taste
1 teaspoon thyme	Dash tamari sauce or soy sauce

Grind the mustard seeds with a mortar and pestle if you desire, and then blend all ingredients together. Store in the refrigerator.

Makes about ¾ cup. Serving size is 1 tablespoon.

Per serving: **5 g. fat,** 42 calories, no cholesterol, no dietary fiber, 48 mg. sodium

Basic Low-Fat Dressing

PREPARATION TIME: 5 MINUTES

To create a basic low-fat, low-calorie dressing, one with about 35 calories per tablespoon, mix equal parts olive oil, vinegar, and water. Then you can begin to get creative! You can make an Italian-style dressing by crushing a small amount of garlic and onion and adding the juice—or by using onion and garlic powder—plus Italian herbs (see our Traditional Italian Herb Blend, p. 333).

If you want to get a feel for the individuality of your herbs, you might try using only one at a time, such as tarragon (as we do here) or basil or oregano. We add a modest amount of salt, as in the recipe below, to help bring out the flavors of the other ingredients, as well as freshly ground black pepper. A tangier dressing is obtained by adding a teaspoon of Dijon mustard, and it gets tangier still with a teaspoon of dry mustard! A dash of cayenne pepper also seems to have a stimulating effect on the other flavorings in the dressing, and we almost always finish our blend with a dash of cayenne or Tabasco.

⅓ cup fine olive oil
⅓ cup water
⅓ cup wine vinegar or fruit
   vinegar
2 cloves garlic, crushed

½ teaspoon salt
1 teaspoon dried tarragon
Fresh-ground black pepper to
   taste

Blend by shaking in a jar and let stand for several hours before using. Shake before using. This will keep for several weeks in the refrigerator, but it won't last nearly that long, because you'll want to eat it! If the oil solidifies in the refrigerator, let the jar sit on the counter to warm before serving or briefly run the jar under lukewarm water.

Makes about 1 cup. Serving size is 1 tablespoon.

Per Serving: **4 g. fat,** 41 calories, no cholesterol, no dietary fiber, 71 mg. sodium

Fennel Dressing

PREPARATION TIME: 5 MINUTES

½ cup water
½ cup olive oil
½ cup red wine vinegar
2 tablespoons lemon juice
2 teaspoons fennel seed,
  ground with mortar and
  pestle

1 teaspoon mustard seed,
  ground with mortar and
  pestle
¼ cup fresh parsley, minced
¼ teaspoon salt
½ teaspoon fresh-ground black
  pepper

Combine all ingredients in a medium-size bowl and store in a jar in the refrigerator.

Makes about 2 cups. Serving size is 1 tablespoon.

Per serving: **3 g. fat,** 31 calories, no cholesterol, no dietary fiber, 17 mg. sodium

Herb and Onion Dressing ✓

PREPARATION TIME: 5 MINUTES

This makes a light, tart dressing that goes equally well with a salad of your favorite greens and vegetables or over a fruit dish.

2 scallions, diced (bulbs and
  green stems)
¼ cup fresh parsley
½ cup plain nonfat yogurt

1 tablespoon light mayonnaise
1 clove garlic, crushed
3 tablespoons red wine vinegar
¼ teaspoon salt

Blend all ingredients in blender or food processor. Store in the refrigerator in an airtight container.

Makes about ¾ cup. Serving size is 2 tablespoons.

Per serving: **1 g. fat,** 21 calories, 1 mg. cholesterol, no dietary fiber, 120 mg. sodium

Red Wine–Bleu Cheese Dressing

PREPARATION TIME: 7 MINUTES   REFRIGERATION TIME: 12 HOURS

It is not possible to make a truly low-fat, low-sodium bleu cheese dressing since bleu cheese is a high-fat, high-sodium cheese. This is our compromise, achieved by using yogurt, rather than sour cream, and light mayonnaise. Bleu cheese dressing, however, cannot be recommended for everyday use except in very small quantities.

¼ cup crumbled bleu cheese
1 clove garlic, crushed
¼ teaspoon salt
¼ teaspoon fresh-ground black
   pepper
1 scallion, minced

3 tablespoons plain nonfat
   yogurt
1 teaspoon light mayonnaise
1 teaspoon red wine
1 teaspoon fresh parsley,
   minced

Combine all ingredients in a small bowl. Chill overnight and serve cold.

Makes about ½ cup. Serving size is 2 tablespoons.

Per serving: **3 g. fat,** 43 calories, 7 mg. cholesterol, no dietary fiber, 267 mg. sodium

THE FAR SIDE. COURTESY CHRONICLE FEATURES, SAN FRANCISCO.

Cottage-Cheese Dressing

PREPARATION TIME: 5 MINUTES

This popular kind of dressing is excellent with salads or on baked potatoes. For variety, add onions or ½ cup bleu cheese.

½ cup 1% low-fat cottage cheese
½ cup plain nonfat yogurt
½ medium green pepper, chopped

4 radishes, sliced
2 tablespoon chives
1 tablespoon poppy seeds
Herb Salt (pp. 332–33) to taste

Mix all ingredients in a blender or food processor.

Makes about 1½ cups. Serving size is 1 tablespoon.

Per serving: **no fat,** 9 calories, no cholesterol, no dietary fiber, 28 mg. sodium (with bleu cheese: **1 g. fat,** 20 calories, 3 mg. cholesterol, no dietary fiber, 72 mg. sodium)

Honey-Mustard Dressing

PREPARATION TIME: 5 MINUTES

Good with a spinach salad or other green salads.

1 teaspoon dry mustard
¼ cup white or fruit vinegar
¼ cup olive oil
1 teaspoon honey
¼ teaspoon ground fennel seed (optional)

1 teaspoon lemon juice
Dash of salt and fresh-ground black pepper to taste
1 tablespoon chopped fresh parsley or watercress

Blend the dry mustard with a small amount of the vinegar, and then combine all ingredients, shake, and serve. Store in the refrigerator.

Makes a little over ½ cup. Serving size is 1 tablespoon.

Per serving: **7 g. fat,** 63 calories, no cholesterol, no dietary fiber, 27 mg. sodium

Dill-Seed and Walnut Dressing

PREPARATION TIME: 3 TO 4 MINUTES

REFRIGERATION TIME:
12 HOURS

This tart-sweet dressing is delicious on a salad of thinly sliced cucumber, or try it with any combination of your favorite greens or raw vegetables.

1 cup plain nonfat yogurt
¼ cup raisins (golden raisins are nice)
1½ teaspoons dill seed
¼ cup chopped walnuts

1 clove garlic, minced
¼ teaspoon salt
⅛ teaspoon fresh-ground black pepper

Combine all ingredients in a small bowl. Chill 12 hours, and serve cold.

Makes about 1½ cups. Serving size is 2 tablespoons.

Per serving: **2 g. fat,** 39 calories, no cholesterol, no dietary fiber, 61 mg. sodium

Paprika Dressing ✓

PREPARATION TIME: 5 MINUTES

This dressing serves double duty as a salad dressing or as a sauce for meats. You can also try using it as a moistener for sandwiches in place of mayonnaise. It's best to use a brand of horseradish with little or no added sugars, dextrose, oils, or mayonnaise.

1 cup plain nonfat yogurt
½ teaspoon salt
¼ teaspoon fresh-ground black pepper
1 clove garlic, crushed

2 teaspoons paprika
1 teaspoon pure horseradish
1 scallion, diced
2 tablespoons light sour cream

Combine all ingredients and chill.

Makes about 1 1/4 cups. Serving size is 1 tablespoon.

Per serving: **no fat,** 10 calories, 1 mg. cholesterol, no dietary fiber, 64 mg. sodium

Vinaigrette

PREPARATION TIME: 4 MINUTES

1 teaspoon dry mustard
2 tablespoons wine vinegar
1/2 cup olive oil
2 tablespoons lemon juice
1/2 cup water

Herb Salt to taste
(pp. 332–33)
Fresh-ground black pepper to
taste

Blend the mustard with a small amount of the vinegar, place all the ingredients in a jar, and shake well.

VARIATIONS: Add other herbs or the juice of pressed garlic or onion.

Makes about 1 1/4 cups. Serving size is 1 tablespoon.

Per serving: **5 g. fat,** 49 calories, no cholesterol, no dietary fiber, 32 mg. sodium (using 1 teaspoon Herb Salt)

No-Fat Salad Dressing

PREPARATION TIME: 4 MINUTES

1 tablespoon fresh parsley, chopped
1 clove garlic, crushed, OR ¼ teaspoon garlic powder
½ cup wine vinegar
½ teaspoon Herb Salt (see pp. 332–33)

Mix all ingredients well. Store in the refrigerator.

VARIATIONS: Use other vinegars and herbs for variety. Tarragon is one of our favorite herbs for salad dressing. If available, try fruit vinegars, such as raspberry and strawberry. Add water to this recipe if you find it too vinegary for your taste.

Makes about ½ cup. Serving size is 1 tablespoon.

Per serving: **no fat,** 2 calories, no cholesterol, no dietary fiber, 13 mg. sodium

Italian Dressing

PREPARATION TIME: 5 MINUTES

⅓ cup water
⅓ cup olive oil
⅓ cup white vinegar
1 tablespoon lemon juice
1 clove garlic, minced
1 teaspoon basil leaves, crushed
¼ teaspoon Worcestershire sauce

Combine all ingredients in a jar, cover, and shake well. Store in the refrigerator. Shake before serving.

Makes about 1 cup. Serving size is 1 tablespoon.

Per serving: **5 g. fat,** 41 calories, no cholesterol, no dietary fiber, 12 mg. sodium

Lime Dressing

PREPARATION TIME: 5 MINUTES

Try this dressing with the Artichoke-Spinach Salad (p. 85).

¼ cup olive oil
¼ cup water
¼ cup lime juice
1 teaspoon coriander
¼ teaspoon basil

⅛ teaspoon ginger
¼ teaspoon salt
¼ teaspoon fresh-ground black
  pepper

Whisk together all ingredients. Store in an airtight container in the refrigerator.

Makes about ¾ cup. Serving size is 1 tablespoon.

Per serving: **5 g. fat,** 42 calories, no cholesterol, no dietary fiber, 45 mg. sodium

Poppy-Seed Dressing

PREPARATION TIME: 4 TO 5 MINUTES

This dressing is both sweet and tart. Pour it over fruit salads or a wedge of honeydew or cantaloupe, or on chicken, tuna, or other seafood salads served with fruit or on a bed of lettuce.

1 cup plain nonfat yogurt
2 teaspoons honey
1 tablespoon poppy seeds

Juice of 1 lime (about 2
  tablespoons)

Combine all ingredients in a bowl. Serve chilled.

Makes about 1¼ cups. Serving size is 2 tablespoons.

Per serving: **no fat,** 23 calories, no cholesterol, no dietary fiber, 19 mg. sodium

Balsamic Dressing

PREPARATION TIME: 5 MINUTES

One of the reasons we seem to understand each other and get along so well with our editor, Starling Lawence, at W. W. Norton, is that we share the same love of fine food and physical activity. He plays a mean game of tennis, and, in addition to testing many of our recipes and providing helpful comments, he occasionally shares one of his recipes with us. Balsamic Dressing is one of his.

If you don't have balsamic vinegar, you may substitute another kind. But, if this is the case, start with water and vinegar in equal proportions.

3/4 cup water
1/4 cup balsamic vinegar
3 teaspoons capers
2 teaspoons Dijon mustard

1 1/2 teaspoons dried basil
1 tablespoon fresh parsley, chopped (optional)

Combine the ingredients. Adjust vinegar to taste, since it has a strong flavor. Store in a covered container in the refrigerator.

Makes about 1 cup. Serving size is 1 tablespoon.

Per serving: **no fat,** 1 calorie, no cholesterol, no dietary fiber, 7 mg. sodium

Beef

Beef receives bad marks from some health experts because it is high in saturated fat, and consumption of saturated fat in large amounts appears to be related to a higher incidence of heart disease and certain forms of cancer.

I have a very simple philosophy when it comes to beef: Use low-fat cuts in moderation. What's moderation? Many authorities suggest once or twice a week, although I don't feel there is strong evidence against eating low-fat cuts of beef three or four times a week, provided your cholesterol level is normal and there is no history of heart disease in your family.

If you like beef in your diet more than once or twice a week, I think you can help protect yourself against possible ill effects by including plenty of dietary fiber, which will help keep you regular and can help lower cholesterol. That is why I place such a strong emphasis on increasing fruits, vegetables, and whole grains in your diet. In addition, you should include fish at least once a week, preferably twice, since the oil contained in certain fatty fish—tuna, mackerel, sardines, bluefish, rainbow trout, salmon, and herring—also seems to help reduce cholesterol levels. As a general dietary principle, no matter what the source of fat in your diet, I think it's best to stay within the limit of 25 percent total calories from fat.

Choose low-fat cuts of beef: top round steaks or roast, eye of round, sirloin tip, flank steak and London broil, tenderloin, and, of course, extra-lean hamburger. But watch out for that hamburger: If it isn't labeled around 95 percent fat free ask your butcher to grind you some from top round, or simply buy Healthy Choice extra lean.

If you don't find well-trimmed beef in the market, don't be shy: Ask the butcher to trim your meat specially. I recommend that you make friends with your butcher, if you haven't already, and explain what you want and why. I have never met a meat manager in a supermarket who did not want to cooperate with me and I think you will find that to be the case, too.

Lean cuts of meat are often not as tender as the fatty cuts. When cooking in a sauce, you may have to simmer longer than the approximate time given in our recipe to achieve the tenderness you desire.

Our Oriental recipes are examples of how to use modest amounts of beef, as well as other meats, more as a garnish or condiment accompanying vegetables and other foods than as the main course. My wife, Enid, and I began doing this several years ago, after a visit to San Francisco. We had such memorable Chinese and Indian dinners there that, before returning to Nashville, we purchased some Chinese and Indian cookbooks that appeared to have recipes for some of the dishes we had eaten.

Sauces and gravies that don't thicken to your liking can be thickened by blending in a tablespoon of cornstarch or increasing the amount originally called for.

Flank Steak

PREPARATION TIME: 12 MINUTES   COOKING TIME: 40 MINUTES

1¼ pounds flank steak
1 tablespoon vegetable oil
1 cup hot water
1 bay leaf
1 large clove garlic, crushed
1 teaspoon salt

4 tablespoons minced celery
⅛ teaspoon fresh-ground black pepper
2 teaspoons lemon juice
1 medium carrot, diced
¼ medium bell pepper, diced

1. Trim away any visible fat from the steak. Sear the steak in the oil over medium to medium-high heat. Remove the

pan from the heat. Place the steak in a casserole dish.

2. For extra flavoring, pour the water into the cooled skillet you seared the meat in, and stir. Pour this over the meat, then add all the other ingredients.

3. Cook uncovered at 350 degrees for 30 minutes, or longer if you prefer your meat well-done.

LIGHT GRAVY (OPTIONAL): To make the roux, heat 1 tablespoon vegetable oil and stir in 2 tablespoons of whole-wheat flour. Take 1 cup of liquid from the meat and stir into the roux. Stir until thickened, and serve over the meat.

4 servings of 3½ ounces each (cooked weight), plus gravy.

Per serving (plus gravy): **10 g. fat**, 249 calories, 83 mg. cholesterol, 1 g. dietary fiber, 607 mg. sodium

"Julia Child was cooking coq au vin and tambour parmentier this evening, and during her pommes en belle vue I burned your filet." DRAWING BY BOOTH; © 1979 THE NEW YORKER MAGAZINE, INC.

Eggplant Beef Casserole

PREPARATION TIME: 15 MINUTES   COOKING TIME: 45 MINUTES

Serve this with a dinner salad for a complete meal.

2 pounds extra-lean ground
  beef
1 medium onion, chopped
1 small green pepper, chopped
1 tablespoon whole-wheat flour
½ teaspoon fresh-ground black
  pepper
½ teaspoon salt

1 teaspoon dried oregano
2 cups tomato sauce (try Real
  Italian Tomato Sauce,
  pp. 288–89)
1 large eggplant
1 cup grated part-skim
  mozzarella or reduced-fat
  cheddar cheese

1. Brown the ground beef. Remove it from the pan, and pour off excess fat, if any, leaving just enough pan juices to sauté the onion and green pepper.
2. When the onion is translucent, return the ground beef to the pan. Add the flour, spices, and tomato sauce, and let simmer until thick.
3. Meanwhile, slice the eggplant into ½-inch rounds, and layer half of them in a 2-quart casserole. Add half the beef mixture, then half the cheese. Repeat layers.
4. Bake covered in a slow oven, around 325 degrees, for 45 minutes.

12 servings. Serving size is 1 cup.

Per serving: **11 g. fat**, 210 calories, 63 mg. cholesterol, 3 g. dietary fiber, 436 mg. sodium

Fajitas

PREPARATION TIME: 15 MINUTES   COOKING TIME: 5 TO 10 MINUTES

You can prepare this Mexican dish (pronounced fah-hee-tuhs) a day ahead of time by dicing your vegetables, grating the cheese, and so on, after you put the meat in to marinate. Store the prepared ingredients in the refrigerator until the next day. Then cook the meat, slice it on a serving platter, put the prepared vegetables and cheese in individual serving bowls, and let everyone make their own fajitas.

1 pound top round, cut ½ inch thick
Juice of 2 limes (about ⅓ cup of juice)
2 cloves garlic, minced
½ teaspoon fresh-ground black pepper
¼ teaspoon chili powder
¼ teaspoon cumin
6 Whole-Wheat Tortillas (see pp. 314–15)

¾ cup lettuce, shredded (don't use a food processor or it will not be the right texture)
¾ cup tomato, diced
6 tablespoons scallions, chopped
6 tablespoons grated reduced-fat cheddar cheese

1. Trim any visible fat from the beef. Pound it with a flat metal meat pounder to about ¼-inch thickness.
2. In a shallow bowl, combine the lime juice, garlic, pepper, chili powder, and cumin. Add the steak, toss lightly, and marinate in the refrigerator overnight or for about 6 or 7 hours, turning the meat occasionally.
3. Broil the steak on a grill over medium-hot coals for about 3 minutes a side, or pan-broil 5 to 10 minutes, turning occasionally. Add some of the marinade if necessary to prevent it from sticking. Meanwhile, warm the tortillas briefly on each side in a dry frying pan, in a warm oven, or in a microwave.
4. Slice the beef across the grain into thin slices. Spread lengthwise in the center of each tortilla equal amounts of beef. Then top each serving with 2 tablespoons each of lettuce and tomato, and 1 tablespoon each of scallions and cheese. Roll the tortillas up lengthwise and serve.

6 servings. Serving size is 1 tortilla with fillings.

Per serving: **9 g. fat,** 279 calories, 55 mg. cholesterol, 3 g. dietary fiber, 216 mg. sodium

Zucchini-Stuffed Flank Steak

PREPARATION TIME: 30 TO 45 MINUTES   COOKING TIME: 1 1/2 HOURS

This is one of those dishes that takes about 45 minutes to prepare the first time, but goes much faster once you get the hang of it. It's so good that I'm sure you will want to prepare it many times, with variations. It lends itself to the use of many different sauces and stuffings. There is enough sauce in this version to cover a side of spaghetti; add a salad for a well-rounded meal.

1 1/4 pounds flank steak
2 large cloves garlic
1 tablespoon olive oil
Salt and fresh-ground black pepper to taste
1 medium zucchini, sliced thin
1/2 cup chopped parsley
1/2 cup coarse-grated part-skim mozzarella

3 teaspoons fresh Parmesan cheese, grated
2 cans (10 ounces each) tomato purée or Real Italian Tomato Sauce (pp. 288–89)
2 medium yellow crookneck squash, sliced thin
1 tablespoon Mrs. Dash or Herb Salt (pp. 332–33)

1. Tenderize and thin out the meat by pounding with a flat metal meat pounder until its thickness is reduced by about one-half. You can use a small section of two-by-four, a pestle, or the bottom of a small wooden salad bowl for this job, but you must thin it out or it will not roll well. (Cover the meat with a piece of waxed paper to prevent your pounder from sticking and the meat from splattering.)
2. Crush the garlic in a garlic press and place it on the meat. Add the olive oil and spread the garlic and oil all over the meat.
3. Salt and pepper to taste (it doesn't take much salt because of the other seasonings).
4. Arrange the sliced zucchini down the center (lengthwise) of the meat, and sprinkle with half the parsley.
5. Add the mozzarella and the Parmesan cheeses.

6. Roll up the whole thing, going with the grain of the meat, so that when you slice it you will be going against the grain. Tie it in four or five places with heavy string (if you have trouble holding it together for tying, run a couple of skewers lengthwise through the meat to hold it together, and then use the string; you can remove the skewers at the table before slicing).
7. Place the rolled steak in a baking dish, pour the sauce or purée over it, add the sliced yellow squash, and sprinkle it with Mrs. Dash or Herb Salt and the remaining parsley.
8. Bake, covered, at 325 degrees for about 1½ hours. Baste two or three times.
9. Remove the roll to a serving dish, with the sauce. Slice, and serve with the sauce.

4 servings of 3½ ounces each of meat (cooked weight), plus sauce.

Per serving: **14 g. fat,** 405 calories, 128 mg. cholesterol, 6 g. dietary fiber, 343 mg. sodium

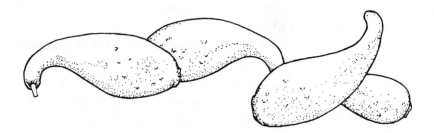

Hungarian Cabbage

PREPARATION TIME: 50 MINUTES   COOKING TIME: 45 TO 50 MINUTES

Hungarian cooking is characterized by the use of paprika, and if you can find a true Hungarian paprika, you're in luck. It is more pungent and has a richer flavor than the kind we usually find in the supermarket. Actually, paprika is a type of chile that apparently originated in South America, not Hungary. Wherever it came from, it is delicious in this dish. Serve with a fresh salad or with a dark green or yellow vegetable on the side. Even with low-sodium beef stock, however, this is rather high in sodium.

1¼ cups low-sodium beef stock
¾ cup brown rice
1 medium onion, chopped
1 tablespoon olive oil
1 pound extra-lean ground beef
2 teaspoons paprika

2 large cloves garlic, crushed
¾ pound low-fat sausage,
   sliced in ¼-inch-thick slices
1 bag (2 pounds) sauerkraut
½ cup light sour cream
½ cup plain nonfat yogurt

1. Bring the beef stock to a boil, add the rice, and bring back to a boil. Reduce the heat to simmer, cover, and let cook for about 45 minutes.
2. Meanwhile, sauté the onions in the olive oil over medium heat until onions are translucent. Set aside.
3. In another pan, brown the ground beef. Drain any excess fat, then add the beef to the onions, along with the paprika and garlic. Mix well and set aside again.
4. In the same pan you used for the ground beef, quickly brown the sausage slices. Drain the sausage on paper toweling, patting well to remove the fat. Set aside.
5. Pour the sauerkraut into a colander, and rinse with water for several minutes. After rinsing, squeeze well to remove excess water.
6. In a small bowl, combine the sour cream and the yogurt, blending well.

7. In a large 2½- to 3-quart casserole dish, layer half the sauerkraut, half the sausage, and half the ground beef. Top with all of the rice, then add half of the sour cream–yogurt mixture. Repeat the layers of sauerkraut, sausage, ground beef, and the sour cream–yogurt mixture.
8. Bake at 350 degrees for 45 to 50 minutes.

8 servings. Serving size is about 1¼ cups.

Per serving: **16 g. fat,** 354 calories, 83 mg. cholesterol, 4 g. dietary fiber, 1295 mg. sodium

Braised Brisket in Tomato Sauce

PREPARATION TIME: 10 MINUTES   COOKING TIME: 1½ HOURS

1¾ **pounds top round roast**
1 **clove garlic, crushed**
½ **teaspoon salt**
½ **teaspoon fresh-ground black pepper**
¼ **teaspoon marjoram**

1 **can (14½ ounces) no-salt-added tomatoes, with juice**
1 **tablespoon lemon juice**
½ **cup chopped onion**
2 **cups sliced carrots**

1. Trim all visible fat from the beef. Combine the garlic, salt, pepper, and marjoram, and rub the mixture all over the beef.
2. Pour the juice from the can of tomatoes into your roasting pan or casserole. Add the meat and lemon juice. Arrange the vegetables around the meat.
3. Cover the pan, place it in a cold oven, and turn the heat to 425 degrees. Bake 1½ hours or until done to your taste.
4. Heat the tomatoes in a pan, and serve alongside the roast.

6 servings of 3½ ounces each (cooked weight), plus vegetables.

Per serving: **5 g. fat,** 220 calories, 83 mg. cholesterol, 3 g. dietary fiber, 265 mg. sodium

Beef Taco Salad

PREPARATION TIME: 15 MINUTES   COOKING TIME: 10 TO 15 MINUTES

1 medium head iceberg lettuce
  (or other lettuce)
½ medium cucumber, sliced
  thin
½ medium bell pepper, sliced
  or diced
1 large tomato, cut in thin
  wedges
4 black olives, diced
½ recipe Quick Tortilla Chips
  (p. 62)
1 pound extra-lean ground beef
  or ground turkey
¼ cup water or stock
1 tablespoon chili powder

½ teaspoon cumin
½ teaspoon fresh-ground black
  pepper
⅛ teaspoon cayenne pepper
¼ teaspoon salt
Dash Tabasco sauce (optional)
1 can (15 ounces) kidney beans,
  drained
1 or more medium jalapeño
  peppers, sliced
¼ cup shredded reduced-fat
  cheddar or Monterey Jack
  cheese
Herb and Onion Dressing (p.
  103) or other low-cal dressing

1. Tear the lettuce into a large serving bowl. Top with the cucumber, bell pepper, tomato, and olives. Slightly crush the tortilla chips over the salad vegetables.
2. In a large skillet, brown the ground meat. Drain off any excess fat. Add the water, seasonings, and beans, stirring well. Cover and cook for about 10 to 15 minutes, until meat is cooked and beans are heated through.
3. Pour the meat mixture over the salad. Top with sliced jalapeño peppers and the cheese. Serve with dressing on the side, so people can help themselves.

6 servings as a main course. Serving size is about 1½ cups.

Per serving: **12 g. fat,** 308 calories, 60 mg. cholesterol, 6 g. dietary fiber, 478 mg. sodium

Steak Marinade

PREPARATION TIME: 3 TO 5 MINUTES

Here are two marinade sauces for flank steak, London broil, or any other lean cut of beef that you might want to use for pan- or oven-broiling, or outdoor grilling. Both the wine and soy sauce have a tenderizing effect, so marinate overnight in the refrigerator, in a large covered bowl or plastic bag. Turn the meat once or twice while it is marinating, to be sure all of it has been well covered.

These amounts will do nicely for 2 pounds of meat.

Basic marinade:
1 tablespoon olive oil
½ cup dry red wine (use white wine for light-colored meats)
¼ teaspoon Herb Salt (pp. 332–33)
1 bay leaf
1 teaspoon chives
1 small onion, minced

Oriental marinade:
1 tablespoon olive oil
¼ cup tamari sauce or soy sauce
¼ cup dry red wine
4 cloves garlic, minced
4 scallions, minced
6 whole peppercorns
⅛ teaspoon ground coriander
1-inch cube fresh gingerroot, peeled and grated or minced

Olive oil contains approximately 14 grams of fat and 120 calories per tablespoon. The other ingredients provide negligible fat and calories, including the wine, since the alcohol evaporates and the sugar content is very low. Soy sauce is quite high in sodium, but it is difficult to predict how much will penetrate or adhere to the meat. Our guess is that the sodium content per serving, that is, 3½ ounces of flank steak, will be about 500 mg.

Japanese Beef Stir-Fry

PREPARATION TIME: 5 TO 10 MINUTES   COOKING TIME: 15 TO 20
                                                                                    MINUTES

Here is an example of Oriental-style cooking in which meat is
only part of the "main course." Serve this dish as soon as it's
ready. If you are making enough for leftovers, use regular or
Chinese cabbage instead of red, as the red cabbage tends to
turn other ingredients purple when cooked and stored.

4 beef tenderloin steaks (about   ¼ inch fresh gingerroot,
  4 ounces each)   minced, OR ground ginger to
1 tablespoon peanut oil   taste
2 packages (6 ounces each)   1 tablespoon saké (optional)
  frozen pea pods, thawed   Dash tamari sauce or soy sauce
¼ head red cabbage, thinly
  sliced

1. Heat a wok or heavy skillet over medium-high heat for
   several minutes. Meanwhile, trim the beef of all visible fat
   and slice the beef into thin slices.
2. Add the oil to the pan, then the beef. Cook, stirring constantly, until browned.
3. Lower the heat to medium, remove the meat from the
   pan, and set aside.
4. Add the pea pods, cabbage, and gingerroot to the wok, and
   cook for five minutes, stirring constantly.
5. Return the meat to the wok, and stir in the saké and the
   soy sauce. Cover, and let simmer for a few more minutes,
   until the vegetables are just tender and the meat is cooked
   the way you like it.

4 servings of 3 ounces each (cooked weight), plus vegetables.

Per serving: **12 g. fat,** 260 calories, 71 mg. cholesterol, 3 g.
dietary fiber, 81 mg. sodium

Goulash

PREPARATION TIME: 15 TO 20 MINUTES   COOKING TIME: 30 TO 40
MINUTES

Serve this with 1 cup of cooked pasta or grain per serving.

2½ pounds top round or sirloin
 tip steak or roast
1 cup diced leeks
1 tablespoon olive oil
2 medium carrots, diced
1 can (16 ounces) no-salt-added
 tomatoes
1 cup low-sodium beef stock
1 tablespoon paprika

1 teaspoon salt
½ teaspoon fresh-ground black
 pepper
¼ teaspoon ground cloves
 (optional)
1 tablespoon cornstarch
¼ cup water
¼ cup light sour cream
¼ cup plain nonfat yogurt

1. Trim the beef of all visible fat, and cut the beef into 1-inch
   chunks. Brown the beef in a skillet, then remove the beef,
   and drain any excess fat. In the same pan, sauté the leeks
   in the oil.
2. When the leeks are tender, return the beef to the pan. Add
   the carrots, tomatoes, stock, paprika, salt, pepper, and
   cloves.
3. Combine the cornstarch with the water, and stir in with
   the beef. Cover, and let simmer until meat is tender. Then
   stir in the sour cream and yogurt and heat through.

8 servings of 3½ ounces each (cooked weight), plus sauce.

Per serving (meat with sauce): **8 g. fat,** 229 calories, 83 mg.
cholesterol, 1 g. dietary fiber, 352 mg. sodium

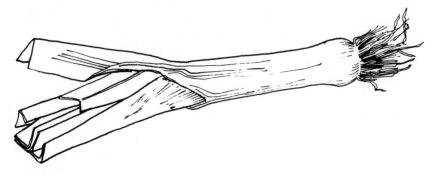

Cheddar Chili Pie

PREPARATION TIME: 30 MINUTES   COOKING TIME: 30 MINUTES

Because this has proven to be one of our best-loved recipes, we didn't want to change it by using reduced-fat cheese. One look at the ingredients will tell you that it is a very nutritious dish, and your taste buds will carry on from there. Serve this with a large salad of greens.

1 pound extra-lean ground beef
1 large onion, chopped
2 cloves garlic, chopped fine
1 can (28 ounces) whole tomatoes
1 can (15 ounces) kidney beans, with juice
1¼ cups cornmeal
1 cup grated cheddar cheese
2 tablespoons chili powder
1 teaspoon cumin
¼ teaspoon cayenne pepper
½ teaspoon crushed red pepper
½ teaspoon fresh-ground black pepper
Dash Tabasco sauce
1¼ cups skim milk
Salt and pepper to taste
2 eggs, lightly beaten

1. Sauté the beef, the onion, and the garlic until the meat is browned. Drain off the fat; add the tomatoes, beans, ¾ cup of the cornmeal, ½ cup of the cheese, and the seasonings. Cook over low heat, stirring occasionally, for about 15 minutes. Pour into a casserole dish.
2. In the same pan, combine the milk, the rest of the cornmeal, and the salt and pepper to taste. Stir over low heat until it thickens a little. Then add the remaining cheese and the eggs, stirring until smooth. Pour this over the ground-beef mixture. Bake uncovered at 375 degrees for 30 minutes or until the crust is lightly browned.

8 servings. Serving size is 1½ cups.

Per serving: **14 g. fat,** 351 calories, 105 mg. cholesterol, 8 g. dietary fiber, 530 mg. sodium

Sauerbraten

PREPARATION TIME: 5 TO 10 MINUTES

COOKING TIME:
2½ TO 3 HOURS

The traditional German recipe for sauerbraten calls for 48 hours of marinating. However, we have found that you can get by with 24 hours and still have a tasty dish.

2½ pounds top round roast
1 teaspoon salt
½ teaspoon fresh-ground black pepper
2 to 3 bay leaves
2 whole peppercorns
4 whole cloves

1 large onion, sliced
1 medium carrot, sliced
1 stalk celery, chopped
1½ cups wine vinegar
2½ cups boiling water
1 tablespoon vegetable oil

1. Trim all visible fat from the beef, and rub the salt and pepper all over the beef. Place the beef in a large pan.
2. Add the remaining ingredients except for the oil and marinate, covered, in the refrigerator for at least 24 hours, turning twice a day.
3. When you're ready to cook the meat, place the oil in a large kettle, add only the meat, and brown over medium heat. Pour in the marinade, cover, and simmer for 2½ to 3 hours, until done.

8 servings of 3½ ounces each (cooked weight).

Per serving: **6 g. fat,** 207 calories, 80 mg. cholesterol, 1 g. dietary fiber, 336 mg. sodium

Thai Stir-Fry

PREPARATION TIME: 15 MINUTES   COOKING TIME: 15 TO 20 MINUTES

Here is an example of how to use nuts or seeds (in this case, sesame) in small amounts as a flavorful garnish. See pages 235–36 for instructions on how to toast them without added fat.

1 pound beef flank steak
¼ cup tamari sauce or soy sauce
3 tablespoons honey
½ inch gingerroot, minced
1 clove garlic, minced or crushed
1 tablespoon oil (preferably peanut)

1 small eggplant, cut in thin strips
¼ to ½ teaspoon crushed red pepper (optional)
¼ cup low-sodium stock
2 tablespoons toasted sesame seeds, ground with mortar and pestle

1. Cut the beef across the grain into strips about ¼ inch thick. Pound lightly with a meat hammer. Place in a bowl or sealable plastic bag with the tamari, honey, ginger, and garlic, and marinate for 30 minutes.
2. Add the oil to a wok or large frying pan, let it heat through, and add the beef after removing it from the marinade. Cook, stirring constantly, until beef is browned, then remove the beef and reserve.
3. Add the eggplant, the crushed red pepper, the marinade, and the stock to the pan. Cover, and steam for 5 to 10 minutes, until the eggplant softens, stirring occasionally.
4. Add the beef, cover, and let simmer for several minutes, until done.
5. Sprinkle with sesame seeds and serve.

4 servings of 3 ounces each (cooked weight), plus vegetables.

Per serving: **15 g. fat,** 331 calories, 57 mg. cholesterol, 5 g. dietary fiber, 891 mg. sodium

Yukon Stew

PREPARATION TIME: 8 TO 10 MINUTES   COOKING TIME: 2¼ HOURS

This recipe originally called for moose or caribou meat. If you have trouble finding these in your local supermarket, substitute beef, as we did! Serve with cooked grain, over whole-wheat noodles, or with boiled potatoes, along with a dark green or yellow/orange vegetable, such as steamed carrots.

2 pounds top round roast, cut into chunks
3 tablespoons lemon juice
½ teaspoon salt
2 teaspoons chili powder
⅓ cup whole-wheat flour
1 tablespoon vegetable oil
Hot water or low-sodium stock to cover
½ cup chopped fresh parsley

1. Sprinkle the meat with the lemon juice. In a shallow bowl, combine the salt, chili powder, and flour, and dredge the meat in the flour mixture.
2. Heat a 3-quart saucepan over medium heat. Add the oil, and brown the meat on all sides. Add water or stock to cover. Simmer, covered, for 2 hours, or until the meat is tender. Then remove the cover and let cook for about 15 minutes to thicken the sauce.
3. Add the parsley, stir, and serve.

6 servings of 4 ounces each (cooked weight).

Per serving: **8 g. fat,** 253 calories, 95 mg. cholesterol, 1 g. dietary fiber, 258 mg. sodium

Easy Beef Stroganoff

PREPARATION TIME: 10 MINUTES   COOKING TIME: 10 MINUTES

1 small onion, diced
3 to 4 ounces fresh mushrooms, diced
1 tablespoon vegetable oil
3 cups cooked beef, either extra-lean ground beef or sliced beefsteak
⅓ cup plain nonfat yogurt

⅓ cup light sour cream
¼ cup plus 2 tablespoons dry white wine
½ teaspoon salt
¼ teaspoon fresh-ground black pepper
½ teaspoon nutmeg

Sauté the onions and mushrooms in the oil over medium-low heat until the onions are translucent. Stir in the remaining ingredients and let simmer for 10 minutes, covered, until heated through. Do not boil.

6 servings. Serving size is about ⅞ cup.

Per serving: **8 g. fat,** 218 calories, 77 mg. cholesterol, 1 g. dietary fiber, 247 mg. sodium

Tarragon Beef

PREPARATION TIME: 15 MINUTES   COOKING TIME: 3¼ HOURS

The combination of tarragon and crushed red pepper in this recipe makes for a slightly exotic variation on a standard "meat-and-potatoes" dish. We suggest you try it the first time with the smaller amount of hot pepper, unless you like spicy hot food.

4 pounds eye of round roast
2 medium onions, quartered
4 medium carrots, cut in chunks
4 medium potatoes, cut in chunks
¾ cup red wine
2 tablespoons dried parsley
2 tablespoons dried tarragon

1 bay leaf
2 cloves garlic, minced or crushed
1 teaspoon salt
1 teaspoon fresh-ground black pepper
¼ to 1 teaspoon crushed dried red pepper

1. Trim any visible fat from the beef, and marinate the beef and the vegetables in all the remaining ingredients in a large roasting pan for at least 2 hours in your refrigerator.
2. Place the roast in a 450-degree oven for 45 minutes, then lower the temperature to 275 degrees and cook for 2½ hours more.

12 servings of about 4 ounces each (cooked weight), plus vegetables.

Per serving: **5 g. fat,** 225 calories, 59 mg. cholesterol, 2 g. dietary fiber, 245 mg. sodium

Easy Beef and Rice

PREPARATION TIME: 10 MINUTES   COOKING TIME: 45 TO 50 MINUTES

With her full schedule as a concert pianist and professor of music at Vanderbilt's Blair School of Music, my wife, Enid, doesn't often have time for elaborate cooking. Here is one of her many quick-and-easy recipes. Serve with a dinner salad for a complete, tasty meal.

2 cups brown rice
4 cups low-sodium stock
4 scallions, chopped
1 pound extra-lean ground beef

2 cans (10¾ ounces each) tomato purée
1 teaspoon Mrs. Dash (or other herb blend)

1. Combine the first 3 ingredients in a 2-quart pot. Bring to a boil, lower the heat, and simmer until tender, about 35 to 40 minutes.
2. In a large frying pan, sauté the ground beef. Drain off any excess fat, then add the purée and seasoning. Add the cooked rice. Heat through, and serve.

8 servings. Serving size is 1 cup.

Per serving: **8 g. fat,** 182 calories, 42 mg. cholesterol, 2 g. dietary fiber, 376 mg. sodium

Lemon-Pepper Beef ✓

PREPARATION TIME: 5 MINUTES   COOKING TIME: 18 TO 20 MINUTES

We first made this dish with ¼ cup of lemon juice (4 table-spoons) and it had a decidedly sharp aftertaste of lemon! So we reduced the amount. Use the lesser amount of lemon juice if you prefer a less intense lemon flavor. Reduce or increase cooking time depending on how you like your meat cooked. This dish goes well with cooked pasta, such as vermicelli, and a dinner salad.

1 pound top round steak, well
  trimmed
¼ cup dry red wine
2 to 3 tablespoons lemon juice
½ teaspoon salt

1 bay leaf
2 yellow or red sweet peppers,
  cut in eighths
Fresh-ground black pepper to
  taste

1. Combine all ingredients in a large bowl or pan, and mari-nate overnight, or at least 6 hours in the refrigerator. Turn beef and peppers occasionally.
2. Place beef on broiler pan about 4 inches from heat and broil about 8 minutes. Turn, and add the pepper pieces to the pan. After six minutes or so, turn the peppers over, then broil about 4 minutes more for medium-well-done beef. Slice the beef thinly across the grain, and serve with the peppers.

4 servings of 3 ounces each (cooked weight), plus peppers.

Per serving: **4 g. fat,** 177 calories, 71 mg. cholesterol, 1 g. dietary fiber, 320 mg. sodium

Veal

The best cut of veal for roasting is the sirloin, but an arm steak, blade, or shoulder cut will be just as tender and almost as lean. Many great chefs love to prepare veal because the delicate flavor makes it such a fine vehicle for carrying the flavors of different sauces.

Look for pale pink-colored flesh and very white fat when you buy veal. Milk-fed veal is more tender and lightly flavored than meat from calves that have been fed solid foods.

We include two recipes for scaloppines (very thin, pounded slices of veal) in sauces, plus a variety of other ways to prepare veal, which can be used in meat loaf, meatballs, stew, and as steak.

Perhaps you will notice that many of our veal recipes seem to be of Italian origin. That's because the Italians have perfected the art of preparing delicate sauces to complement the delicacy of veal. In fact, the per-capita consumption of veal in Italy is at least two or three times that of the United States.

Because veal is such a lean and delicate meat, many cooks add an unconscionable amount of butter and oil in its preparation, in the mistaken belief that adding fat is the way to enhance the flavor. From our recipes, you will discover that preparing veal requires very little fat; we find a judicious use of herbs, spices, and wine is the best way to bring out veal's flavor. Our Herb Salt (pages 332–33) and Traditional Italian Herb Blend (page 333) complement veal; keeping some ready-made herb blends on hand for the times when you don't care to start from scratch will save on preparation time.

But veal invites experimentation and every one of the following herbs and spices, alone or in combination, will enhance your pleasure of this delicate meat: rosemary, thyme, sage, bay leaf, chervil, parsley, mustard seed, coriander, tarragon, chives, basil, allspice, or, in place of allspice, a blend of cinnamon, nutmeg, and cloves, which is especially good in meatballs.

Experiment with wine in the sauces: dry sherry, Marsala, Madeira, dry vermouth, and white with the scaloppine, and dry red when you want a richer marinade. White wines add little color to the pale meat, while reds, of course, darken it.

When you pound veal to make scaloppine, place it on a wooden board and cover it with wax paper to prevent your pounder from sticking and the meat from splattering. I have used everything from a piece of two-by-four to the bottom of a wooden salad bowl to pound meat, but your best implement is a metal pounder made especially for that purpose. I have one that has a flat side for veal and a waffle-edge side for tenderizing tougher cuts of beef. You can find one at a cookware shop.

Brochette of Veal

PREPARATION TIME: 50 MINUTES   COOKING TIME: 10 MINUTES

Though we recommend grilling for this recipe, you can also oven-broil.

1½ pounds boneless veal roast, well trimmed, cut into 1-inch cubes
12 ounces white mushrooms
1 tablespoon olive oil
½ teaspoon salt
Fresh-ground black pepper to taste
3 tablespoons dry red wine

Juice of ½ lemon
¼ teaspoon thyme
1 bay leaf, crushed
1 teaspoon tarragon
3 cloves garlic, minced
2 medium sweet red peppers or any other sweet peppers, cut into 1-inch pieces

1. Place the cubed veal in a large mixing bowl and add all the remaining ingredients. Cover and marinate in the refrigerator for about 2 hours. Stir the mixture at least twice.

2. About ½ hour before grilling time, prepare a charcoal fire.
3. While the coals are warming, arrange the cubed veal, mushrooms, and peppers on 6 skewers.
4. When the charcoal fire is hot, place the skewered veal on the grill and cook, turning occasionally, until done (about 10 minutes, depending upon the heat of the grill).

6 servings of 3 ounces each (cooked weight), plus vegetables.

Per serving: **8 g. fat,** 193 calories, 89 mg. cholesterol, 2 g. dietary fiber, 254 mg. sodium

Veal Scaloppine Piccata

PREPARATION TIME: 10 TO 12 MINUTES   COOKING TIME: 5 TO 10 MINUTES

1 pound veal, sliced thin (8 slices)
Fresh-ground black pepper to taste
1 tablespoon olive oil
¼ cup low-sodium chicken stock

¼ cup dry white wine
Juice of 1 lemon (or 1 tablespoon of reconstituted lemon juice)
2 tablespoons chopped fresh parsley

1. Pound the veal to about ½ its original thickness, or as thin as possible without tearing the meat. Sprinkle the meat with pepper.
2. Heat the olive oil in a large nonstick frying pan and, when it is quite hot, brown the veal 1 minute per side.
3. Add the chicken stock, wine, lemon juice, and parsley and continue to cook the veal, occasionally turning the slices, until the sauce has reduced to desired consistency (5 to 10 minutes).

4 servings of 3 ounces each (cooked weight), plus sauce.

Per serving: **9 g. fat,** 187 calories, 89 mg. cholesterol, no dietary fiber, 79 mg. sodium

Roast Veal with Italian Seasoning ✓

PREPARATION TIME: 25 MINUTES   COOKING TIME: 1¼ HOURS

1 3-pound boneless veal roast,
   well trimmed
2 cloves garlic, minced
1 teaspoon Traditional Italian
   Herb Blend (p. 333)
½ teaspoon salt
Fresh-ground black pepper to
   taste

1 tablespoon olive oil
4 medium onions, cut into
   quarters
½ cup dry white wine
1½ cups chicken stock
8 medium carrots, quartered

1. Preheat the oven to 400 degrees.
2. Place the meat in a shallow roasting pan. Rub the garlic and the Herb Blend all over the meat. Sprinkle it with salt and pepper and rub it with oil.
3. Place the roasting pan on a low shelf in the oven and brown at 400 degrees for about 10 minutes. Pour off all the fat from the roasting pan. Place onions around the meat. Brown the meat and onions for about 5 minutes.
4. Add the wine and chicken stock, and cover tightly with foil. Reduce heat to 350 degrees and bake for about 45 minutes. Add carrots and bake for an additional 30 minutes, or until a meat thermometer reaches 170 degrees. Skim away the fat and serve the meat with its own sauce and the vegetables.

8 servings of 3½ ounces each (cooked weight), plus vegetables.

Per serving: **8 g. fat,** 250 calories, 103 mg. cholesterol, 3 g. dietary fiber, 297 mg. sodium

Veal (or Chicken) Florentine

PREPARATION TIME: 25 MINUTES   COOKING TIME: 25 MINUTES

"Florentine" indicates that a dish is made with spinach. It is an Italian style of cooking that works well with veal, chicken, or fish. This is good served with cooked pasta.

1 pound veal cutlets (4 slices)
   OR 4 chicken breasts,
   skinned, boned
¼ teaspoon fresh-ground black
   pepper
1 package (10 ounces) frozen
   chopped spinach, thawed,
   drained
1 egg OR 2 egg whites

¼ cup part-skim ricotta cheese
2 tablespoons grated Parmesan
   or sapsago cheese
1 clove garlic, minced or
   crushed
½ teaspoon oregano
2 tablespoons olive oil
1 cup dry white wine

1. Pound the veal or chicken to ¼-inch thickness. Sprinkle
   with the pepper.
2. In a medium bowl, combine the spinach, egg, cheeses,
   garlic, and oregano. Spread this mixture over the veal.
3. Roll the veal, jelly-roll fashion, around the spinach filling,
   securing the rolls with toothpicks or twine.
4. Add the oil and meat to a small skillet, over medium to
   medium-low heat, and lightly brown the rolls on all sides.
   Place the rolls in a casserole dish, add the wine, and bake
   at 350 degrees for 25 minutes.

*4 servings (1 roll) of 3 ounces each (cooked weight), plus
vegetables.*

Per serving (with veal): **13 g. fat,** 296 calories, 140 mg.
cholesterol, 2 g. dietary fiber, 204 mg. sodium

Per serving (with chicken): **10 g. fat,** 283 calories, 127 mg.
cholesterol, 2 g. dietary fiber, 206 mg. sodium

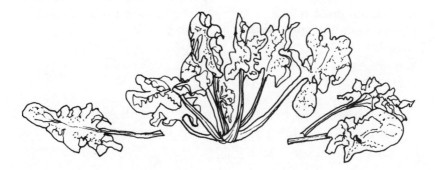

Veal Stew

PREPARATION TIME: 30 MINUTES   COOKING TIME (WITHOUT BROWNING):
1¾ HOURS

Although our Yukon Stew (p. 127) is a delicious exception to the rule, I generally prefer not to brown my meat when I make stews. Skipping the browning step results in a lighter gravy and you save a couple hundred calories of fat content in the total recipe. I also don't normally add any flour or cornstarch to thicken the gravy. It will thicken somewhat during the final minutes of cooking in an uncovered pot.

If you wish to brown the meat (which will take out some of the moisture in the meat, but won't really "seal in" the juices), do it in the same stewpot, using a minimum of oil, say one tablespoon. As for a gravy, if you prefer it thick, make a roux (p. 290) and blend it in during the last 30 minutes of cooking, or simply sprinkle a bit of flour into the stew, about a minute before it finishes cooking, and stir frequently until done.

1 tablespoon oil (optional, for browning)
3 pounds veal roast, cut into 1½-inch cubes
3 medium onions, chopped
4 cloves garlic, chopped
½ teaspoon salt
Fresh-ground black pepper to taste
1 bay leaf
½ teaspoon dried thyme
4 tablespoons chopped fresh parsley

¼ teaspoon rosemary
1 cup dry white wine
3 cups low-sodium chicken stock
4 medium ripe tomatoes, cut into eighths
5 medium carrots
5 small zucchini
4 celery stalks
5 small yellow summer squash
¼ cup chopped fresh parsley for garnish

BROWNING METHOD

1. If you want to brown the meat, heat the oil in a large stewpot or Dutch oven and add the veal cubes, turning until brown.

2. Add onions and garlic; heat until translucent. Add all seasonings, wine, stock and tomatoes. Cover and simmer for 30 minutes.
3. As the stew is simmering, cut the carrots, zucchini, celery, and squash into bite-size pieces (about 1 inch long; for the zucchini and squash, halve in the other direction as necessary), add to the pot, cover, and simmer another 45 minutes. Uncover and continue to simmer until the gravy is reduced to the desired consistency.
4. Skim any fat that appears on the surface of the liquid, and serve, garnished with the extra parsley.

TO OMIT BROWNING

Prepare the vegetables, and then add all the ingredients to the pot, except for the parsley garnish, cover, and bring to the boiling point. Immediately reduce heat and simmer for about 1½ hours on low heat. Uncover to reduce liquid and skim off the fat. When gravy is of desired consistency, serve with parsley garnish.

10 servings. Serving size is about 2 cups.

Per serving (without oil): **7 g. fat,** 265 calories, 106 mg. cholesterol, 5 g. dietary fiber, 253 mg. sodium (oil will add 9 calories per serving in the form of another gram of fat)

Veal Roast with Fennel and Leeks

PREPARATION TIME: 15 MINUTES   COOKING TIME: 1½ TO 2 HOURS

1 3-pound veal roast, bone in
3 bulbs fennel
4 leeks
16 small new potatoes
½ teaspoon sage
½ teaspoon rosemary

¼ teaspoon coriander
Fresh-ground black pepper to
  taste
1 tablespoon lemon juice
¼ cup white wine or water

1. Trim all visible fat from the roast and place it in a Dutch oven or large casserole dish.
2. Trim the tough outer leaves from the fennel. Wash and core the bulbs and cut in chunks. Arrange around the veal roast.
3. Carefully wash and trim the leeks. Cut the white portion in large pieces and add to the roasting pan, along with the washed new potatoes.
4. Sprinkle with seasonings, lemon juice, and wine. Cover and bake at 350 degrees for about 1½ to 2 hours.

8 servings of 3½ ounces each (cooked weight), plus vegetables.

Per serving: **7 g. fat,** 337 calories, 103 mg. cholesterol, 7 g. dietary fiber, 150 mg. sodium

Veal Marsala

PREPARATION TIME: 10 TO 12 MINUTES   COOKING TIME: 3 MINUTES

1½ pounds thinly sliced veal
  (12 slices)
¼ teaspoon salt
Fresh-ground black pepper to
  taste

1 tablespoon olive oil
¼ cup Marsala wine
2 tablespoons chopped fresh
  parsley

1. Between wax paper, pound the meat to ¼-inch thickness and sprinkle with the salt and pepper.
2. Heat the oil in a large nonstick frying pan. When it is hot, brown half the veal for 1 minute on each side, then remove

to an oven-proof plate warmed in the oven, and hold in reserve. Brown the other half of the veal and then immediately return the meat from the platter to the pan.
3. Add the Marsala and parsley and cook for 3 minutes. Serve at once.

6 servings of 3 ounces each (cooked weight).

Per serving: **8 g. fat,** 170 calories, 89 mg. cholesterol, no dietary fiber, 163 mg. sodium

Veal-Steak Milano

PREPARATION TIME: 10 MINUTES   COOKING TIME: 2 MINUTES

4 thinly sliced, boneless veal steaks (about ½ pound each, no more than ½ inch thick)
1 teaspoon Herb Salt (pp. 332–33)
Fresh-ground black pepper to taste

1 tablespoon olive oil or other vegetable oil
2 tablespoons chopped fresh parsley
4 lemon wedges

1. Pound the veal with a flat meat mallet until it is about ¼-inch thick.
2. Rub meat on both sides with Herb Salt and pepper, and then brush with oil.
3. Preheat a heavy frying pan until it is hot, then place the meat in it. Sear the meat for about 1 minute on each side, testing for doneness by cutting into the center of a slice with a knife. Cook until done the way you like it.
4. Remove the meat to a warmed serving plate, sprinkle it with parsley, and serve with the lemon wedges.

4 servings of 6 ounces each (cooked weight).

Per serving: **12 g. fat,** 355 calories, 246 mg. cholesterol, no dietary fiber, 222 mg. sodium

Pork

Pork, like lamb, is not a regular part of our diet. We include a few favorite recipes for pork as a main course that we occasionally make, plus three others that illustrate how you can use pork as a condiment in combination with other vegetables.

Contrary to what most people think, pork can be a lean meat! The tenderloin has only about 1 gram of fat per ounce, while top loin roasts and chops have about 2 grams. Even picnic roasts and legs, well trimmed, have only about 3 to 4 grams of fat per ounce. But be sure to trim all visible fat from these basically lean cuts because even a small amount of fat can double or triple the total fat count if you don't.

We calculate the nutritional values for serving sizes of 3½ ounces. We slice our meat thinly, averaging three slices of meat for a serving of that size. A good-size rib or loin chop, about 1 inch thick before cooking, will have 2 to 3 ounces of meat and contain about 5 grams of fat and 130 calories.

Pork is normally priced below beef, and it's just as full of the B vitamins and iron, so it's a good substitute from a nutritional standpoint.

You will rarely see bacon or fatback in our recipes. Bacon, broiled or fried, contains 14 grams of fat and 160 calories an ounce. Whenever bacon is called for in your own recipes, try using Canadian bacon (about 2 grams of fat and 50 calories per ounce) or extra-lean ham (about 1 gram of fat and 35 calories per ounce).

Because the names of the various cuts of pork vary around the country, be sure to ask your butcher for his recommendations for the leanest cuts at your market, and remember that the internal temperature of a pork roast should reach 170°F for health reasons. Place your meat thermometer in the center of the thickest part of the meat.

Dijon Pork Roast ✓

PREPARATION TIME: 10 MINUTES   COOKING TIME: 1½ HOURS

1 lean pork roast, about 2½ to 3 pounds with bone
2 cups low-sodium stock
½ teaspoon garlic powder
½ teaspoon dry mustard
1 teaspoon thyme
½ cup chopped leeks

1 medium carrot, sliced into ¼-inch rounds
1 medium zucchini, sliced into ¼-inch rounds
1 stalk celery, sliced
Dijon mustard or Dijon Sauce (p. 296)

1. Trim all visible fat from the roast, and place the roast in a baking pan. Pour the stock over it.
2. Combine the garlic powder, dry mustard, and thyme, and rub the mixture over all sides of the roast. Arrange the chopped vegetables around the roast.
3. Bake at 350 degrees for 1½ hours, or until the roast is cooked through and tender (170°F), basting occasionally. Serve each slice of pork with a teaspoon or two of Dijon mustard or Dijon Sauce, plus vegetables.

6 servings of 3½ ounces each (cooked weight), plus vegetables.

Per serving: **8 g. fat,** 227 calories, 78 mg. cholesterol, 1 g. dietary fiber, 146 mg. sodium

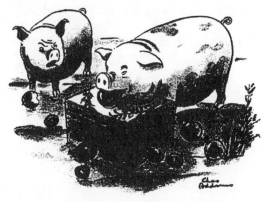

"You certainly have a peculiar sense of humor." DRAWING BY CHAS. ADDAMS; © 1939, 1967 THE NEW YORKER MAGAZINE, INC.

Pork Loin Stir-Fry

PREPARATION TIME: 12 TO 15 MINUTES   COOKING TIME: 15 TO 20 MINUTES

This stir-fry is mild and very good. Serve it over cooked grain or whole-wheat pasta.

2 pounds boneless top loin or roast
1 tablespoon peanut oil
1 clove garlic, minced or crushed
½ inch fresh gingerroot, minced, OR 1 teaspoon ground ginger

1 medium onion, cut in chunks
1 medium apple, chopped
1 medium green pepper, sliced in thin strips
4 medium carrots, cut in thin strips, 1 inch long
½ cup water or low-sodium stock

1. Trim all visible fat from pork, and cut into strips about 2 inches by ½ inch.
2. Heat the oil in a wok or large frying pan over medium-high heat. Add the pork and brown it, stirring constantly. Remove pork and drain on paper towels.
3. Add the garlic, ginger if using fresh, and onion to the wok, cover, and sauté/steam until onions are translucent.
4. Add the apple, green pepper, carrots, and water. Stir, cover, and reduce the heat to medium low. Cook for about 3 minutes, and return the pork to the pan.
5. If you're using ground ginger, add it to the stir-fry when the apples are just tender. Let sauté/steam for a few more minutes, until pork is cooked through.

6 servings of 3½ ounces each (cooked weight), plus vegetables.

Per serving: **10 g. fat,** 248 calories, 78 mg. cholesterol, 2 g. dietary fiber, 69 mg. sodium

Pork Chops Parmesan

PREPARATION TIME: 8 TO 10 MINUTES   COOKING TIME: 30 MINUTES

3 tablespoons cornmeal, whole-wheat flour, or bread crumbs
1 tablespoon grated Parmesan cheese
½ teaspoon fresh-ground black pepper
½ teaspoon salt
½ teaspoon basil
4 top loin chops, about ½ inch thick
1 tablespoon vegetable oil
3 scallions, chopped
1 clove garlic, minced
¼ teaspoon fennel seeds, crushed

1. Combine the cornmeal, Parmesan cheese, pepper, salt, and basil.
2. Trim the pork chops of all visible fat, pat them dry, and dredge in the cornmeal mixture.
3. Heat a skillet over medium heat, and add the oil. When the oil is hot, place the chops in the skillet, and reduce the heat to low.
4. Fry the chops for 10 minutes on each side. Then add the scallions, garlic, and fennel, and continue frying for another 10 minutes, turning as necessary to keep from sticking.

4 servings of 2½ ounces each (lean meat only, cooked weight).

Per serving: **9 g. fat,** 194 calories, 52 mg. cholesterol, 1 g. dietary fiber, 341 mg. sodium

Roast Pork with Vegetables

PREPARATION TIME: 10 MINUTES   COOKING TIME: 2 TO 2½ HOURS

1 lean pork roast, about 2½ to
   3 pounds, with bone
1 teaspoon garlic powder
1 teaspoon fresh gingerroot,
   minced
1 teaspoon sage
2 large potatoes, sliced ½ inch
   thick

1 large onion, sliced
4 ounces fresh mushrooms
1 cup low-sodium beef or
   vegetable stock
2 teaspoons tamari sauce or soy
   sauce

1. Trim the roast of all visible fat. Place the roast in a baking pan, and rub all sides with the garlic powder, ginger, and sage.
2. Arrange the vegetables around the roast. Combine the stock and the tamari sauce, and pour over the roast and vegetables.
3. Bake at 375 degrees for 30 minutes, then reduce the heat to 350 and bake an additional 1½ to 2 hours, or until pork is cooked, and appears gray throughout. Baste every 40 minutes.

6 servings of 3½ ounces each (cooked weight), plus vegetables.

Per serving: **7 g. fat,** 284 calories, 78 mg. cholesterol, 2 g. dietary fiber, 153 mg. sodium

Baked Pork Chops

PREPARATION TIME: 5 TO 10 MINUTES   COOKING TIME: 1 HOUR

4 top loin pork chops, 4–6
   ounces each
⅛ teaspoon garlic powder
¼ teaspoon Traditional Italian
   Herb Blend (p. 333)
Dash of salt and fresh-ground
   black pepper

1 can (16 ounces) no-salt-added
   tomatoes
4 ounces fresh mushrooms,
   sliced
¼ cup grated cheese (Jarlsberg
   Lite or low-fat Swiss is good)

1. Trim the chops of all visible fat and place them in a roasting pan. Sprinkle with the seasonings.
2. Drain the juice from the tomatoes into the pan, over the pork chops. Reserve the tomatoes.

3. Bake the chops at 375 degrees for 30 minutes.
4. Cover the chops with the mushrooms, the reserved tomatoes, and the cheese, and bake an additional 30 minutes.

4 servings of 2½ ounces each (lean meat only, cooked weight), plus vegetables.

Per serving: **6 g. fat,** 181 calories, 54 mg. cholesterol, 3 g. dietary fiber, 213 mg. sodium

Oriental Pork Chops

PREPARATION TIME: 5 MINUTES   COOKING TIME: 35 MINUTES

Serve this with cooked grain or a baked potato and a vegetable stir-fry, such as Chinese Cabbage Stir-Fry (p. 278).

4 top loin pork chops, 4–6
  ounces each
1 tablespoon tamari sauce or
  soy sauce
½ teaspoon fresh-ground black
  pepper

½ teaspoon salt
1 slice fresh gingerroot, about
  ¼ inch thick, minced
3 tablespoons white wine
¼ cup low-sodium beef stock

1. Trim the chops of all visible fat and place them in a baking pan.
2. Combine the remaining ingredients, except for the stock, in a small bowl. Brush the sauce mixture over each chop, reserving any remaining sauce.
3. Bake the chops at 350 degrees for 20 minutes.
4. Pour the stock over the chops, along with any remaining sauce. Bake an additional 10 to 15 minutes, basting occasionally, until chops are cooked (gray all the way through the center).

4 servings of 2½ ounces each (lean meat only, cooked weight), plus sauce.

Per serving: **5 g. fat,** 145 calories, 51 mg. cholesterol, no dietary fiber, 516 mg. sodium

Jambalaya

PREPARATION TIME: 25 MINUTES   COOKING TIME: 20 MINUTES

Jambalaya is good served hot over brown rice or other cooked grain for a complete meal. Check your supermarket for specially marked packages of *lean* ham and low-fat sausage. Lean ham will have 1 gram of fat per ounce, while low-fat sausage will have about 2 grams of fat per once. Be sure to check the labels since regular sausage may have 10 grams of fat per ounce!

10 ounces cooked lean ham, diced

½ pound smoked low-fat sausage, cut into ¼-inch-thick slices

2 medium onions, diced

1 large clove garlic, crushed

1 teaspoon vegetable oil (optional)

2 cans (16 ounces each) no-salt-added tomatoes

1 can (4 ounces) oysters, plus their liquid, OR 4 ounces fresh oysters

1 tablespoon whole-wheat flour

2 packages (6 ounces each) mini-shrimp

1. Brown the ham and the sausage in a skillet. Drain off any fat, and place the meat on paper towels, patting dry to remove excess fat.
2. In the same pan, sauté the onions and garlic, adding the teaspoon of vegetable oil if necessary to keep them from sticking.
3. In a large pot, heat the tomatoes, cutting the larger ones in half. When the tomatoes are hot, add the onions and garlic, ham and sausage, and simmer over low heat.
4. Drain the oysters, reserving their juice. Mix the flour with a little bit of the juice to make a thick roux. Add this roux to the pot, stirring well.
5. Add the oysters and the shrimp, and let simmer for 20 minutes.

8 servings. Serving size is about 1½ cups.

Per serving: **6 g. fat**, 186 calories, 121 mg. cholesterol, 2 g. dietary fiber, 979 mg. sodium

Pork Chops à la Grecque

PREPARATION TIME: 15 MINUTES   COOKING TIME: 35 MINUTES

4 top loin pork chops, 4–6
  ounces each
½ teaspoon salt
2 medium onions, sliced
1 tablespoon olive oil or
  vegetable oil
4 ounces fresh mushrooms,
  sliced
¼ cup unsweetened orange
  juice

¼ cup water or low-sodium
  beef stock
¼ cup Greek or other black
  olives, diced
1 tablespoon lemon juice
¼ teaspoon fresh-ground black
  pepper

1. Trim all visible fat from the chops. Place the chops in a
   baking pan and sprinkle with the salt.
2. Bake at 350 degrees for 20 minutes.
3. While the chops are baking, prepare the sauce by sautéing
   the onions in the oil. When onions are translucent, add the
   mushrooms, cover, and cook two to three minutes more.
   Add the remaining ingredients, and heat through.
4. Spoon the sauce over the chops. Bake another 10 to 15
   minutes or longer, depending on the thickness of the
   chops. Baste occasionally, until the chops are cooked
   through (gray all the way through the center).

*4 servings of 2½ ounces each (lean only, cooked weight), plus
sauce.*

Per serving: **10 g. fat,** 207 calories, 57 mg. cholesterol, 2 g.
dietary fiber, 370 mg. sodium

Roast Pork Tenderloin

PREPARATION TIME: 10 MINUTES   COOKING TIME: 45 MINUTES

Pork tenderloin makes a memorable roast. One and a half pounds of meat will reduce in cooking and yield about six 3½-ounce servings.

½ teaspoon thyme
½ teaspoon marjoram
½ teaspoon sage
½ teaspoon garlic powder
½ teaspoon onion powder
½ teaspoon ground ginger

Fresh-ground black pepper to taste
2 tablespoons soy sauce
1 tablespoon Worcestershire sauce
1½ pounds pork tenderloin

1. Place all dry ingredients in a small bowl.
2. Add soy sauce and Worcestershire sauce and mix well.
3. Spread mixture evenly over meat and allow to marinate for an hour or two in the refrigerator.
4. Roast at 350 degrees until internal temperature reaches 170°F (about 45 minutes).
5. To serve, slice in ¼-inch pieces and arrange on a platter with rice or vegetables.

VARIATIONS: 1. If you wish, you can add 1 teaspoon olive oil to the marinade. The oil helps the marinade stick to the meat, and since some of the marinade cooks away during roasting and some sticks to the pan, you will add only a couple of grams of fat to the entire roast.
2. Company version: Use 4 cloves of minced garlic, 3 chopped green onions, and a 1-inch piece of ginger, minced, in place of the dry ingredients.
3. When you are in a hurry for a roast, one of my friends who is a master chef recommended that you forget everything else and just rub the meat with 2 tablespoons of Dijon mustard and 2 cloves of garlic, minced, before roasting.

6 servings of 3½ ounces each.

Per serving: **5 g. fat,** 169 calories, 92 mg. cholesterol, no dietary fiber, 67 mg. sodium

Lamb

Although I have never had much of a preference for fatty meats in general and have never regretted the close trimming of any other meat, lamb is an exception. I can remember, as a child, gnawing and sucking every gram of meat, fat, and marrow from my serving of two little ribs of broiled lamb chops. I could never get enough of them, nor could the rest of the family. Always expensive, they were served only when we decided that it was time for a treat.

Indeed, the source of a never-to-be-forgotten memory is the first night I brought my future wife, Enid, to meet my parents.

As my mother approached the dinner table with a platter laden with luscious double-thick chops, my brother and father rose from their chairs to a near-standing position to spear a chop before the platter could be set upon the table. Enid, the slowest eater of the group, was still at work carefully cutting and trimming her second chop after everyone else had finished and cleaned their bones. About halfway through, Enid made the fatal error of pausing and putting her fork down. Before Enid's hand could come to rest, my mother reached across the table and speared the remainder of the meat. As she stabbed the plump little chop, Mother said to Enid, "You don't want this?" It was more a statement than a question.

Whenever lamb chops were served at my family's dinner table, Enid rightly felt she had to be on guard.

Like most Americans, we do not eat lamb on a regular basis. In fact, in the United States, lamb runs a poor fourth in consumption to beef, pork, and veal. In the eastern and western

regions of the country, where consumption is high, good-quality lamb is easier to come by than in others parts of the United States. There is a big difference between young lamb, under six months old, and that which has reached six months to a year.

Most of our lamb recipes, such as Lamb Shanks and Lentils (pages 152–53), one of our most special entrées, have their origin in Middle Eastern cooking, where lamb is a preferred meat. We guarantee both Sesame-Ginger Lamb Chops (page 158) and Surprise Lamb Chops (page 160) are two dishes worth keeping in your "special dinner" category.

But, yes, lamb is truly a fat meat. The chops that I trimmed to the bone with my teeth as an overweight child averaged 27 grams of fat and 430 calories for just 3½ ounces! But lamb doesn't have to be that fatty. The leg roast and loin chops are the leanest cuts, and if you thoroughly trim your roast or chops before eating, you can still enjoy the wonderful flavors in our recipes, and end up with lamb at 2 to 3 grams of fat and 55 to 65 calories per ounce. So don't pass up the recipes in this chapter.

Lamb Roast with Savory Tomato Sauce ✓

PREPARATION TIME: 10 MINUTES   COOKING TIME: 2 HOURS

1 boneless leg of lamb, about
  2½ pounds
1 medium white onion,
  chopped in chunks
2 medium tomatoes, cut in
  quarters
1 medium bell pepper, cut in
  chunks

2 cloves garlic, crushed
⅓ cup dry red wine
1 can (6 ounces) tomato paste
Fresh-ground black pepper to
  taste
1 teaspoon dried thyme
½ teaspoon dried savory
1 bay leaf

1. Trim all visible fat from the leg of lamb. Place it in a large roasting pan or Dutch oven. Arrange the cut-up vegetables around the lamb. Spread the crushed garlic on top of the meat.
2. Pour the wine over the lamb, then top with the tomato paste, black pepper, thyme, and savory. Float the bay leaf in the bottom of the pan.
3. Cover and bake at 325 degrees for about 2 hours, basting occasionally. The internal temperature should reach 175°F for a well-done roast or 160°–165°F for a barely rare to medium roast.

8 servings of 3½ ounces each (cooked weight).

Per serving: **8 g. fat,** 240 calories, 88 mg. cholesterol, 3 g. dietary fiber, 241 mg. sodium

Lamb Shanks and Lentils

PREPARATION TIME: 55 MINUTES TO 1 HOUR   COOKING TIME: 40 MINUTES

1½ cups lentils
1 medium onion, stuck with 2 whole cloves
1 bay leaf
3 cups beef stock
4 lamb shanks

¼ to ⅓ cup whole-wheat flour
2 cloves garlic, chopped
1 tablespoon vegetable oil
½ cup low-sodium beef stock
½ cup white wine

The following to taste: ground ginger, dry mustard, oregano, tarragon, salt, pepper

1. Overnight, soak the lentils, the onion stuck with the cloves, and the bay leaf in the 3 cups of stock. (Add a little more stock or water if necessary to completely cover the lentils.)
2. Next day, bring this mixture to a boil, then reduce heat and simmer until the lentils are tender, about 35 to 40 minutes. Remove from the heat and let cool.
3. Dust the lamb shanks with the flour (we shake them together in a bag). Set aside.
4. In a skillet, brown the garlic in the oil. Remove the garlic, then brown the lamb shanks in the same pan. Sprinkle them with ginger, dry mustard, oregano, and tarragon as they brown. Then pour in the ½ cup of beef stock and the ½ cup of wine and sprinkle in a little salt and pepper. Simmer, covered, until tender.
5. With a slotted spoon, remove the lentils from their broth, and put them in a large baking dish. Remove the cloves from the onion and discard; also discard the bay leaf.
6. Chop the cooked onion, and mix in with the lentils. Place the lamb shanks on top, and pour in the juice from the lamb. Then pour in the broth from the lentils until it just comes to the top of the lentils.

7. Bake at 375 degrees for 40 minutes.

4 servings of 1 lamb shank each (about 3 ounces of meat after cooking), plus about 1 cup of lentils.

Per serving: **11 g. fat,** 503 calories, 89 mg. cholesterol, 10 g. dietary fiber, 135 mg. sodium

Sweet-Pepper Lamb

PREPARATION TIME: 10 MINUTES   COOKING TIME: 1¼ HOURS

If you can't find the red peppers that make this dish so attractive, try the yellow variety. Green or purple peppers are fine, too.

2½ pounds lean lamb meat (leg roast preferred)
2 cups low-sodium stock
2 large cloves garlic, minced or crushed
2 tablespoons dried parsley
2 teaspoons rosemary
1 teaspoon sage
Salt and fresh-ground black pepper to taste
2 whole fresh red peppers, cut into strips

1. Preheat oven to 350 degrees.
2. Trim the visible fat from the lamb, and place the lamb in a roasting pan. Pour the stock over the lamb, and add the seasonings. Arrange the strips of red pepper on top of the meat.
3. Cover and bake for 1 hour and 15 minutes.

8 servings of 3½ ounces each (cooked weight), plus peppers.

Per serving: **8 g. fat,** 207 calories, 88 mg. cholesterol, 1 g. dietary fiber, 154 mg. sodium

Lamb Stew

PREPARATION TIME: 8 TO 10 MINUTES   COOKING TIME: 1½ HOURS

This goes well with a side dish of pasta and fresh cooked spinach or other greens, such as kale, collard, mustard, or turnip greens.

1 pound lean lamb, cubed
1 tablespoon vegetable oil or
  olive oil
1 medium tomato, diced
1 tablespoon parsley

1 teaspoon oregano
2 or 3 scallions, diced
1 tablespoon lemon juice
1 teaspoon salt

1. Trim the lamb of all visible fat, and brown the lamb in the oil in a large saucepan or skillet over medium-high heat.
2. Add the remaining ingredients, stirring well. Cover, and reduce heat to low. Simmer for at least 1½ hours, stirring occasionally.

4 servings of 3 ounces each (cooked weight), plus sauce.

Per serving: **10 g. fat,** 204 calories, 76 mg. cholesterol, 1 g. dietary fiber, 596 mg. sodium

Rolled Lamb Roast

PREPARATION TIME: 10 MINUTES   COOKING TIME: 45 TO 60
MINUTES

For a simple and delicious treat, have your butcher bone and trim a leg of lamb and tie a rolled roast for you. I think the roast is most tender when cooked in a slow oven, around 300 degrees, until my meat thermometer reaches 170 degrees. If you don't have a meat thermometer, figure about 20 minutes or so per pound.

1 2½-pound rolled lamb roast
1 teaspoon each of rosemary,
   thyme, sage, marjoram,
   ground ginger, and
   fresh-ground black pepper

1 or 2 cloves garlic, crushed
½ teaspoon salt
1 tablespoon olive oil
1 tablespoon soy sauce

1. Use the tip of a sharp knife to make gashes about an inch apart in the meat.
2. In a bowl or cup, mix together the remaining ingredients to make a paste. Rub the paste well into the roast, covering all exposed meat and pushing it into the gashes you have made.
3. Place in a 300-degree oven for about 45 minutes to 1 hour, until the roast is cooked the way you like it.

8 servings of 3½ ounces each (cooked weight).

Per serving: **10 g. fat,** 204 calories, 88 mg. cholesterol, no dietary fiber, 330 mg. sodium

Curried Lamb with Vegetables

PREPARATION TIME: 20 MINUTES   COOKING TIME: 40 MINUTES

In countries where curries are popular, every great cook creates a curry powder out of a variety of spices, such as the ones in this recipe. Even if you've never liked curry, you'll probably like this—it's quite mild.

4 lamb loin or shoulder chops, about ¾ inch thick (4–6 ounces each)
2 cloves garlic, minced
1 tablespoon vegetable oil
1 cup water or low-sodium stock
1 teaspoon cumin
½ teaspoon ground ginger
¼ teaspoon ground coriander

¼ teaspoon cayenne pepper
½ teaspoon turmeric
1 medium zucchini, cut in chunks
2 medium carrots, sliced
1 medium onion, cut in chunks
Fresh-ground black pepper to taste
1 package (10 ounces) frozen green peas

1. Trim any visible fat from the chops, and brown them with the garlic in the vegetable oil in a large skillet.
2. Remove the lamb, and add the remaining ingredients except the peas. Cover and bring to a boil. Reduce heat to simmer, and put the lamb back in the pan. Cover, and simmer for 30 minutes.
3. Add the peas, and simmer another 10 minutes, until the vegetables are tender and the lamb is cooked.

4 servings of 2½ ounces each (lean only, cooked weight), plus vegetables.

Per serving: **8 g. fat,** 221 calories, 44 mg. cholesterol, 6 g. dietary fiber, 136 mg. sodium

Moroccan Stew

PREPARATION TIME: 20 MINUTES   COOKING TIME: 2½ HOURS

Serve this stew over cooked semolina, the grain often used in Moroccan couscous, or any other of your favorite cooked grains. Or serve it alone as a soup.

3 cups water
1 leg of lamb, about 2½–3 pounds
1 can (16 ounces) tomatoes, with juice
2 medium onions, sliced or quartered
2 cups carrots, sliced about ¼ inch thick
1 piece fresh gingerroot, about ½ inch thick

2 cinnamon sticks
3 whole cloves
½ teaspoon saffron threads
1 teaspoon salt
½ teaspoon fresh-ground black pepper
½ teaspoon ground coriander
1 cup cooked garbanzo beans
1 medium zucchini, diced
¼ cup raisins

1. Bring the water to a boil in a large pot. Meanwhile, trim the lamb of any visible fat. Add the lamb to the boiling water, along with the tomatoes and their juice, the onions, and the carrots. Bring to a boil again. Reduce the heat to low, cover, and let simmer, turning the meat and basting it occasionally to cook evenly.
2. Put the ginger, cinnamon sticks, and cloves in a cheesecloth bag and add to the stew. (You can add these without the bag, but the bag makes them easier to remove.)
3. Combine the saffron, salt, pepper, and coriander, and add to the stew after it has been simmering for about 1½ hours.
4. Add the garbanzos, zucchini, and raisins, and continue cooking for another hour.
5. Remove the cheesecloth spice bag or individual spices, and serve.

8 servings of 3½ ounces of meat (cooked weight), plus vegetables.

Per serving: **9 g. fat,** 272 calories, 88 mg. cholesterol, 4 g. dietary fiber, 439 mg. sodium

Sesame-Ginger Lamb Chops

PREPARATION TIME: 5 TO 10 MINUTES   COOKING TIME: 23 TO 26 MINUTES

Prepare the marinade early in the morning (before work, for example) or the night before. Then almost all that remains to be done to prepare this main dish for dinner is to broil it. See pages 235–36 for instructions on how to toast seeds.

4 lamb chops, 4–6 ounces each
3 tablespoons tamari sauce or soy sauce
¼ cup water
1 teaspoon lemon juice
1 teaspoon honey

1 slice fresh gingerroot, ½ inch thick, minced
4 teaspoons toasted sesame seeds, crushed with mortar and pestle

1. Trim the chops of all visible fat. Arrange the chops in a shallow pan.
2. In a small bowl, combine the tamari, water, lemon juice, honey, and ginger. Pour this mixture over the lamb and cover. Marinate in the refrigerator overnight or for about 8 hours.
3. When you're ready to cook the meal, remove the chops from the marinade and arrange on a broiler pan. Broil about 5 inches from the heat at your oven's lowest broiler setting for 10 minutes. Turn and broil another 8 minutes.
4. Sprinkle the chops with the sesame seeds, and broil 5 to 8 minutes more.

4 servings of 2½ ounces each (lean meat only, cooked weight).

Per serving: **6 g. fat,** 130 calories, 44 mg. cholesterol, no dietary fiber, 647 mg. sodium

Roast Herbed Leg of Lamb

PREPARATION TIME: 15 MINUTES   COOKING TIME: 3½ HOURS

1 bone-in leg of lamb, 4 pounds
Salt and pepper to taste
4 cloves garlic, cut in slivers
1 teaspoon dried thyme
1 teaspoon dried rosemary
Juice of 2 lemons
1 tablespoon olive oil

8 small whole onions, peeled
16 small new potatoes, washed
2½ pounds yellow squash
1 cup water (optional)
2 teaspoons cornstarch
   (optional)
2 tablespoons water (optional)

1. Trim the lamb of all visible fat. Lightly sprinkle the lamb with salt and pepper. Cut small slits in the meat, and insert the garlic slivers. Sprinkle the herbs over the meat. Place the lamb in a roasting pan.
2. In a small bowl, combine the lemon juice and olive oil. Pour this mixture over the meat.
3. Bake at 325 degrees for about 2½ hours.
4. Arrange the vegetables around the roast, cutting the larger squash in half. Return the roast to the oven for another hour.
5. Optional: To make a gravy, remove the completely cooked lamb and vegetables to a large serving platter. Skim off any fat in the pan. Add the cup of water to the pan, and stir constantly on the stove top over low heat. Dissolve the cornstarch in the 2 tablespoons of water, and add to the gravy to thicken, if desired.

8 servings of 3½ ounces each (cooked weight), plus vegetables.

Per serving: **10 g. fat,** 352 calories, 88 mg. cholesterol, 4 g. dietary fiber, 146 mg. sodium

Surprise Lamb Chops ✓

PREPARATION TIME: 12 TO 15 MINUTES   COOKING TIME: 1 HOUR

This recipe is so named because each serving comes wrapped in its own foil "surprise package."

4 lamb loin chops, 4–6 ounces each
1 teaspoon salt
½ teaspoon fresh-ground black pepper
1 teaspoon oregano
3 small potatoes, sliced ¼ inch thick
1 large carrot, sliced ¼ inch thick
½ medium zucchini, sliced
4 fresh mushrooms, sliced
4 teaspoons crumbled feta cheese (or other cheese of choice)
2 teaspoons lemon juice
Aluminum foil

1. Trim the chops of all visible fat. Place each chop on a *doubled over* piece of foil (or use heavy-duty foil) large enough to fold over the chop and vegetables.
2. Combine the salt, pepper, and oregano, and sprinkle each chop with one-quarter of the mixture. Then cover each chop with a layer of each different vegetable, a teaspoon of cheese, and a sprinkling of lemon juice.
3. Bring the longest edges of the foil together and roll down until it fits well across the top of the chop and vegetables, sealing them. Roll up the ends securely so that you have a neat package.
4. Place the 4 packages in a baking pan, in order to catch any juices. Bake at 350 degrees for 1 hour.
5. Serve in the package if you like; just be careful when unwrapping—it will be hot!

4 servings of 2½ ounces each (lean only, cooked weight), plus vegetables.

Per serving: **6 g. fat,** 207 calories, 48 mg. cholesterol, 3 g. dietary fiber, 642 mg. sodium

Poultry

Chicken in one form or another is about the most frequent main course for dinner in my home and in Terri's. One reason is that it is so simple to prepare. Buy extra and freeze it, if you like. If you forget to defrost the night's dinner before you leave the house in the morning and you have a microwave oven, a cut-up fryer will defrost in just a few minutes in the microwave when you get home. Then you can pop it in the oven with very little fuss. Look, for example, at the variations of Baked Chicken (pages 162–63) or, for a spicy treat, our Oven-Fried Chicken (page 166). Talk about ease of preparation!

In comparison with red meats, chicken is a low-fat source of protein. We knew there was a difference between the fat levels of beef and chicken, but it was not until we had to look up some information about the relative nutrient content of each that we became fully aware of some incredible differences. A half breast of chicken—about 3 ounces of cooked white meat without skin—might contain 3 grams of fat and about 120 to 140 calories. A *small* rib-eye steak—about 3½ ounces cooked, and not well trimmed—might contain over 25 grams of fat and 440 calories.

While we still like our chicken prepared as a main course according to the recipes we include in this chapter, we have also begun using chicken as a condiment in combination with other foods. Check out our various chicken combination dishes, such as Chicken with Broccoli and Carrot (page 167), with Cashews and Broccoli (page 174), and with Leeks and Mushrooms (page 169). Remember to save the carcass from roasted chicken to make soups and stock.

Our nutritional analyses assume half white meat, half dark,

when whole chickens are called for. When our recipes call for chicken breasts, we mean split breasts; that is, 4 chicken breasts equal 4 half breasts unless otherwise specified. Skinned white meat contains roughly 1 gram of fat and 40 calories per ounce, while skinned dark meat contains about 2 grams of fat and 55 calories per ounce.

Watch out for ground turkey! Regular ground turkey averages 4 grams of fat per ounce. You can obtain ground turkey with only 1 gram of fat per ounce in extra-lean brands or by asking your butcher to grind skinless breast on special order.

Neither Terri nor I has ever made a duck. The thought of all the fat is a turn-off. So you can imagine our surprise when Chef Sylvain Le Coguic at Julian's, which was one of Nashville's most noted restaurants, responded to our request to illustrate a dish that he might serve to someone interested in keeping fat and calories low with a recipe for duck! It isn't, of course, possible to prepare duck so that it ends up containing as little fat as the white meat of chicken, but Julian's Grilled Duck Breast (page 181) ends up at fewer than 4 grams of fat and about 60 calories an ounce. The entire main course, prepared as directed, is only about 350 calories. If you like duck and thought you might have to deprive yourself because it's so high in fat, try preparing it this way. For that special occasion it will be a pleasure to look at, as well as to eat.

Finally, for health reasons, it is a good idea to rinse poultry in cold water before cooking, pat it dry with paper towels, and, if you need to slice or chop it, do this on a non-wooden cutting board.

Baked Chicken

PREPARATION TIME: 5 TO 10 MINUTES   COOKING TIME: 25 MINUTES

For days when you really want a low-calorie entrée or need something quick to throw in the oven, baked chicken is a simple yet delicious solution.

Try the following seasoning combinations for variety:

VARIATION 1: Sprinkle liberally with onion and garlic powder, and Herb Salt (pp. 332–33). Or make your own selection of herbs, using one or more of the following: marjoram, oregano, rosemary leaves, tarragon, or thyme leaves. Add fresh-ground black pepper.

VARIATION 2: Sprinkle liberally with chili powder, paprika, and a dash of cayenne pepper. Add salt at the table after tasting.

VARIATION 3: Fat and calories are significantly reduced if the chicken is skinned *before* baking. But skinning prior to cooking creates a problem since the meat is likely to dry out. You can prevent this by coating the skinned chicken with a basting sauce made from ½ cup of ketchup, 2 tablespoons of tamari sauce or low-sodium soy sauce, and 2 ounces of sherry. Then sprinkle with herbs of your choice. Loosely cover the chicken with a piece of aluminum foil for about half the cooking time and it will stay moist.

Here are the basic directions for baking chicken.

1 small frying chicken, about 3 to 3½ pounds, cut up	Your favorite seasonings Aluminum foil

Line a baking pan with foil and lay out the pieces of the fryer. Season as desired and bake at 400 degrees for approximately 25 minutes. Skin before eating. (Much of the flavor of the seasonings will have penetrated to the flesh of the chicken during baking; however, add more at the table, if desired.)

6 servings of about 3 ounces each (cooked weight).

Per serving (half light, half dark meat): **3 g. fat,** 155 calories, 72 mg. cholesterol, no dietary fiber, 63 mg. sodium

Barbecued Chicken ✓

PREPARATION TIME: 5 MINUTES   COOKING TIME: 45 TO 50 MINUTES

You can use this recipe with our Barbecue Sauce (p. 288) or your own variation. Or substitute store-bought sauce if you wish. Look for the one lowest in sugar and salt.

2½ pounds chicken pieces   1 cup barbecue sauce

1. Preheat oven to 350 degrees.
2. Skin the chicken. Place the pieces "skin" side down in a large, shallow baking pan. (You may wish to line the pan with foil for easy cleaning.)
3. Baste the chicken liberally with barbecue sauce, and place in the oven.
4. Bake 20 minutes, basting halfway through. Then turn the chicken over and bake another 25 to 30 minutes, or until chicken is tender, basting occasionally.

6 servings of about 3½ ounces each (cooked weight), plus sauce.

Per serving: **5 g. fat,** 193 calories, 88 mg. cholesterol, 0 dietary fiber, 373 mg. sodium

Patti's Roast Chicken ✓

PREPARATION TIME: 10 MINUTES   COOKING TIME: 1 HOUR AND
                                                           50 MINUTES

Patti Bereyso is a video producer and writer who helped produce a home video several years ago based on *The Rotation Diet*. Ever energetic, she cheerfully handed us this recipe as soon as she heard we were writing a cookbook.

Prepare this a day in advance, then discard the fat, reheat, and serve with its own rich-tasting gravy over cooked grain.

4 chicken breasts, skinned   1 teaspoon garlic powder
  (about 5 ounces each)   1 teaspoon dried rosemary
¾ cup water   1 bay leaf
¼ cup tamari sauce or soy
  sauce

1. Preheat the oven to 375 degrees. Rinse the chicken with cold water and pat dry with paper towels.
2. Place the chicken in a roasting pan. Pour the ¾ cup water into the bottom of the pan. Pour the tamari sauce or soy sauce over the chicken, then sprinkle with garlic powder and rosemary. Float the bay leaf in the water in the bottom of the pan.
3. Bake at 375 degrees for 1½ hours, basting frequently, until chicken is tender and well browned. Add more water (and soy sauce, if you like) as needed.
4. Cool and refrigerate overnight. The fat will harden when chilled. Carefully spoon out the fat, leaving the jelled water-soy mixture in the pan. Place the pan in a 325-degree oven for about 20 minutes, or until thoroughly heated.

4 servings of 3½ ounces each (cooked weight).

Per serving: **4 g. fat,** 176 calories, 84 mg. cholesterol, no dietary fiber, 885 mg. sodium

Oven-Fried Chicken ✓

PREPARATION TIME: 15 MINUTES   COOKING TIME: 1 HOUR

1 tablespoon vegetable oil
1 teaspoon lemon juice
3 pounds chicken pieces,
  skinned
About ⅓ cup skim milk
  or low-fat milk
  or buttermilk
½ cup flour (all-purpose,
  whole-wheat, or combination)

1½ teaspoons paprika
¼ teaspoon salt
¼ teaspoon fresh-ground black
  pepper
¼ teaspoon onion powder
¼ teaspoon garlic powder
⅛ teaspoon cayenne pepper
¼ teaspoon marjoram
¼ teaspoon oregano

1. Combine the oil and lemon juice, and brush each piece of skinned chicken with the mixture.
2. Place the milk in a shallow bowl, and set aside. Combine the flour(s) and seasonings in another bowl, mixing well.
3. Dip the chicken into the milk, coating all sides. Then coat with the flour mixture.
4. Place the chicken "skin" side down in a foil-covered baking pan. Cover loosely with foil, and bake at 350 degrees for 30 minutes. Turn the chicken pieces over, and bake 30 minutes more, or until cooked through.

6 servings of 3½ ounces each (cooked weight).

Per serving: **7 g. fat,** 233 calories, 89 mg. cholesterol, 1 g. dietary fiber, 180 mg. sodium

Chicken with Broccoli and Carrot

PREPARATION TIME: 12 MINUTES   COOKING TIME: 10 MINUTES

Here we try to replicate one of Chef Wang Chia Hsin's creations from Nashville's Peking Garden restaurant. It was the first dish in which we ever used the Chinese technique of dipping the cut-up chicken in egg white and sprinkling with cornstarch before stir-frying. It's a technique worth using.

2 chicken breasts, skinned, boned (about 5 ounces each after boning), and cut into 1-inch pieces
1 egg white
½ teaspoon cornstarch
1 large stalk fresh broccoli
1 small carrot
2 teaspoons vegetable oil
½ cup low-sodium chicken stock
¼ teaspoon cornstarch, dissolved in a small amount of water

1. Dip the chicken pieces in the egg white, and place them on a dish. Sprinkle with the ½ teaspoon of cornstarch.
2. Cut the broccoli and carrot into bite-size pieces and steam over hot water until tender.
3. While the vegetables are cooking, heat a wok or large skillet until hot; add the oil and the chicken. Cook for about 3 minutes on high heat, or until nearly done, stirring frequently. Reduce heat to medium.
4. Remove the broccoli and carrot from the steamer and add to the wok or skillet.
5. Add the chicken stock and the dissolved cornstarch. Bring to a boil, stirring constantly. Reduce heat and continue to stir, cooking only until sauce is just slightly thickened. Then immediately remove from the heat and serve.

2 servings of 1 cut-up breast each, plus vegetables.

Per serving: **8 g. fat,** 227 calories, 75 mg. cholesterol, 2 g. dietary fiber, 130 mg. sodium

Happy Heart Chicken

PREPARATION TIME: 10 MINUTES   COOKING TIME: 1 HOUR

The layer of vegetables in this recipe helps keep the skinned chicken moist. Notice that no oil is necessary!

3 pounds chicken pieces, skinned
2 teaspoons dried basil
3 tablespoons lemon juice
4 green scallions

1 large zucchini
2 medium carrots
1 can (14 ounces) hearts of palm or artichoke hearts

1. Arrange the chicken in a large casserole dish. Sprinkle with the basil and lemon juice. Chop the scallions and spread over the chicken.
2. Scrub the zucchini and carrots clean—do not peel—then cut each vegetable in half. Quarter them lengthwise to make 8 pieces out of each vegetable. Arrange the vegetables in an alternating pattern on top of the chicken, along with the hearts of palm.
3. Cover and bake at 350 degrees for 1 hour, or until the carrots are just tender.

8 servings of 3½ ounces each (cooked weight), plus vegetables.

Per serving: **5 g. fat,** 202 calories, 88 mg. cholesterol, 3 g. dietary fiber, 116 mg. sodium

Greek Chicken

PREPARATION TIME: 4 MINUTES   COOKING TIME: 35 MINUTES

Try serving this with warmed whole-grain pita bread, rice, or Tabbouli (p. 98) and Greek Salad (pp. 94–95).

4 chicken breasts OR 8 drumsticks, skinned
Juice of 2 lemons
1 tablespoon olive oil

3 cloves garlic, crushed
1 teaspoon oregano
Salt and pepper to taste

1. Place the chicken in a shallow pan. Combine all remaining ingredients, and pour over the chicken. Cover and refrigerate at least 3 hours, preferably overnight.
2. Place the chicken on a broiler pan, barbecue grill, or on a rack in a baking pan in a 450-degree oven, and cook for about 35 minutes.

4 servings of 3 1/2 ounces of meat (cooked weight).

Per serving: **7 g. fat,** 179 calories, 73 mg. cholesterol, no dietary fiber, 198 mg. sodium (analysis is for chicken breasts; drumsticks will contain about 30 calories more than breasts, with a total of about 9 grams of fat)

Chicken with Leeks and Mushrooms ✓

PREPARATION TIME: 10 MINUTES   COOKING TIME: 1 1/2 HOURS

Mild and tasty, and easy to prepare.

2 cups low-sodium stock
1 cup brown rice
4 chicken breasts, skinned, about 6 ounces each

6 ounces fresh mushrooms, quartered
2 whole leeks
Mrs. Dash to taste

1. Put the stock and the rice in a large casserole dish, and place the chicken breasts on top. Spread the mushrooms over the chicken.
2. Wash the leeks thoroughly, separating the leaves to get all the dirt out. Then slice the leeks in 1-inch pieces, and place on top of the chicken and mushrooms. Sprinkle with Mrs. Dash.
3. Bake at 325 degrees for 1 1/2 hours.

4 servings of 3 1/2 ounces meat (cooked weight), plus vegetables and rice.

Per serving: **6 g. fat,** 380 calories, 74 mg. cholesterol, 4 g. dietary fiber, 117 mg. sodium

Chicken Divan ✓

PREPARATION TIME: 30 MINUTES   COOKING TIME: 20 MINUTES

If you wish, you may substitute ¾ cup of canned evaporated skim milk for the regular skim milk and nonfat dry milk combination in this recipe. The sapsago cheese is a hard cheese, low in fat, which is similar to Parmesan.

6 chicken breasts, boned and skinned, 5 ounces each
1½ cups low-sodium chicken stock
4 tablespoons whole-wheat flour
¾ cup skim or low-fat milk
¼ cup nonfat dry milk
¼ cup white wine
¼ teaspoon fresh-ground black pepper
1 large bunch fresh broccoli OR 2 packages (10 ounces each) frozen broccoli spears
½ cup sapsago cheese or Parmesan, grated
1 tablespoon fresh parsley, chopped

1. Wrap the chicken breasts in aluminum foil and bake at 350 degrees for 30 minutes.
2. Meanwhile, bring the chicken stock to a boil.
3. In another pan over low heat, combine ¼ cup of the boiling broth and the flour. Cook and stir until smooth. Gradually add the rest of the broth, stirring until thickened. Remove from heat.
4. Combine the skim and nonfat dry milk, and add to the broth, along with the wine and pepper.
5. Place the broccoli spears in a shallow baking dish. Top with half the sauce. Arrange the cooked chicken breasts on top of the broccoli. Combine half the cheese with the rest of the sauce, and pour over the chicken. Sprinkle with parsley and the remaining cheese, and bake at 350 degrees for 20 minutes.

6 servings of 1 breast, plus vegetables.

Per serving: **6 g. fat,** 260 calories, 81 mg. cholesterol, 3 g. dietary fiber, 292 mg. sodium

Baked Lemon Chicken with Vegetables

PREPARATION TIME: 8 MINUTES   COOKING TIME: 30 MINUTES

It seems every low-fat cookbook has a recipe for lemon-baked chicken. In fact, two of my other books have slightly different versions of it, so this time we were going to leave it out and substitute our Lime-Light Chicken (the next recipe). But this variation is so good, we gave in to tradition. It is excellent served with brown rice or any other cooked whole grain.

4 chicken breasts, skinned and boned, about 4½–5 ounces each
1 clove garlic, crushed
½ teaspoon oregano
Dash of salt (optional)
Fresh-ground black pepper to taste

2 medium zucchinis, sliced
1 medium green pepper, sliced in strips
½ cup low-sodium chicken stock
3 tablespoons lemon juice
1 tablespoon white wine

1. Place the chicken in a casserole dish. Top with the garlic, the other seasonings, and the vegetables. Pour in the stock, lemon juice, and wine.
2. Cover tightly and bake at 350 degrees for 30 minutes or until chicken is cooked through.

4 servings of about 3½ ounces meat (cooked weight), plus vegetables.

Per serving: **3 g. fat,** 172 calories, 73 mg. cholesterol, 2 g. dietary fiber, 76 mg. sodium

Lime-Light Chicken

PREPARATION TIME: 5 MINUTES   COOKING TIME: 50 TO 55 MINUTES

This is good hot, and for some reason, even better cold. Make it ahead of time for a picnic lunch: Chill it in the refrigerator for several hours or overnight, then skim off any fat that has risen to the top. Add a small amount of salt at the table if you like.

4 chicken breasts, skinned (about 6 ounces each)	1 teaspoon dried thyme
1 bay leaf	¼ teaspoon ground coriander
1 tablespoon vegetable oil	Fresh-ground black pepper to taste
1 tablespoon white vinegar	1 lime, cut into thin rounds
1 tablespoon lime juice	

1. Preheat the oven to 325 degrees. Place the chicken breasts and the bay leaf in a casserole dish. Pour the vegetable oil, vinegar, and lime juice over the top.
2. Sprinkle with the seasonings, cover, and bake in the oven for 45 minutes.
3. Remove the chicken from the oven, and arrange the lime slices on top of the chicken. Return the chicken to the oven and bake uncovered for another 5 to 10 minutes, until chicken is cooked through.

4 servings of 3½ ounces each (cooked weight).

Per serving: **7 g. fat,** 180 calories, 73 mg. cholesterol, 1 g. dietary fiber, 64 mg. sodium

Easy Indian Chicken Stir-Fry

PREPARATION TIME: 12 MINUTES   COOKING TIME: 20 MINUTES

We tried this with chicken, but it would do just as well with any leftover cooked meat, or even as a vegetarian stir-fry. It's also a great way to use up any extra raw or cooked vegetables you may have on hand. Use any vegetables you like, to make 2 cups, and always remember to start cooking the ones which take the most time first, adding the others as you go along. If you use cooked vegetables, they will need only a quick warming up.

For a "make-ahead" dish, simply dice the meat and vegetables the night before or in the morning, and store in the refrigerator.

Have ready:

1 tablespoon peanut oil
1 clove garlic, crushed
2 scallions, diced
1 medium zucchini, thinly sliced
8 ounces mushrooms, sliced

1 tomato, diced
2 cups cooked chicken, skinned, diced
2 tablespoons tamari sauce or soy sauce

Spices:

½ teaspoon cumin
½ teaspoon fresh gingerroot, minced
¼ teaspoon ground coriander
¼ teaspoon cayenne pepper
½ teaspoon turmeric

¼ teaspoon fresh-ground black pepper
(Or substitute 2¼ teaspoons of Indian Spice Blend, p. 332, for these spices)

1. Heat the oil in a wok or large skillet over medium heat. Add the garlic and scallions, and cook for 2 to 3 minutes, stirring constantly. Add the zucchini, and stir-fry for about 6 or 7 minutes. Add the mushrooms and tomato, and stir-fry until zucchini is almost tender.
2. Add the chicken, and heat through, still stirring. Then add the tamari sauce and the spices, mix well, and serve.

4 servings. Serving size is 1 cup.

Per serving: **9 g. fat,** 197 calories, 58 mg. cholesterol, 3 g. dietary fiber, 464 mg. sodium

Chicken with Cashews and Broccoli

PREPARATION TIME: 15 MINUTES   COOKING TIME: 10 TO 15 MINUTES

Assemble all of your ingredients ahead of time, so you can follow the steps of this Oriental dish quickly and easily. Serve with steaming-hot brown rice.

1 tablespoon cornstarch
1 cup low-sodium chicken stock
3 tablespoons dry sherry
2 tablespoons tamari sauce or soy sauce
½ teaspoon Tabasco sauce
1 tablespoon peanut oil
3 whole chicken breasts, skinned, boned, and cut in 1-inch chunks
2 slices fresh gingerroot, ¼ inch thick each

3 cups broccoli flowerets
1 medium sweet red pepper, cut in 1-inch squares
½ pound fresh mushrooms, sliced
1 bunch scallions (about 5 or 6), slivered
1 clove garlic, crushed or minced
⅓ cup roasted, unsalted cashews or peanuts

1. Combine the cornstarch, chicken stock, sherry, tamari sauce, and Tabasco in a small bowl.
2. Heat the oil in a hot skillet or wok. When the oil is very hot, add the chicken and ginger. Cook, stirring constantly, until chicken turns white. Remove the ginger and push the chicken aside.
3. Place the broccoli, red pepper, mushrooms, scallions, and garlic in the skillet or center of the wok. Cook 3 minutes, stirring constantly.
4. Combine the broth mixture with the vegetables and continue stirring until the sauce thickens slightly. Stir in the chicken from the sides of the wok.
5. Sprinkle with nuts and serve immediately.

6 servings of ½ breast each (about 3½ ounces of meat, cooked weight), plus vegetables.

Per serving: **9 g. fat,** 250 calories, 73 mg. cholesterol, 3 g. dietary fiber, 366 mg. sodium

White-Wine Worcestershire Chicken

PREPARATION TIME: 15 MINUTES   COOKING TIME: 45 TO 60 MINUTES

This very easy recipe uses Lea and Perrins White Wine Worcestershire sauce, which, along with a dry white wine, is the primary seasoning. Check your supermarket for this fine Worcestershire sauce.

3 pounds chicken pieces, skinned
3 medium potatoes, cut in chunks
2 medium onions, cut in chunks

4 ounces mushrooms, whole
1 pint cherry tomatoes, whole
½ cup white wine
2 tablespoons White Wine Worcestershire sauce
1 bay leaf

1. Place the skinned chicken in a casserole dish and cover with the vegetables. Pour in the wine and the Worcestershire sauce, and float the bay leaf in the bottom of the dish.
2. Bake, covered, at 350 degrees for 45 minutes to 1 hour, until the chicken is cooked through and tender.

6 servings of 3½ ounces each (cooked weight), plus vegetables and sauce.

Per serving: **5 g. fat,** 280 calories, 88 mg. cholesterol, 3 g. dietary fiber, 152 mg. sodium

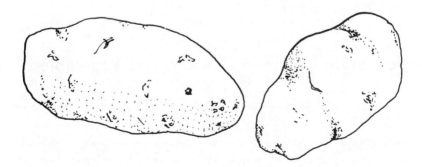

Quick Chicken Stir-Fry with Bulgur

PREPARATION TIME: 12 MINUTES   COOKING TIME: 10 TO 15 MINUTES

3/4 cup bulgur wheat, uncooked
Water to cover
1 tablespoon peanut oil
2 scallions, minced
1 clove garlic, crushed or
   minced
1/4 green bell pepper, diced
1 stalk celery, diced
6 fresh mushrooms, sliced

2 cups cooked chicken, diced
1/4 teaspoon salt
1/2 teaspoon fresh-ground black
   pepper
1/4 cup unsalted, dry-roasted
   peanuts
1/4 cup plain nonfat yogurt
1 tablespoon tamari sauce or
   soy sauce

1. Soak the bulgur in water to cover for 3 to 4 hours. When
   the bulgur is ready—puffy and chewable—drain off any
   remaining water.
2. Heat the oil in a large skillet or wok over medium heat.
   Add the scallions, garlic, bell pepper, and celery, and stir-
   fry for 2 minutes. Add the mushrooms, and stir-fry until
   vegetables are tender.
3. Add the chicken, salt, and pepper, and stir-fry until
   chicken is heated through.
4. Stir in the peanuts, yogurt, and tamari sauce, mixing well.
   Serve over the bulgur.

8 servings of about 1 cup each.

Per serving: **7 g. fat,** 160 calories, 29 mg. cholesterol, 3 g. dietary
fiber, 206 mg. sodium

New-Style Creamed Chicken and Vegetables

PREPARATION TIME: 20 MINUTES   COOKING TIME: 35 TO 40 MINUTES

This recipe is based on an old Shaker recipe—a traditional
American dish with a "new-style" lower-calorie twist that pro-

vides another complete meal-in-one when served with corn-bread as suggested below.

1 large diced potato
1 cup green peas or green
  beans
1 large diced carrot
Water
1 tablespoon butter or
  margarine
1 large onion, chopped
2 stalks celery, chopped
6 tablespoons whole-wheat
  flour

½ teaspoon salt
2 teaspoons marjoram
½ teaspoon fresh-ground black
  pepper
Up to 1 cup water
  or low-sodium stock
2 cups low-fat milk
3 cups cooked chicken, skinned
  and chopped
⅓ cup chopped fresh parsley
½ teaspoon dried rosemary

1. Place the potato, peas, and carrot in a steamer over water, and steam until just tender. Reserve the liquid used for steaming.
2. Meanwhile, melt the butter in a large saucepan and sauté the onion and celery in it until the onion is translucent. Remove from the heat and stir in the flour, 5 tablespoons of the reserved liquid, the salt, marjoram, and pepper. Blend until smooth.
3. Return to the stove on medium heat. Add enough water or stock to the remaining reserved liquid to make one cup, and gradually stir the liquid and the milk into the flour-onion mixture. Bring to a slow boil over medium heat, stirring frequently.
4. Add the chicken, steamed vegetables, parsley, and rosemary. Heat through, and serve over warm Buttermilk Corn Bread (p. 310).

6 servings. Serving size is about 1¾ cups.

Per serving (not including cornbread): **8 g. fat,** 272 calories, 66 mg. cholesterol, 4 g. dietary fiber, 311 mg. sodium

Chicken Italian Style

PREPARATION TIME: 25 MINUTES   COOKING TIME: 25 MINUTES

1 tablespoon olive oil
2 large tomatoes, diced
1 clove garlic, crushed
½ teaspoon salt
¼ teaspoon fresh-ground black
  pepper
½ teaspoon dried parsley
½ teaspoon dried basil

1 egg, beaten
¼ cup skim milk
4 chicken breasts, skinned and
  boned, about 4½–5 ounces
  each
About 1 teaspoon olive oil
1 cup Whole-Wheat Bread
  Crumbs (p. 305)

1. Heat the tablespoon of oil in a skillet over medium heat, then add the tomatoes, garlic, and other seasonings. Simmer on low for 10 minutes, stirring occasionally. Set aside.
2. Beat together the egg and milk. Pound the chicken breasts between wax paper until thin.
3. Brush another skillet with the 1 teaspoon of olive oil. Turn heat on to medium. Dip the chicken in the egg batter and then in the bread crumbs. Sauté a couple of minutes on each side until lightly browned.
4. Place the chicken in a baking dish, and top with the tomato sauce. Bake at 350 degrees for 25 minutes.

4 servings of 1 breast each, plus sauce.

Per serving: **10 g. fat,** 323 calories, 120 mg. cholesterol, 2 g. dietary fiber, 576 mg. sodium

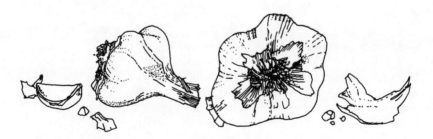

Tandoori Chicken ✓

PREPARATION TIME: 40 MINUTES   COOKING TIME: 40 MINUTES

This simple version of Tandoori Chicken should be prepared a day in advance, as it must marinate for 24 hours before cooking. Serve with cooked grain and curried vegetables.

4 chicken breasts, skinned (about 6 ounces each)
1½ teaspoons chili powder
3 tablespoons lemon juice
1 cup plain nonfat yogurt
5 cloves garlic, roughly chopped

1 tablespoon raisins
1 slice gingerroot, 1½ inches thick, roughly chopped
½ teaspoon ground cumin
1 teaspoon ground coriander
½ teaspoon crushed red pepper
¼ teaspoon salt

1. Place the chicken in a large shallow pan. Slash each chicken breast a few times. Mix together the chili powder and lemon juice, and brush over the chicken breasts with a pastry brush. Let stand 30 minutes.
2. Combine all other ingredients in a blender or food processor, and purée until smooth. Pour over the chicken, cover, and refrigerate for 24 hours.
3. Bake the chicken at 450 degrees for about 40 minutes.

4 servings of about 3½ ounces each (cooked weight).

Per serving: **4 g. fat,** 200 calories, 74 mg. cholesterol, 1 g. dietary fiber, 255 mg. sodium

Baked Horseradish Chicken

PREPARATION TIME: 7 MINUTES   COOKING TIME: 50 TO 60 MINUTES

½ cup white wine
4 chicken breasts, skin
  removed, about 6 ounces
  each
1 tablespoon vegetable oil
2 tablespoons plain horseradish

1¼ teaspoons mustard seed
½ teaspoon onion powder
½ teaspoon garlic powder
¼ teaspoon dried thyme
2 tablespoons fresh parsley,
  chopped fine

1. Pour the wine into a casserole dish, then add the chicken breasts.
2. Using a pastry brush, baste each piece of chicken with the oil. Spread ½ tablespoon of horseradish on each breast.
3. Bake covered at 350 degrees for about 30 minutes. While chicken is baking, grind the mustard seed and combine it with the remaining ingredients.
4. After 30 minutes, baste the chicken with the wine sauce in the pan. Then pour the mustard-seed mixture over the chicken, and bake uncovered another 20 to 30 minutes, until chicken is tender.

4 servings of about 3½ ounces each (cooked weight).

Per serving: **7 g. fat, 202 calories, 73 mg. cholesterol, 1 g. dietary fiber, 73 mg. sodium

Almond Chicken

PREPARATION TIME: 10 MINUTES   COOKING TIME: 20 TO 25
                                                MINUTES

⅓ cup tamari sauce or soy
  sauce
1 teaspoon ground ginger
1 teaspoon garlic powder
3 pounds chicken, skinned and
  boned

½ cup whole-wheat flour
½ cup finely ground almonds
½ teaspoon salt
½ teaspoon fresh-ground black
  pepper
2 tablespoons peanut oil

1. In a large bowl, combine the tamari sauce, ginger, and garlic powder. Cut the chicken into bite-size chunks, and

marinate it in the tamari-sauce mixture while preparing the other ingredients.
2. In another bowl, combine the flour, almonds, salt, and pepper.
3. Heat the oil in a wok or large saucepan on high heat. When the oil is hot, coat the chicken pieces with the flour mixture, and add to the wok. Reduce the heat to medium.
4. Cover and cook, stirring often, until the chicken is done, about 20 minutes.

8 servings of 3 1/2 ounces each (cooked weight).

Per serving: **12 g. fat,** 275 calories, 88 mg. cholesterol, 2 g. dietary fiber, 487 mg. sodium

Grilled Duck Breast (Julian's)

PREPARATION TIME: 10 MINUTES   COOKING TIME: 30 TO 40 MINUTES

1 ounce wild rice
Herbs to taste
1 duck breast
1/2 fresh tomato

2 ounces fresh spinach
1 teaspoon unsalted butter
Pinch nutmeg
1 bunch watercress

1. Cook the wild rice in water along with your favorite herb or herbs.
2. Grill the duck breast, skin side down, until medium-well-done. At the same time, grill the half tomato. When cooked, peel the skin off the tomato if desired.
3. Just before the duck breast is ready to serve, thoroughly wash the spinach. Heat the butter in a sauté pan, add the spinach and nutmeg, and toss until tender.
4. Remove the skin from the duck breast, and slice the breast. Arrange the slices on a platter with the tomato, the rice, and the wilted spinach. Garnish with watercress.

1 serving of 3 1/2 ounces meat (cooked weight), plus vegetables.

Per serving: **12 g. fat,** 349 calories, 138 mg. cholesterol, 5 g. dietary fiber, 158 mg. sodium

Chicken à l'Orange

PREPARATION TIME: 15 MINUTES   COOKING TIME: 45 TO 50 MINUTES

2½ pounds chicken pieces,
  skinned
1 cup orange juice
½ cup white wine
Traditional Italian Herb Blend
  (p. 333) to taste

Paprika to taste
1 teaspoon peanut oil
1 medium onion, diced
1 large tomato, diced
4 ounces fresh mushrooms,
  diced

1. Preheat oven to 375 degrees. Place chicken pieces in a shallow baking pan. Combine the orange juice and white wine and pour them over the chicken.
2. Sprinkle seasonings over chicken.
3. Bake at 375 degrees for 35 minutes.
4. While chicken is baking, prepare the sauce by brushing a skillet with the peanut oil and heating over medium-high heat. Add the onions, tomato, and mushrooms, and sauté, stirring constantly.
5. When onions are translucent, spoon the sauce over the chicken and bake an additional 10 to 15 minutes.

6 servings of 3½ ounces each (cooked weight), plus sauce.

Per serving: **6 g. fat,** 232 calories, 88 mg. cholesterol, 2 g. dietary fiber, 268 mg. sodium

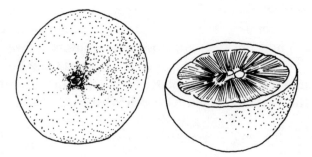

Turkey Meatballs with Tomato Sauce

PREPARATION TIME: 12 TO 15 MINUTES   COOKING TIME: 15 TO
                                                        20 MINUTES

Many meatball recipes start out with raw ground meat, to
which you then add your other ingredients. In this recipe,
however, you brown and drain the meat first, thereby reducing the cooking time of the meatballs. If you want to use homemade tomato sauce, try Fresh Tomato Sauce with White Wine
(pp. 296–97) or Real Italian Tomato Sauce (pp. 288–89).

1 pound lean ground turkey,
  cooked
½ cup bread crumbs
1 tablespoon olive oil
1 medium onion, minced
2 garlic cloves, minced
1 large egg, lightly beaten
½ cup low-sodium chicken
  stock

1 teaspoon dried basil
¼ teaspoon salt
Fresh-ground black pepper to
  taste
1 can (15 ounces) tomato sauce
  OR 2 cups homemade tomato
  sauce
¼ cup chopped fresh parsley

1. Combine the turkey and bread crumbs in a mixing bowl.
2. In a frying pan, sauté the onion and garlic in the olive oil
   until translucent.
3. Keeping the fat, carefully remove the onions and garlic
   from the pan and blend them, together with the egg, stock,
   basil, salt, and pepper, in the mixing bowl with the turkey
   and bread crumbs.
4. Shape the mixture into approximately 24 little meatballs.
5. Place the meatballs in the frying pan and brown evenly
   over medium heat (about 5 minutes). Drain whatever fat
   remains visible at this time. Add the tomato sauce to the
   pan and bring to a simmer. Sprinkle with fresh parsley and
   serve.

6 servings of 4 meatballs each, plus sauce.

Per serving: **11 g. fat**, 233 calories, 93 mg. cholesterol, 2 g.
dietary fiber, 669 mg. sodium

Turkey-Apple Stir-Fry

PREPARATION TIME: 15 MINUTES   COOKING TIME: 15 MINUTES

This may sound like an odd combination at first, but the apple in this recipe won't taste too sweet, and it will blend well with the onion and celery. A great way to use up leftover cooked turkey.

As always when stir-frying, be sure to have all your vegetables and the turkey chopped and ready to toss in the pan.

1 tablespoon peanut
  or vegetable oil
1 medium apple, chopped
1 small onion, chopped
1 clove garlic, minced or
  crushed
½ cup green pepper, diced
2 stalks celery, chopped
1 tablespoon butter
  or margarine
1 tablespoon whole-wheat flour

1 cup low-sodium chicken stock
¼ teaspoon curry powder (try
  Indian Spice Blend,
  p. 332)
½ teaspoon lime juice
¼ teaspoon minced fresh
  gingerroot
2 cups cooked turkey breast,
  diced
½ teaspoon salt

1. Heat the oil in a wok or medium-sized skillet over medium heat. Add the apple, onion, and garlic, and cook, stirring often, until tender.
2. Add the green pepper and celery and stir-fry 2 minutes more. Remove from the heat and set aside.
3. In another large skillet, melt the butter or margarine, and stir in the flour. Cook, stirring, for a minute or two, until the flour is golden brown.
4. Slowly stir in the chicken stock, curry powder, lime juice, and ginger. Then add the apple mixture and the turkey, and simmer until heated through. Stir in the salt, and serve.

4 servings. Serving size is about 1½ cups.

Per serving: **8 g. fat,** 205 calories, 68 mg. cholesterol, 2 g. dietary fiber, 371 mg. sodium

South American Turkey Stew

PREPARATION TIME: 15 MINUTES   COOKING TIME: 1 HOUR AND
                                                            20 MINUTES

¼ cup red wine vinegar
2 cloves garlic, crushed or
   minced
½ teaspoon salt
½ teaspoon fresh-ground black
   pepper
2 turkey drumsticks, skinned
1 green bell pepper, sliced

1 can (10¾ ounces) tomato
   purée
Water
2 tablespoons capers
3 medium potatoes, sliced
¼ cup black olives, sliced
½ cup frozen green peas

1. Combine the vinegar, garlic, salt, and pepper. Marinate the turkey in the mixture for 1 hour.
2. Place the turkey in a heavy pot, with the bell pepper and tomato purée, and add water to cover. Simmer, covered, over medium-low heat for 1 hour.
3. Add the capers, potatoes, and olives, and simmer for 20 more minutes. Add the peas, and simmer another 15 minutes.
4. Remove the turkey and cut the meat off the bones. Chop into chunks, and return the meat to the stew. Heat thoroughly and serve.

4 servings of 3½ ounces meat each (cooked weight), plus vegetables.

Per serving: **8 g. fat,** 348 calories, 87 mg. cholesterol, 6 g. dietary fiber, 735 mg. sodium

Australian Shepherd's Pie

PREPARATION TIME: 45 MINUTES   COOKING TIME: 1 HOUR AND
                                                   5 MINUTES

The original Australian recipe calls for beef, but we have substituted ground turkey with the same delicious results. This is another "meal-in-one" recipe.

Nonstick vegetable cooking
  spray
2 pounds extra-lean ground
  turkey or extra-lean ground
  beef
1 tablespoon olive oil
  or other vegetable oil
1 medium onion, chopped
2 leeks OR 4 scallions, chopped
  fine
1 large carrot, chopped
2 stalks celery, chopped fine
6 medium potatoes, cut in
  chunks

Water for boiling
1 teaspoon thyme
½ teaspoon salt
Fresh-ground black pepper to
  taste
1 tablespoon Worcestershire
  sauce
¾ cup tomato purée
¾ cup low-sodium chicken
  stock
½ cup skim milk or plain
  nonfat yogurt
Dash salt and pepper (optional)
¾ cup frozen green peas

1. Spray a skillet with cooking spray and brown the meat over medium heat. Pour off any fat.
2. In another large skillet, heat the oil. Add the onion, leek, carrot, and celery. Turn the heat to low, and cook covered, for 20 minutes, stirring occasionally.
3. Meanwhile, boil the potatoes in water until tender.
4. Add the meat, thyme, salt, pepper, Worcestershire sauce, tomato purée, and stock to the cooked vegetables, and stir well. Pour into a casserole dish.
5. Cover and bake at 350 degrees for 20 minutes.
6. Meanwhile, mash the cooked potatoes with the milk or yogurt to make stiff mashed potatoes. Add a little more salt and pepper if you wish.
7. Stir the peas into the meat mixture. Spread the mashed potatoes on top. Make a crisscross pattern with a fork for decoration.

8. Bake at 375 degrees for 45 minutes or until brown and bubbly on top.

6 servings of 4 ounces meat (cooked weight), plus vegetables.

Per serving: **9 g. fat**, 431 calories, 86 mg. cholesterol, 7 g. dietary fiber, 488 mg. sodium

Golden Turkey Breast

PREPARATION TIME: 5 MINUTES   COOKING TIME: 2 HOURS

We usually omit sugar whenever it is called for in sauces or meats that simply don't require it. However, this recipe is so good with the sugar that we are leaving in the option of using a little.

1 turkey breast, about 3 pounds
1 cup low-sodium stock
½ cup white wine
1 tablespoon lime juice

1 tablespoon sugar (optional)
2 medium onions, sliced
⅓ cup golden raisins

1. Place the turkey breast in a shallow baking pan. Pour the stock, wine, and lime juice over it. Sprinkle the sugar, if you're using it, over the turkey and into the liquid. Arrange the onion slices around the turkey.
2. Bake at 375 degrees for 2 hours, or until the turkey is tender, basting every ½ hour. Add the raisins for the last 10 minutes of cooking. Remove the skin before serving.

10 servings of 3½ ounces each (cooked weight), plus sauce.

Per serving (with sugar): **1 g. fat**, 179 calories, 85 mg. cholesterol, 1 g. dietary fiber, 65 mg. sodium

Turkey Loaf

PREPARATION TIME: 10 MINUTES   COOKING TIME: 1 HOUR

Ground turkey is becoming increasingly accepted as a substitute for ground beef in loaves and meatballs. Here we have used it alone, but you can blend it with other meats, such as veal. In this recipe we get a bit more elaborate than absolutely necessary by sautéing our mushrooms, onions, and garlic before blending with the other ingredients, but you can whip up a quick version, with different herbs, such as we illustrate in the next recipe, Quick Turkey Loaf. If you are really in a hurry, do this one with canned mushrooms, and use onion and garlic powder instead of the fresh onion and garlic cloves.

1 tablespoon butter
  or margarine
½ pound mushrooms, sliced
1 medium onion, chopped
2 garlic cloves, chopped
1½ pounds extra-lean ground
  turkey
1 tablespoon soy sauce

Fresh-ground black pepper to
  taste
¾ cup dry bread crumbs
¼ cup low-sodium chicken or
  turkey stock
4 tablespoons chopped fresh
  parsley OR 2 teaspoons dried
1 large egg, lightly beaten

1. Preheat the oven to 350 degrees.
2. Melt the butter in a frying pan and sauté the mushrooms, onion, and garlic until the onions are translucent.
3. Transfer the mixture to a bowl and combine with the turkey, soy sauce, pepper, bread crumbs, stock, parsley, and egg. Blend thoroughly.
4. Bake uncovered in a 9 × 5 × 3-inch loaf pan for 1 hour. Let stand for 10 minutes before serving.

6 servings, each slice 1½ inches thick.

Per serving: **8 g. fat,** 245 calories, 105 mg. cholesterol, 2 g. dietary fiber, 339 mg. sodium

Quick Turkey Loaf

PREPARATION TIME: 5 MINUTES   COOKING TIME: 1 HOUR

1½ pounds extra-lean ground
  turkey
¾ cup dry bread crumbs
1 tablespoon soy sauce
¼ cup low-sodium chicken
  or turkey stock
1 teaspoon Worcestershire sauce

Fresh-ground black pepper to
  taste
½ teaspoon each thyme,
  marjoram, and basil
1 teaspoon dried parsley
1 large egg, lightly beaten

1. Preheat the oven to 350 degrees.
2. Blend all the ingredients thoroughly in a mixing bowl and
   bake uncovered in a 9 × 5 × 3-inch loaf pan for 1 hour.
   Let stand for 10 minutes before serving.

6 servings, each slice 1½ inches thick.

Per serving: **6 g. fat,** 211 calories, 100 mg. cholesterol, 1 g.
dietary fiber, 316 mg. sodium

Turkey-Sage Sausage or Meatballs

PREPARATION TIME: 12 MINUTES

COOKING TIME:
SAUSAGE—8 TO 10 MINUTES
MEATBALLS—55 MINUTES

The sage and fennel seeds conjure up the taste of Italian sausage. In the form of meatballs, this dish goes well with spaghetti.

1 pound extra-lean ground turkey
½ cup rolled oats
1 egg
1 medium onion, chopped fine
1 or 2 cloves garlic, minced or crushed
½ teaspoon sage

2 tablespoons fresh parsley, chopped
1 teaspoon ground thyme
½ teaspoon fresh-ground black pepper
1 teaspoon fennel seeds, crushed
¼ teaspoon salt (optional)

1. In a large bowl, combine all ingredients, blending well.
2. For sausage patties, shape into a dozen rounds, flattening them with your palms. Place the patties on a nonstick baking sheet, or cover a baking sheet with foil and spray with nonstick cooking spray. Broil at about 3 inches from heat source for 5 minutes or until lightly browned. Then turn and broil 3 minutes more.
3. For meatballs, shape into a dozen balls and brown lightly in a pan heated over medium-high heat, with no added fat. Then add to your favorite tomato sauce, and let cook in the sauce for about 45 minutes.

6 servings (2 sausage rounds each or 2 meatballs each).

Per serving: **4 g. fat,** 146 calories, 78 mg. cholesterol, 1 g. dietary fiber, 141 mg. sodium

Fish

Fish is not only an excellent, low-calorie source of protein, but there are certain fatty acids in fish, called omega-III fatty acids, that can reduce the risk of heart disease. One of these, eicosapentanoic acid (EPA), has been shown to lower serum cholesterol and triglycerides, and to increase high-density lipoproteins (HDL). Higher HDL levels, like lower total cholesterol, are associated with a reduction in the risk of cardiovascular disease. EPA also brings about some changes in the red blood cells and the platelets in the bloodstream, which are responsible for clotting, so that the risk of blood clots and stroke is reduced.

The best sources of omega-III fatty acids are fatty fish such as salmon, mackerel, pollock (bluefish), albacore tuna, and herring. Halibut, red snapper, swordfish, and shellfish have medium amounts, and cod, monkfish, and orange roughy a little less.

I eat fish at least twice a week when I am in Nashville, and when I travel, I tend to search out restaurants that feature seafood. I probably eat fish three or four times a week on the road, and much prefer it to meat.

I didn't always enjoy fish and my consumption went up from almost zero to the present high level when my wife, Enid, and I learned how to prepare it! Up until about a dozen years ago, all of our efforts at cooking fish seemed to turn out badly. Then, on a trip to Miami, a relative introduced us to a former commodore of the New York Yacht Club, Jim Foster. As he drove us back to our relative's home after a sightseeing trip to the Everglades, the conversation turned to plans for dinner. I commented on our poor luck preparing fish. Jim snorted and said, "Well, I think I can take care of that!" Without further comment, he made a heart-stopping U-turn in order to head for his favorite fish market. He bought three different varieties of fish, which he prepared by tossing together into a large covered baking dish and poaching to perfection in a broth containing sliced fresh tomatoes, onions, and a fifty-fifty mixture of water and dry white wine. Along with one of the best dinners we had ever eaten, we had a lesson in how to prepare fish. Here are the rules we learned.

The first rule is: DO NOT OVERCOOK FISH. Follow cooking times closely.

Second, to keep your interest and appetite at a high level, learn the many different ways of preparing fish: broil, steam, bake, and grill, as well as poach.

Third, learn to use herbs and spices appropriately, together with various sauces. Fish is mild flavored and at its best when fresh. As with veal, this mildness permits a creative, delicate approach to seasoning. Fresh fish is firm to the touch, does not have a strong, unpleasant odor, and, if you are buying the whole fish rather than fillets, has bulging eyes and reddish gills.

Of course, buy fresh fish whenever possible and cook it the same day. But if you happen to find a bargain, then purchase an extra, wrap it well in freezer paper so it won't suffer "freezer burn," and store it for special occasions. We have kept whole salmons frozen for six months or more, and they were still excellent when defrosted and either wrapped in foil and baked in a court bouillon or grilled over a charcoal fire. Remember: If you want to freeze fresh fish and have it hold up well, your freezer *must* be kept at 0 degrees Fahrenheit or lower, and the fish must be wrapped in airtight freezer paper. (This applies to fresh meat, too.) When we know at the time of purchase that meat or fish is to go in our freezer, we ask the meat or fish manager at our grocery to wrap it for us especially for freezing. The market has the equipment for double wrapping and heat sealing the meat or fish in plastic.

If we had to pick just a few recipes that we think can make you as enthusiastic about fish as we are, we advise starting with Royal Indian Salmon (page 200). I published this recipe of Terri's before, but it is SO good, and such a fine example of how to broil fish steaks in general, that we could not think of omitting it from this cookbook. Then, give Steamed Trout (pages 194–95) a try, using any other fish fillets if trout is not available or if you feel inadequate to do the difficult job of filleting a trout. This Oriental preparation method was demonstrated for us by Chef Wang Chia Hsin at the Peking Garden in Nashville, and once you try it, we think you, too, will adopt this way of preparing fish as part of your stock in trade. Finally, there's Arthur's Court Bouillon (below), designed for poaching halibut steaks as part of a five-course, low-fat, 600-calorie gourmet dinner. It can become your standard for poaching.

Court Bouillon (Arthur's)

PREPARATION TIME: 10 MINUTES   COOKING TIME: 30 MINUTES

This is the Court Bouillon used at Arthur's, one of Nashville's finest restaurants, and recommended especially for the Poached Halibut (pp. 196–97) as well as other fish fillets and steaks.

1 quart water	2 teaspoons salt
¼ cup wine vinegar	6 whole peppercorns, crushed
or lemon juice	1 bay leaf
1 small onion, sliced	Pinch of thyme
1 stalk celery, sliced	3 or 4 fresh parsley sprigs
1 medium carrot, sliced	

Combine all ingredients in a stock pot or saucepot and bring to a boil. Reduce the heat and simmer 30 minutes. Strain and cool. (This makes a fat-free, virtually calorie-free strained bouillon.)

Steamed Trout

PREPARATION TIME: 10 TO 15 MINUTES   COOKING TIME: 10 MINUTES

You can steam just about any fish, and fillets of various kinds are perfect for the style of preparation we present here.

In order to preserve the sauce that develops as you cook the fish, this recipe is served on the dish or platter that you will use for steaming, so prepare your dishes and pans in advance. You can invert one dish in the bottom of a pan, put enough water in it to just cover that dish, and place the fish platter on top. The pan or pot must be deep enough so that it can be covered. The first time I prepared fillets this way, I used a roasting pan with a rack inside, and fashioned a platter from heavy-duty aluminum foil by folding up the sides. I heated it on top of the stove over low heat, after bringing the water to a boil, and it worked perfectly.

¼ cup dried black mushrooms (or white, if you cannot find black in the international or Oriental food section of your market)
2 rainbow trout, filleted, OR ¾ pound fillets
Dash of salt
2 scallions
2 inches fresh gingerroot
Fresh-ground black pepper to taste
1 teaspoon rice wine or dry white wine
1 teaspoon vegetable oil

1. Soak the black mushrooms for about 30 minutes in warm water.
2. Score the trout with a sharp knive every inch or so on the back side. Sprinkle this side with salt and place the fish back-side down on the platter you will use for steaming and serving.
3. Use only the bottom 4 inches of the scallions and cut these pieces in half. Peel the ginger. Remove the mushrooms from the water and pat dry with a paper towel. Remove the stems from the mushrooms and discard. Then, slice the scallions and ginger lengthwise, julienne style, and do the

same in the longest direction with the mushrooms. The closer you get to matchstick thinness the better, but it will taste fine even if your matchsticks are pretty thick.

4. Spread the scallions, ginger, and mushrooms evenly over the fish. Sprinkle the pepper, wine, and oil evenly over the fish.
5. Place in the steamer and bring the water to a boil. Cover, reduce the heat, and steam for 10 minutes. Carefully remove the platter so as not to lose the sauce, and serve.

VARIATIONS: Add 1 carrot and/or 1 ounce boiled ham, sliced julienne style.

2 servings of about 4½ ounces each (cooked weight).

Per serving: **10 g. fat,** 221 calories, 86 mg. cholesterol, 1 g. dietary fiber, 206 mg. sodium

Baked Bass with Lemon-Wine Bouillon

PREPARATION TIME: 5 MINUTES   COOKING TIME: 30 MINUTES

4 bass fillets, about 1 pound raw
½ teaspoon dried chives
¼ teaspoon dried chervil or dried parsley
¼ teaspoon dried tarragon
1 tablespoon lemon juice (fresh is best!)

½ cup dry white wine
½ cup Whole-Wheat Bread Crumbs (p. 305)
1 tablespoon butter or margarine

1. Place the fillets in a shallow baking dish. Sprinkle with seasonings and lemon juice. Pour the wine over the fish.
2. Bake at 400 degrees for 15 minutes. Then sprinkle the bread crumbs on top, and dot with butter. Bake 15 minutes more, or until fish flakes easily with a fork.

4 servings of 3½ ounces each (cooked weight).

Per serving: **7 g. fat,** 209 calories, 75 mg. cholesterol, 1 g. dietary fiber, 208 mg. sodium

"Fish, without complications." DRAWING BY W. B. PARK; ©
1986 THE NEW YORKER MAGAZINE, INC.

Poached Halibut in Court Bouillon (Arthur's)

PREPARATION TIME: 5 MINUTES   COOKING TIME: 5 MINUTES

Poaching the fish in the wonderful Court Bouillon is seasoning
enough and no additional sauce is necessary. Serve the fish
with Poached Vegetables with Shallots (p. 276).

1 teaspoon butter
1 or 2 chopped shallots
6 ounces halibut (or other fish
    fillets or steaks such as sole,

turbot, haddock, cod, pike,
    perch, or salmon)
Court Bouillon to cover
    (p. 193)

1. Lightly butter the bottom of a pan with low sloping sides, such as a pie pan. Sprinkle with chopped shallots. Place fish on top in a single layer, and cover with the Court Bouillon.
2. Cover and place in a preheated, 350-degree oven. This takes just a few minutes to cook—no more than 5. Remove from the heat and place on a serving plate.

1 serving of 4½ ounces (cooked weight).

Per serving: **8 g. fat,** 241 calories, 63 mg. cholesterol, no dietary fiber, 132 mg. sodium

Vegetable-Simmered Fish Steaks ✓

PREPARATION TIME: 10 MINUTES   COOKING TIME: 15 TO 20 MINUTES

1 medium onion, chopped
1 clove garlic, chopped
1 tablespoon butter
   or margarine
4 medium tomatoes, cut into
   eighths
8 ounces fresh mushrooms,
   thickly sliced

8 fresh basil leaves, coarsely
   shredded, OR ½ teaspoon
   dried basil
¼ teaspoon salt
Fresh-ground black pepper to
   taste
1½ pounds fish steaks, cut into
   4 servings

1. Sauté the onion and garlic in the butter, covered, over low heat, until golden. Add the tomatoes and simmer, covered, until the tomatoes soften. Add the mushrooms and seasonings, and simmer for about 3 minutes.
2. Add the fish, spoon some sauce over each portion, and simmer, covered, for 5 to 10 minutes, until fish flakes easily with a fork.

4 servings of 4½ ounces each (cooked weight), plus vegetable sauce.

Per serving (with haddock): **5 g. fat,** 220 calories, 102 mg. cholesterol, 3 g. dietary fiber, 288 mg. sodium

Simple Salmon ✓

PREPARATION TIME: 5 MINUTES   COOKING TIME: 10 TO 12 MINUTES

Most recipes for poached fish are simple to prepare and this one is no exception.

4 salmon steaks, 1 inch thick (about 6 ounces each)
½ cup white wine
½ cup lemon juice
1 bay leaf

1 medium onion, sliced into rounds
Fresh-ground black pepper to taste
Water

1. Place steaks in a large shallow saucepan, preferably one you can use to cook in later. Add remaining ingredients except the water, and marinate, covered, in the refrigerator, for 1 hour or more.
2. Remove from refrigerator and add enough water to cover the steaks. Heat on medium-high heat until just under a boil, then turn to low and poach (simmer) for about 10 minutes, until fish flakes easily with a fork.

4 servings of about 4½ ounces each (cooked weight).

Per serving: **8 g. fat,** 221 calories, 70 mg. cholesterol, 1 g. dietary fiber, 59 mg. sodium

Teriyaki Salmon

PREPARATION TIME: 4 MINUTES   COOKING TIME: 14 TO 20 MINUTES

This dish vies with Royal Indian Salmon for ease of preparation and elegant taste.

Nonstick vegetable cooking spray
1½ pounds salmon fillets OR 4 steaks, about 6 ounces each

1 tablespoon tamari sauce or soy sauce
1 tablespoon honey
¼ teaspoon ground ginger
⅛ teaspoon mace (optional)

1. Spray a foil-lined broiler pan with nonstick cooking spray.
2. Arrange the salmon on the pan. In a small bowl, combine the remaining ingredients to make a teriyaki sauce.
3. Brush the salmon with the teriyaki sauce. Broil about 7 to 10 minutes a side, basting frequently with the sauce.

4 servings of 4½ ounces each (cooked weight).

Per serving: **8 g. fat,** 200 calories, 70 mg. cholesterol, no dietary fiber, 259 mg. sodium

Poached Sweet-Pepper Salmon ✓

PREPARATION TIME: 7 MINUTES   COOKING TIME: 7 TO 8 MINUTES

The sweet, or bell, pepper is a mild-mannered relative of the hot chile pepper. You can use green, yellow, red, or purple bell peppers interchangeably in almost any recipe, to add color and flavor. Here, they enhance the already marvelous taste of salmon, in another "serve-hot-or-cold" recipe.

⅓ cup dry white wine
1½ pounds salmon fillets
  OR 4 steaks, about 6 ounces
  each

1 bell pepper, diced fine
½ teaspoon salt
2 teaspoons dried parsley
2 teaspoons lime juice

1. Pour the wine into a large skillet, and add the fish fillets.
2. Sprinkle the fillets evenly with the remaining ingredients.
3. Cover and bring almost to a boil, then reduce heat to low. Let cook for about 7 to 8 minutes, until fish flakes easily with a fork.

4 servings of 4½ ounces each (cooked weight).

Per serving: **8 g. fat,** 187 calories, 70 mg. cholesterol, no dietary fiber, 324 mg. sodium

Royal Indian Salmon ✓

PREPARATION TIME: 5 MINUTES   COOKING TIME: 16 TO 20 MINUTES

We couldn't resist including this recipe, which first appeared in *The Rotation Diet*. It is one of our all-time favorites, delicately flavored and very easy to prepare.

4 salmon steaks, 1 inch thick
  (about 6 ounces each)
¼ cup low-sodium chicken
  or vegetable stock
2 tablespoons lemon juice
¼ teaspoon cumin

½ teaspoon fennel seeds,
  crushed
¼ teaspoon ground coriander
Dash of salt and fresh-ground
  black pepper

1. Place the steaks in a shallow baking pan. Pour the stock and the lemon juice over the steaks. Add the seasonings. Marinate, covered, in the refrigerator for at least two hours, turning the steaks occasionally.
2. To cook, place the steaks on a foil-covered broiling pan. Spoon 2 teaspoons of the marinade on top of each steak. Place under the broiler on low broil for 8 to 10 minutes, or until slightly brown on the edges. Turn steaks over, spoon on the remaining marinade, and broil for an additional 8 to 10 minutes.

4 servings of about 4½ ounces each (cooked weight).

Per serving: **8 g. fat,** 187 calories, 70 mg. cholesterol, no dietary fiber, 61 mg. sodium

Broiled Cod with Shallots

PREPARATION TIME: 10 MINUTES   COOKING TIME: 10 MINUTES

2 pounds cod fillets
Nonstick vegetable cooking
  spray
2 teaspoons butter
  or vegetable oil
3 shallots, chopped
1 clove garlic, minced

1 tablespoon lemon juice
1 teaspoon dried dillweed
3 tablespoons fresh parsley,
  minced
Salt and fresh-ground black
  pepper to taste

1. Place fillets on foil-covered broiler pan that has been sprayed lightly with vegetable spray.
2. Heat saucepan over medium heat, add butter or oil, and shallots. Cover and let cook, stirring occasionally, for about a minute, then add garlic, lemon juice, dillweed, and parsley. Let cook until onions are translucent.
3. Spread shallot mixture over fish. Add salt and pepper to taste.
4. Broil for about 5 minutes, turn, baste, and broil for an additional 5 minutes, or until fish flakes easily with a fork.

6 servings of 4 ounces each (cooked weight).

Per serving: **2 g. fat,** 140 calories, 66 mg. cholesterol, no dietary fiber, 193 mg. sodium

Easy Mushroom and Shrimp Dinner

PREPARATION TIME: 5 MINUTES   COOKING TIME: 15 MINUTES

Try this dish over cooked grain (½ cup of grain per serving). It's especially good with brown rice or bulgur wheat.

2 teaspoons peanut oil
8 ounces mushrooms, sliced
2 scallions, diced
¼ green or red pepper, diced
2 packages (6 ounces each)
   frozen mini-shrimp

2 tablespoons white wine
½ teaspoon Traditional Italian
   Herb Blend (p. 333)

1. Heat the oil in a skillet on medium heat. Add the mushrooms, scallions, and green or red pepper. Sauté 5 to 7 minutes, stirring constantly.
2. Add the shrimp, wine, and Herb Blend. Reduce heat to low, cover, and simmer for 5 minutes.

4 servings. Serving size is about ¾ cup.

Per serving: **4 g. fat,** 146 calories, 129 mg. cholesterol, 2 g. dietary fiber, 398 mg. sodium

Curried Shrimp

PREPARATION TIME: 7 MINUTES   COOKING TIME: 12 TO 15 MINUTES

Serve this over cooked grain, whole-grain English muffins, or toast.

1 teaspoon vegetable oil
½ medium red onion, diced
1 small apple, diced
1 tablespoon butter
  or margarine
1 tablespoon whole-wheat flour
1 cup low-sodium chicken
  stock
3 tablespoons skim or low-fat
  milk

½ teaspoon salt
Fresh-ground black pepper to
  taste
½ teaspoon Indian Spice Blend
  (p. 332) or other curry
  powder
¼ teaspoon ground ginger
2 packages (6 ounces each)
  frozen mini-shrimp

1. Brush a skillet with the 1 teaspoon of oil, and heat over medium-low heat. Add the diced onion and apple, and sauté, covered, until onions are translucent. Add a little water if necessary to prevent sticking.
2. In another small pan, melt the butter or margarine over medium heat. Stir in the flour. Cook, stirring constantly, until nicely browned. Stir in the chicken stock, and cook a couple more minutes.
3. Add the chicken-stock mixture to the onion-apple mixture, along with the remaining ingredients. Blend well. Cover and let simmer until thickened and heated through.

4 servings. Serving size is about 1 cup.

Per serving: **6 g. fat**, 172 calories, 137 mg. cholesterol, 1 g. dietary fiber, 446 mg. sodium

Crab Quiche with Crumb Topping

PREPARATION TIME: 8 TO 10 MINUTES   COOKING TIME: 45 MINUTES

You can halve this recipe and make only one quiche, but we usually make two and freeze one for another time.

2 packages (6 ounces each) frozen crabmeat, thawed, drained
2 cups skim milk
2 cups grated light sharp cheddar cheese
1½ cups Egg Beaters OR 6 eggs, beaten
2 teaspoons dried parsley
½ teaspoon salt

¼ teaspoon fresh-ground black pepper
¼ teaspoon marjoram
¼ teaspoon garlic powder
¼ teaspoon nutmeg
2 cups Pepperidge Farm seasoned bread crumbs
½ tablespoon butter or margarine

1. Layer the crab on the bottom of two empty pie pans.
2. Combine all other ingredients except the bread crumbs and butter, and pour half of the mixture into each pie pan.
3. Bake at 350 degrees for 30 minutes. Then top each quiche with 1 cup of bread crumbs and dot with ¼ tablespoon of butter. Bake 15 minutes more.
4. Remove from the oven and let stand for about 3 to 5 minutes.
5. Cut each quiche into quarters and serve.

8 servings. Serving size is ¼ quiche.

Per serving: **8 g. fat**, 278 calories, 158 mg. cholesterol, 1 g. dietary fiber, 468 mg. sodium

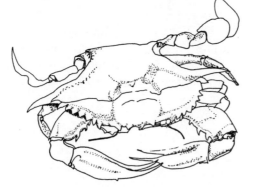

Oriental Shark Steaks

PREPARATION TIME: 8 MINUTES   COOKING TIME: 20 MINUTES

3 scallions, minced
3 tablespoons tamari sauce or
  soy sauce
3 tablespoons orange juice
1 tablespoon vegetable oil
1 tablespoon honey

½ teaspoon ground ginger
½ teaspoon fresh-ground black
  pepper
2 pounds shark steaks
1 medium orange, cut in thin
  rounds

1. Combine all the ingredients except the shark steaks and
   orange slices. Cut the steaks into 6 individual portions, and
   place in a shallow baking dish.
2. Baste the steaks with about half the sauce, and broil for 10
   minutes. Turn the fish over and cover with the remaining
   sauce. Top with orange slices and broil for another 10
   minutes, or until fish flakes easily with a fork.

6 servings of 4½ ounces each (cooked weight).

Per serving: **9 g. fat,** 249 calories, 64 mg. cholesterol, 1 g. dietary
fiber, 553 mg. sodium

Steamed Fish Fillets Oriental

PREPARATION TIME: 5 MINUTES   COOKING TIME: 4 TO 5 MINUTES

Remember one of the basic tricks to Oriental cooking: Have
everything chopped and ready to go, because the food cooks
quickly.

1 pound fish fillets
5 tablespoons scallions,
  chopped fine
1 small clove garlic, minced

1 slice gingerroot, ¼ inch thick,
  minced
2 tablespoons tamari sauce or
  soy sauce

1. Place the fish on a steamer rack over boiling water, and sprinkle with the scallions.
2. Combine the garlic, ginger, and tamari sauce in a small bowl, and spread all of the mixture over the fish.
3. Steam, covered, for about 4 to 5 minutes, or until fish flakes easily with a fork.

4 servings of 3 ounces each (cooked weight).

Per serving: **1 g. fat,** 84 calories, 22 mg. cholesterol, no dietary fiber, 475 mg. sodium

Fillet of Roughy Espagnole

PREPARATION TIME: 10 MINUTES   COOKING TIME: 15 TO 20 MINUTES

For a complete meal, serve this over cooked grain with a salad on the side.

2 medium onions, chopped
1 tablespoon butter
  or margarine
1 large clove garlic, chopped
3 stalks celery, sliced
1 green pepper, chopped
1 teaspoon dried cilantro
  or tarragon

1 teaspoon dried basil
¼ teaspoon crushed red pepper
¼ teaspoon dried thyme
1 tablespoon dried parsley
1 can (15 ounces) tomato sauce
1½ pounds orange roughy
  or other thick fish fillets

1. Sauté the onions in the butter or margarine until translucent. Add the next 8 ingredients and sauté a few moments more.
2. Add the tomato sauce and simmer until the vegetables are tender. Add the fish, and simmer just until fish flakes easily with a fork, about 5 to 10 minutes.

4 servings of 4½ ounces each (cooked weight), plus sauce.

Per serving: **4 g. fat,** 204 calories, 41 mg. cholesterol, 4 g. dietary fiber, 806 mg. sodium

Seafood Stove-Top Casserole ✓

PREPARATION TIME: 12 MINUTES   COOKING TIME: 15 TO 20 MINUTES

You can serve this over brown rice, or pour it into a baking dish, bake for 10 minutes or so in a 350-degree oven, and serve as is.

2 cups low-sodium stock
1 cup dry white wine OR 1 cup
  1% milk
1 bay leaf
1 cup sliced fresh mushrooms
2 red peppers, sliced into strips
1 tablespoon dried parsley
  OR ⅓ cup fresh, minced
Fresh-ground black pepper to
  taste

4 cups cooked lobster, crab,
  scallops, or monkfish, cut
  into chunks
2 eggs
2 teaspoons cayenne pepper
1 tablespoon dry mustard
4 pimiento strips (optional)

1. Bring the stock and wine to a boil in a large saucepan. (If you're using milk instead of wine, add the milk to the eggs later; just boil the stock now.)
2. Add the bay leaf, mushrooms, sliced peppers, parsley, and black pepper to the stock, reduce the heat, and let simmer for about 5 to 10 minutes, until the vegetables are just tender. Add the seafood, and simmer 5 minutes more.
3. In the meantime, blend the egg, milk if used instead of wine, cayenne pepper, and dry mustard together. Add to the seafood, and let simmer for a couple more minutes. Garnish with pimiento strips, if desired.

8 servings. Serving size is about 1¼ cups.

Per serving (with wine): **2 g. fat,** 123 calories, 99 mg. cholesterol, 1 g. dietary fiber, 310 mg. sodium

Per serving (with milk): **3 g. fat,** 126 calories, 100 mg. cholesterol, 1 g. dietary fiber, 325 mg. sodium

Mexican Red Snapper

PREPARATION TIME: 10 MINUTES　　　COOKING TIME: 25 MINUTES

The fresh coriander in this recipe is available in most Oriental or international markets, and really makes this dish special. If you absolutely can't find it, you may substitute an equal amount of fresh parsley, or 1 or 2 tablespoons of dried cilantro.

2 medium onions, sliced
2 pounds red snapper fillets
1/4 teaspoon salt
1/4 teaspoon fresh-ground black pepper

1/3 cup lime or lemon juice
3 jalapeños, chopped
1 bunch fresh coriander, leaves only (about 1 cup)

1. In an oblong casserole or baking dish, layer half the sliced onions, followed by the fish, then the rest of the onions. Sprinkle with salt and pepper. Pour the lime juice over the fish, and let sit for 1 to 2 hours in the refrigerator.
2. Top the fish dish with the jalapeños and the coriander.
3. Cover and bake at 350 degrees for 25 minutes, or until tender.

4 servings of 6 ounces each (cooked weight), plus vegetables.

Per serving: **3 g. fat,** 249 calories, 80 mg. cholesterol, 1 g. dietary fiber, 279 mg. sodium

Fish Fillets Veronique ✓

PREPARATION TIME: 15 TO 20 MINUTES   COOKING TIME: 7 MINUTES

1 cup seedless grapes
2 tablespoons white wine
1 tablespoon lemon juice
2 pounds fish fillets (flounder,
  sole, or snapper)
1 teaspoon grated lemon peel
1 tablespoon lime juice
1 tablespoon fresh gingerroot,
  julienned in small strips

½ medium bell pepper,
  julienned
¼ teaspoon salt
Fresh-ground black pepper to
  taste
Fresh parsley or coriander for
  garnish
Lemon and/or lime wedges for
  garnish

1. Slice the grapes in half, and place them in a bowl with the wine and the lemon juice, tossing gently.
2. Line a broiling pan with foil, and arrange the fish in the pan. Sprinkle the lemon peel and lime juice over the fish. Top with the ginger, bell pepper, and seasoning, except for the garnish.
3. Broil the fish for about 5 minutes, until the fillets begin to turn golden. Pour the grape-wine mixture over the fish, arranging the grapes cut-side down. Broil a couple more minutes, until fish flakes easily with a fork. Serve with the garnishes.

6 servings of 4 ounces each (cooked weight), plus grapes and vegetables.

Per serving: **2 g. fat,** 162 calories, 77 mg. cholesterol, 1 g. dietary fiber, 209 mg. sodium

Fish Florentine

PREPARATION TIME: 8 MINUTES   COOKING TIME: 15 TO 20 MINUTES

This Italian style of cooking (with spinach) works as well with fish as it does with veal and chicken.

1 pound fish fillets (try flounder or sole)

1 package (10 ounces) frozen chopped spinach, thawed and drained

10 whole-wheat crackers, crushed

2 tablespoons wheat germ

3 tablespoons Parmesan or sapsago cheese

1. Arrange the fillets in the bottom of a shallow baking dish.
2. Cover the fish with the well-drained spinach.
3. Combine the cracker crumbs, wheat germ, and cheese, and pour over the fish and spinach.
4. Bake, uncovered, at 400 degrees for 15 to 20 minutes.

4 servings of 3 ounces each (cooked weight), plus spinach.

Per serving: **4 g. fat,** 184 calories, 62 mg. cholesterol, 2 g. dietary fiber, 306 mg. sodium

Shrimp Skimpy

PREPARATION TIME: 5 MINUTES   COOKING TIME: 4 MINUTES

2 tablespoons tamari sauce or soy sauce

2 tablespoons lemon juice

2 tablespoons oil

2 cloves garlic, finely chopped

Bay seasoning or seasonings of your choice, to taste

1½ pounds shelled, deveined, uncooked shrimp

1. Combine all the ingredients, except the shrimp, in a bowl and mix well. Add the shrimp and marinate for an hour or so in the refrigerator, stirring occasionally.
2. Broil in a shallow pan for about 4 minutes, turning pieces midway during cooking.

4 servings of 4½ ounces each (cooked weight).

Per serving: **8 g. fat,** 167 calories, 193 mg. cholesterol, no dietary fiber, 627 mg. sodium

Mock Crabmeat and Pasta ✓

PREPARATION TIME: 20 MINUTES   COOKING TIME: 10 MINUTES

Mock or imitation crabmeat is often made from bluefish, and presents a cheaper alternative to the real crab. Of course you may substitute frozen or canned crabmeat.

1 medium onion, diced
4 cloves garlic, minced
1 medium green pepper, diced
2 stalks celery, sliced thin
1 tablespoon butter
  or margarine
1 tablespoon water
6 ounces fresh mushrooms,
  sliced
½ teaspoon marjoram
½ teaspoon thyme

¼ teaspoon salt
¼ teaspoon fresh-ground black
  pepper
2 carrots, diced
6 ounces fresh mushrooms,
  quartered
2 cups 1% milk
1 pound imitation crabmeat,
  diced
8 ounces vermicelli, cooked
  and drained

1. Sauté/steam the onion, garlic, green pepper, and celery in the combined butter and water, covered, over medium-low heat, until the celery and green pepper are tender. Stir occasionally.
2. Add the sliced mushrooms and the seasonings. Remove from the heat, and set aside.
3. In a small amount of water, cook the carrots and the quartered mushrooms until the carrots are tender. Drain, and purée in a blender or food processor. Combine with the milk, and add to the sautéed vegetables, along with the imitation crab.
4. Combine the cooked pasta and the crab mixture. Place in a casserole dish, and bake at 350 degrees for about 10 minutes, or until heated through.

8 servings. Serving size is about 1½ cups.

Per serving: **3 g. fat**, 152 calories, 15 mg. cholesterol, 2 g. dietary fiber, 208 mg. sodium

Lime-Steamed Fish Fillets

PREPARATION TIME: 3 TO 5 MINUTES   COOKING TIME: 5 MINUTES

If you have a wok, you may have a metal or bamboo steamer rack that came with it. If not, use any other steamer or rack you have on hand, or use the "plate" method, as described in the recipe for Steamed Trout (pp. 194–95).

1½ pounds fish fillets (try flounder or sole)
Juice of 1 lime

¼ cup shallots, minced
Fresh-ground black pepper to taste

1. Arrange fillets in foil or on a plate, and place on a steamer rack over boiling water.
2. Squeeze the lime juice over the fish, and top with shallots and pepper.
3. Cover and steam for about 5 minutes, until fish flakes easily with a fork.

4 servings of 4½ ounces each (cooked weight).

Per serving: **2 g. fat**, 126 calories, 68 mg. cholesterol, no dietary fiber, 105 mg. sodium

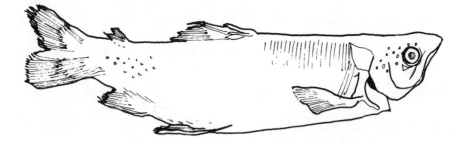

Blackened Fish

PREPARATION TIME: 5 MINUTES   COOKING TIME: 5 MINUTES

The recent rise in popularity of this spicy, Cajun-style dish in restaurants is a testimonial to what spices can do to disguise the flavor of less palatable (and often cheaper!) varieties of fish. At home, you can start out with any kind of firm-fleshed fish you want.

1 teaspoon salt
1 tablespoon garlic powder
2 teaspoons thyme
1 tablespoon dried parsley
   flakes
1 tablespoon dried basil
1 to 2 teaspoons cayenne
   pepper

¼ teaspoon fresh-ground black
   pepper
4 fillets of redfish, red snapper,
   or other firm fish, about 1½
   pounds raw
1 tablespoon olive oil
   or corn oil

1. Combine the spices on a flat plate. Press the fish fillets firmly into the spices, coating both sides.
2. Heat the oil to almost smoking in a heavy skillet. Cook the fish about 2½ minutes on each side, for fillets not more than ¾ inch thick. Serve immediately.

4 servings of 4½ ounces each (cooked weight).

Per serving: **5 g. fat,** 137 calories, 42 mg. cholesterol, 1 g. dietary fiber, 609 mg. sodium

Oyster Stew

PREPARATION TIME: 15 MINUTES   COOKING TIME: 10 MINUTES

4 cups low-fat milk
1 large potato, unpeeled, diced
   fine
1 tablespoon butter
   or margarine
2 leeks, washed, trimmed, and
   diced

1 pint fresh oysters, undrained
½ teaspoon salt
⅛ to ¼ teaspoon cayenne
   pepper

1. Heat the milk along with the potatoes in a double boiler over medium heat. Do not boil.
2. In a large saucepan or kettle, melt the butter over medium heat. Add the leeks and sauté, covered, stirring often.
3. Add the oysters, and sauté, covered, until the edges of the oysters begin to curl.
4. Pour the hot milk and potatoes into the saucepan with the oysters. Add the salt and cayenne.

8 servings. Serving size is about 1 cup.

Per serving: **4 g. fat,** 150 calories, 42 mg. cholesterol, 1 g. dietary fiber, 348 mg. sodium

Halibut Steaks

PREPARATION TIME: 15 MINUTES   COOKING TIME: 15 TO 20 MINUTES

This dish is good hot or cold.

1 tablespoon olive oil
1 small onion, diced
½ medium bell pepper (green, red, purple, or yellow), diced
8 fresh mushrooms, chopped fine
2 pounds halibut steaks, 1 inch thick

½ teaspoon salt
½ teaspoon fresh-ground black pepper
½ teaspoon dried marjoram
1 medium tomato, sliced as thinly as possible

1. Preheat oven to 400 degrees.
2. Heat oil in skillet on medium heat, and sauté onions, bell pepper, and mushrooms, covered, stirring occasionally, until onions are translucent.
3. Place steaks in baking dish, and season with salt, pepper, and marjoram. Spread sautéed vegetables over the top.
4. Bake at 400 degrees for 10 minutes, then cover with a layer of tomato slices. Bake an additional 5 minutes, or until fish flakes easily with a fork.

6 servings of 4½ ounces each (cooked weight).

Per serving: **6 g. fat,** 215 calories, 52 mg. cholesterol, 1 g. dietary fiber, 269 mg. sodium

Poached Grouper with Clams

PREPARATION TIME: 15 MINUTES   COOKING TIME: 20 MINUTES

The bouillon in this recipe is so good that the first time we made it, we couldn't resist eating our main course out of bowls, as a soup. Try it that way—it's delicious!

1 medium onion, thinly sliced	2 cans (6½ ounces each)
1 clove garlic, minced	minced clams, with juice
1 tablespoon butter	4 ounces dry white wine
or margarine	1 teaspoon dried basil
1½ pounds grouper fillets	Dash of salt and fresh-ground
1 large tomato, thinly sliced	black pepper
3 thin slices lemon	

1. Lightly sauté the onions and garlic in the butter in a large frying pan, until onions are translucent. Place fish fillets on top; then layer tomato slices, lemon slices, clams and clam juice, and wine on top of the fish. Sprinkle with basil, salt, and pepper.
2. Cover the pan, bring to a boil, then turn down the heat and simmer for about 20 minutes, or until fish flakes easily with a fork. Serve in bowls with the bouillon.

4 servings of 4½ ounces each (cooked weight).

Per serving: **6 g. fat,** 292 calories, 100 mg. cholesterol, 1 g. dietary fiber, 318 mg. sodium

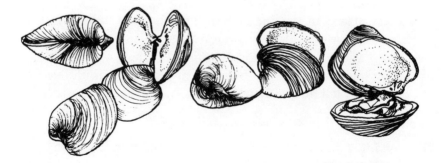

Monkfish Italian Style

PREPARATION TIME: 8 MINUTES   COOKING TIME: 15 TO 20 MINUTES

1 medium onion, sliced
½ pound mushrooms, sliced
1 medium green pepper, diced
1 tablespoon vegetable oil
2 cloves garlic, minced or
   crushed

½ cup dry white wine
1 can (10¾ ounces) tomato
   purée
2 teaspoons dried basil
2 pounds monkfish fillets

1. Sauté the onion, mushrooms, and green pepper in the oil over medium-low heat, covered, until the onions are translucent.
2. Add the remaining ingredients, cover, and let simmer for about 12 to 15 minutes, or until fish flakes easily with a fork.

VARIATION: For a quick version of this recipe, you can use our Real Italian Tomato Sauce (pp. 288–89), if you have any pre-made. Pour 2½ cups of sauce into a saucepan on medium heat, add the fish, and cook until done.

6 servings of 4 ounces each (cooked weight), plus sauce.

Per serving: **5 g. fat,** 186 calories, 36 mg. cholesterol, 2 g. dietary fiber, 228 mg. sodium

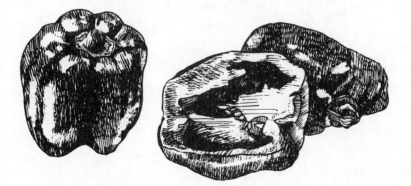

Really Orange Roughy

PREPARATION TIME: 25 MINUTES   COOKING TIME: 25 TO 30 MINUTES

Nonstick vegetable cooking
  spray
1 pound orange roughy fillets
1 onion, chopped
1 green pepper, chopped
1 clove garlic, minced
1 tablespoon butter
  or margarine

2 medium carrots, diced
1 cup plain nonfat yogurt
Grated rind and juice of ½
  orange
1 teaspoon Dijon mustard
¼ teaspoon tarragon
Salt and pepper to taste

1. Spray a casserole dish with nonstick cooking spray. Place the fish in the casserole.
2. Sauté the onion, green pepper, and garlic in the butter until onion is slightly golden in color. Spoon this mixture on top of the fillets.
3. Meanwhile, lightly steam the carrots in another pan.
4. In a blender or food processor, blend the yogurt, cooked carrots, orange rind and juice, mustard, tarragon, salt, and pepper. Pour over the fish.
5. Bake at 350 degrees for 25 to 30 minutes until bubbly around the edges and fish flakes easily with a fork.

4 servings of 3 ounces each (cooked weight), plus vegetables.

Per serving: **4 g. fat,** 177 calories, 31 mg. cholesterol, 2 g. dietary fiber, 242 mg. sodium

Pasta

Pasta used to be considered fattening, along with bread and potatoes, but now that carbohydrates are getting "better press" and people are realizing their healthful attributes, we find a surge of interest in new and attractive pasta dishes. There are some restaurants that serve only pasta: pasta salads, pasta entrées, and even pasta desserts. (No one has gone so far as to process pasta into a beverage—yet!)

Pasta can be made from wheat, soy, rice, corn, buckwheat, other grains, or a wide variety of other ingredients, including legumes and even seaweed. Pastas come in many colors: You can sometimes even find black or brown noodles; green noodles are colored with spinach. The kind of noodle most of us in America are used to is an egg noodle made from durum-wheat semolina that is often enriched to provide extra nutrients. One cup of cooked egg noodles contains about 50 milligrams of cholesterol; we normally use pasta (spaghetti, vermicelli, etc.) made from enriched semolina that contains no eggs or cholesterol.

Look in health-food stores or international markets for more exotic noodles. Oriental noodles, such as soba noodles, are especially delicate in texture and flavor. Whole-wheat pasta is higher in fiber, but has a somewhat stronger flavor than egg noodles or regular semolina, so you may want to combine it with other kinds of pasta until you get used to it, or as a way to add color.

One cup of cooked spaghetti contains about 1 gram of fat

and 160 calories. With a low-calorie sauce, a fresh garden salad, a beverage, and a fruit for dessert, you have a complete meal. Although spaghetti is mentioned here, pasta comes in dozens of shapes and sizes, from shells and corkscrews (fusilli) to the wide noodles used in fettuccine and lasagna. One of the delights of discovering pasta is determining by experiment which pasta forms go best with your favorite sauces.

In addition to serving our tomato sauces with pasta, be sure to try our delicious meatball recipes as well (Turkey Meatballs with Tomato Sauce, page 183, and Turkey-Sage Sausage or Meatballs, page 190). Also see our tofu section for several more pasta recipes that use tofu as a principal ingredient.

As you experiment with cooking different types of pasta, keep in mind the amount of time you'll need to cook your pasta *al dente*—that is, it should be slightly firm, not mushy, when you bite into it. If you make a lot of pasta, a multi-cooker/steamer, sometimes called simply a "pasta cooker," can be very handy. An 8-quart stockpot will contain a 6-quart colander insert that automatically drains your pasta when you remove it. The gadget is also useful for cooking clams, shrimp, or anything else that requires draining. There is also a shallow insert for steaming.

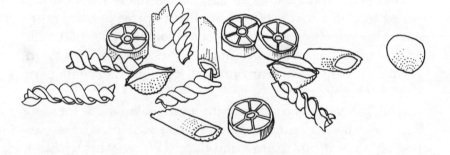

Pasta with Garlic-and-Clam Sauce

PREPARATION TIME: 8 MINUTES   COOKING TIME: 15 MINUTES

This unusual but very tasty garlic-and-clam sauce combines vegetables with the clams so that a large serving can use less spaghetti or linguine and more sauce, with fewer calories per portion.

1 medium onion, chopped
1 green pepper, chopped
4 cloves garlic, minced
1 tablespoon olive oil
½ pound mushrooms, sliced
2 cans (6½ ounces each) minced clams, plus their liquid
1½ teaspoons dried thyme leaves

Salt and fresh-ground black pepper to taste
2 tablespoons chopped fresh parsley
Dash of cayenne pepper
4 cups cooked spaghetti or linguine (about 8 ounces uncooked)
Parmesan cheese (optional)

1. Sauté the onion, green pepper, and garlic in the olive oil until onions are translucent. Add a little water and cover if necessary to prevent sticking. Add the mushrooms, cover, and continue heating for about 3 minutes.
2. Add the remaining ingredients except for the pasta and cheese, and heat until hot in the covered saucepan. Serve with the pasta and sprinkle with Parmesan cheese if desired.

4 servings. Serving size is 1 cup pasta, plus 1 cup sauce.

Per serving (with 1 tablespoon grated Parmesan cheese): **8 g. fat,** 364 calories, 38 mg. cholesterol, 4 g. dietary fiber, 336 mg. sodium

"Once in a while couldn't we just have some pasta?" *THE FAR SIDE.*
COURTESY CHRONICLE FEATURES, SAN FRANCISCO.

Spinach Roll-Ups

PREPARATION TIME: 30 MINUTES   COOKING TIME: 30 MINUTES

6 lasagne noodle strips
1 package (10 ounces) frozen chopped spinach
4 ounces fresh mushrooms, diced
2 tablespoons water
2 eggs, slightly beaten
1 cup 1% low-fat cottage cheese
⅛ teaspoon garlic powder
⅛ teaspoon onion powder
Fresh-ground black pepper to taste

1 tablespoon butter or margarine
2 tablespoons whole-wheat flour
1 cup 1% milk
⅛ teaspoon salt
2 tablespoons grated Parmesan cheese
Nonstick vegetable cooking spray

1. Cook the lasagne noodles according to the package directions. Then place them in cool water until ready to use.

2. Cook the frozen spinach and mushrooms in the 2 tablespoons of water until the spinach is completely defrosted and the mushrooms are just beginning to look cooked. Drain well.

3. In a medium to large bowl, combine the eggs, cottage cheese, garlic and onion powders, pepper, and spinach and mushrooms, mixing well.

4. In a saucepan, melt the butter slowly over medium-low heat. Stir in the flour, mixing until it is thoroughly moistened. Add the milk slowly, stirring constantly. Add the salt and the Parmesan cheese, and cook over very low heat, stirring frequently, until the sauce just begins to thicken. Remove from the heat and cover.

5. Spray a casserole dish with the cooking spray. On a plate, cut each lasagne strip in half crosswise. Place about a tablespoonful of the spinach mixture on each strip and fold the ends over, leaving the sides open. Place the roll-ups folded-side down in the casserole dish. Fill in the empty spaces in the dish with any leftover spinach mixture. Cover with the cheese sauce.

6. Bake at 325 degrees for about 30 minutes, or until bubbly.

4 servings of 3 roll-ups each.

Per serving: **8 g. fat,** 292 calories, 109 mg. cholesterol, 4 g. dietary fiber, 497 mg. sodium

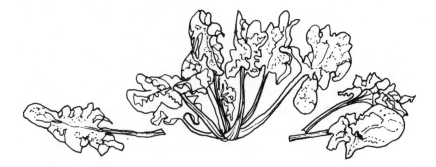

Linguine al frutti di mare
(Linguine with Shellfish)

PREPARATION TIME: 30 TO 40 MINUTES   COOKING TIME: 15 MINUTES

Here is another fine recipe from the Villa Romano, again with
reduced oil. Though you may use canned or frozen shellfish
and squid that are already cleaned and ready for cooking, use
fresh if you can; directions follow on how to clean them, and
the extra trouble is worth it if you have the time.

Clams in the shell: Scrub and wash in several bowls of water
or under running water to remove as much sand as possible.
Soak them in a large pot filled with 1 gallon of water and ⅓
cup of salt. Throw out any clams that have broken shells or that
float. Shells should be tightly closed or should close at a touch
if barely open. The shells will open as they cook. It's very
difficult to get all the sand out; some people even wash the
clams in cold running water once they're cooked.

Mussels in the shell: Throw out any mussels with broken
shells. Again, the shells should be tightly closed. If a mussel is
open, put it in a freezer for a couple of minutes. The shell
should close; if it won't, throw it out. If the two sides of the shell
can be slid back and forth against each other, discard it—it may
be more mud than mussel. Clean as for clams. Clip the "beard"
off the mussel before cooking.

Squid: Be sure the squid is dead! A strong blow to the head
is a good precautionary measure. Then firmly hold the head
section just underneath the eyes and pull the outer portion of
the tail and fin section away. You will find the gray ink sac,
which should be removed and discarded. (Though some
recipes use the ink from the sac for coloring and flavoring
sauces, this recipe does not.) Cut away the tentacles just above
the eyes. Throw out the eye section, innards, and the small
roundish cartilage at the base of the tentacles (this should be
easy to remove with your fingers). Throw away the cuttlebone
inside the tail, then rub off the red membrane covering most

of the squid. If the squid is over 8 inches long, pound well with a mallet to tenderize. Now the tentacles, arms, and body meat are ready for slicing.

1 tablespoon olive oil
2 to 3 shallots, chopped
4 to 5 cloves garlic, minced
1 dozen littleneck clams, washed and scrubbed
2 dozen mussels, washed and scrubbed
¾ pound squid, cleaned and sliced in rings ¼ to ½ inch thick (you'll end up with about 2 cups squid)
¼ cup white wine

2 cups Basil-Tomato Sauce (pp. 294–95)
¼ teaspoon crushed red pepper
Pinch of saffron threads
Chopped fresh parsley to taste
Dash of salt and fresh-ground black pepper if needed
12 large fresh shrimp, shelled and deveined
8 ounces linguine, cooked and drained

1. Heat olive oil over medium heat. Add the shallots and garlic. Sauté until soft, being careful not to burn.
2. Add the clams and stir, cooking for about 1 minute. Add the mussels and squid. Cook, stirring constantly, over medium-high heat for 1 more minute. Add the wine, Basil-Tomato Sauce, and the rest of the spices. Cover and cook 4 to 5 minutes, until the clams and mussels have fully opened.
3. Add the shrimp. Cover and cook for 1 to 1½ minutes, just until the shrimp is pink. Serve in flat soup bowls or on plates over cooked linguine. Chef Ramovich suggested another way to serve this dish: Arrange the pasta, topped with the shrimp and sauce, in the middle of the plate and put the other shellfish around the pasta.

4 servings. Serving size is 1 cup pasta, plus sauce.

Per serving: **12 g. fat**, 425 calories, 326 mg. cholesterol, 3 g. dietary fiber, 571 mg. sodium

Sunflower Pasta Salad

PREPARATION TIME: 20 MINUTES   REFRIGERATION TIME: 1 HOUR

Although slightly different in taste, black and white pepper may be used interchangeably, as in this recipe. White pepper is actually the fully ripened pepper berry with the dark outer shell removed. Black pepper is underripe, and is fermented and dried in the sun before grinding. Often, cooks choose one or the other depending on color preference for a given recipe—white pepper is used in white sauces, for example.

For variety, try one or more of the following herbs in this salad: parsley, rosemary, thyme, oregano, or chives. Or choose your own favorite herbs. As always, fresh is best, but dried is often easier to obtain for those of us who don't grow our own herbs.

4 ounces bow-tie
   or twist pasta
2 tablespoons lemon juice
1 tablespoon sunflower, olive,
   or safflower oil
1 clove garlic, crushed
¼ teaspoon salt
Fresh-ground black
   or white pepper to taste
1 cup cherry tomatoes
   or tomato wedges

3 tablespoons black olives
   (Greek olives are best), pitted
   and sliced
½ medium cucumber, thinly
   sliced
4 radishes, thinly sliced
2 tablespoons dry-roasted,
   unsalted sunflower seeds
1 tablespoon fresh
   OR 1 teaspoon dried of your
   favorite herb combination

1. Cook the pasta according to the package directions, without added salt.
2. Meanwhile, combine the lemon juice, oil, garlic, salt, and pepper in a jar. Cover and shake.
3. Combine all the other ingredients, including the cooked, drained pasta, in a large bowl. Add the dressing, and toss.
4. Refrigerate, covered, for at least 1 hour before serving.

2 servings as a main course. Serving size is about 2 cups.

Per serving: **14 g. fat,** 346 calories, no cholesterol, 5 g. dietary fiber, 363 mg. sodium

Spinach Lasagne

PREPARATION TIME: 30 MINUTES   COOKING TIME: 30 MINUTES

2 pounds fresh spinach
4 tablespoons grated Parmesan cheese
1 cup part-skim ricotta cheese
1/4 teaspoon nutmeg
1/4 teaspoon salt
Fresh-ground black pepper to taste
1 tablespoon vegetable oil or olive oil

2 cloves garlic, crushed
1/2 cup chopped onion
1/2 cup chopped bell pepper
2 cups tomato sauce
1/2 teaspoon basil
1/2 teaspoon oregano
1/2 teaspoon thyme
1/2 pound lasagne noodles

1. Wash the spinach carefully to remove grit, then steam until just limp, about 1 or 2 minutes. Chop the spinach, and mix with 2 tablespoons of the Parmesan and all of the ricotta, nutmeg, salt, and pepper.
2. Heat the oil in a large saucepan, and sauté the garlic, onion, and bell pepper until the onions are translucent. Stir in the tomato sauce, basil, oregano, and thyme. Cover and let simmer until ready to use.
3. Cook the noodles according to the package directions.
4. Preheat the oven to 350 degrees.
5. Layer the noodles alternately with the cheese-spinach mixture and the tomato sauce in an 8 × 13-inch baking dish. Sprinkle the top with the remaining Parmesan.
6. Bake at 350 degrees for 30 minutes, until bubbly.

8 servings. Serving size is about 1 1/2 cups.

Per serving: **6 g. fat,** 221 calories, 12 mg. cholesterol, 6 g. dietary fiber, 624 mg. sodium

Triple-Cheese Manicotti

PREPARATION TIME: 25 MINUTES

COOKING TIME: 25 MINUTES

8 manicotti shells
1 tablespoon vegetable oil
   or olive oil
½ cup chopped onion
2 cloves garlic, crushed
½ cup chopped bell pepper
2 cups tomato sauce
½ teaspoon basil
½ teaspoon oregano

½ teaspoon thyme
¼ teaspoon fresh-ground black
   pepper
1½ cups shredded part-skim
   mozzarella
1 cup 1% low-fat cottage cheese
⅓ cup grated Parmesan cheese
2 eggs, beaten

1. Cook the manicotti shells according to the package directions, and drain. While they are cooking, heat the oil in a large saucepan, and sauté the onion, garlic, and bell pepper until the onions are translucent. Stir in the tomato sauce, basil, oregano, thyme, and pepper. Cover and let simmer until needed, stirring occasionally.

2. Combine 1 cup of the mozzarella with the cottage cheese, Parmesan, and beaten eggs. Stir gently.

3. Stuff the cheese mixture into the cooked, drained shells, using about ¼ cup per shell.

4. Pour ½ cup of the tomato-sauce mixture into a shallow 2-quart casserole dish. Arrange the stuffed manicotti shells on top, then pour the remaining sauce over them. Sprinkle with the remaining ½ cup of mozzarella.

5. Bake uncovered at 350 degrees for 25 minutes, or until sauce is bubbly and cheese is melted.

4 servings. Serving size is 2 shells each, plus sauce.

Per serving: **15 g. fat,** 356 calories, 125 mg. cholesterol, 4 g. dietary fiber, 601 mg. sodium

Mock Lasagne

PREPARATION TIME: 25 MINUTES   COOKING TIME: 45 MINUTES

This can be prepared early in the day and refrigerated. It may take a little more cooking time if you put it in the oven cold. Serve with a spinach salad or other fresh greens on the side.

4 cups elbow macaroni,
  uncooked
Nonstick vegetable cooking
  spray
1½ pounds extra-lean ground
  beef, ground turkey,
  or ground veal
2 cloves garlic, minced
½ teaspoon ground ginger

3 cups canned tomato sauce
  or Real Italian Tomato Sauce
  (pp. 288–89)
1 pound 1% low-fat cottage
  cheese
1 pound Neufchâtel cheese
½ cup plain nonfat yogurt
1 medium bell pepper, chopped
6–8 scallions, chopped
½ teaspoon oregano

1. Cook the macaroni in water according to the package directions. Drain.
2. Spray a 4-quart casserole dish with the cooking spray. Put in half the cooked macaroni.
3. In a skillet, brown the ground meat and remove it from the pan with a slotted spoon. Sauté the garlic in the skillet, then return the meat to the pan. Sprinkle in the ginger, and stir in the tomato sauce. Remove from the heat.
4. In a bowl, combine the cottage cheese, Neufchâtel, yogurt, bell pepper, and scallions. Spread this mixture over the macaroni in the casserole dish. Add the remaining macaroni, spreading evenly. Spread the meat-tomato sauce over the top, and sprinkle with the oregano.
5. Bake at 375 degrees for 45 minutes.

12 servings. Serving size is about 1⅓ cups.

Per serving: **12 g. fat,** 307 calories, 71 mg. cholesterol, 2 g. dietary fiber, 715 mg. sodium

Capellini di angelo al filetto di pomodoro
(Angel Hair Pasta with Basil-Tomato Sauce)

PREPARATION TIME: 15 MINUTES   COOKING TIME: 15 TO 20 MINUTES

The original recipe for this dish from the Villa Romano restaurant in Nashville called for four times the amount of olive oil used here. Olive oil has about 14 grams of fat and 120 calories per tablespoon, so this version has over 40 fewer grams of fat and 360 fewer calories.

The basil-tomato sauce given here is a basic sauce used in other recipes, including *Linguine al frutti di mare.* (The sauce recipe alone appears in the sauce section, on pp. 294–95.) Though tomato skins contain fiber, vitamins, and minerals, more elegant recipes, such as this one, generally say to remove them. If you wish to remove the skins, drop the tomatoes in boiling water for about 1 minute. Remove them from the pot and run them under cold water; the skins should now peel off easily. Fresh basil will give the richest flavor, but the dried herb can be substituted.

Villa Romano's proprietor and chef, Kem Ramovich, suggested serving this delicate pasta as an appetizer or as a light main course. In restaurants that prepare pasta fresh when ordered, as was the case at the Villa Romano, you should ask for a low-fat version of your favorite sauce. Most chefs can cut the quantity of fat on request.

1 tablespoon olive oil
  (extra-virgin if available)
4 to 5 cloves garlic, minced
1 large shallot, minced
3 large ripe tomatoes, skinned,
  seeded, and chopped, OR 1
  can (28 ounces) Italian plum
  tomatoes, quartered

Salt and coarse fresh-ground
  black pepper to taste
¼ cup fresh basil, chopped,
  OR 4 teaspoons dried basil
8 ounces angel hair pasta
3 quarts water
4 tablespoons grated Parmesan
  cheese

1. Heat the oil over medium heat. Add the garlic and shallot, and sauté until the garlic is golden and the shallot wilted. Add the tomatoes. Season with salt, pepper, and basil.

2. Meanwhile, cook the pasta in an uncovered pot in rapidly boiling water for about 1 to 2 minutes. Test it after 1 minute for *al dente* ("firm to the bite") texture.
3. Drain the pasta, reserving 2 tablespoons of the water it was cooked in. Add the pasta and the reserved water to the tomato sauce. Stir gently to coat the pasta with the sauce. Remove to a serving platter, sprinkle with the Parmesan cheese, and serve immediately.

4 servings. Serving size is about 1 cup pasta with ½ cup sauce.

Per serving: **7 g. fat,** 297 calories, 5 mg. cholesterol, 5 g. dietary fiber, 221 mg. sodium

Tuna-Pasta Salad

PREPARATION TIME: 20 TO 25 MINUTES

Combine whole-wheat and regular macaroni for a pleasing color and taste combination, and do try the caraway seeds.

1 package (8 ounces) macaroni
1 package (10 ounces) frozen peas
2 small cans (6½ ounces each) water-packed tuna, drained
1 or 2 scallions, minced
2 tablespoons light mayonnaise
¾ cup plain nonfat yogurt
1 tablespoon Dijon mustard
1 teaspoon garlic powder
Fresh-ground black pepper to taste
1 teaspoon caraway seeds (optional)
½ teaspoon salt

1. Cook the macaroni according to the package directions, without added salt. Drain and reserve.
2. In another saucepan, cook peas according to directions.
3. In a large bowl, combine remaining ingredients. Add drained macaroni and drained peas, and mix lightly. Chill.

8 servings. Serving size is about 1 cup.

Per serving: **3 g. fat,** 217 calories, 19 mg. cholesterol, 3 g. dietary fiber, 405 mg. sodium

Crabmeat-Filled Macaroni Shells

PREPARATION TIME: 25 MINUTES   COOKING TIME: 30 MINUTES

You may substitute frozen crab for canned.

1 package (12 ounces) jumbo
  macaroni shells
2 cans (6½ ounces each)
  crabmeat, drained
1¼ cups 1% low-fat cottage
  cheese or part-skim ricotta
  cheese

¼ teaspoon dried marjoram
¼ teaspoon dried rosemary
½ teaspoon garlic powder
¼ cup fresh parsley, minced
3 cups Real Italian Tomato
  Sauce (pp. 288–89)
  or other tomato sauce

1. Cook the shells according to the package directions but without the salt. Drain, and spread the shells in a single layer on foil to prevent them from sticking together.
2. In a medium bowl, combine the crab, cheese, and seasonings, blending well. Then fill each shell with about 1 tablespoon of the crab-cheese mixture.
3. Pour half the tomato sauce into the bottom of a 9 × 13-inch baking pan. Place the shells, open-side down, in a single layer on top of the sauce. Cover with the remaining sauce.
4. Bake covered at 350 degrees for about 25 minutes. Remove the cover and bake about 5 minutes longer, until bubbly.

8 servings. Serving size is about 1½ cups.

Per serving: **3 g. fat,** 273 calories, 43 mg. cholesterol, 3 g. dietary fiber, 543 mg. sodium

Meatless Main Courses

Most Americans eat twice as much protein each day as necessary to meet the body's daily protein needs. Much of this protein comes from meat.

Yet there is a wide variety of protein sources in the plant world: Beans and other legumes, grains, and seeds provide endless possibilities for tasty, protein-filled dishes.

I recommend that you try at least one meatless day a week. Begin to think of meat as a seasoning or special condiment to your main recipe ingredients from the plant world, which are generally lower in fat, cholesterol, chemical additives, and cost than meat.

If you think going a whole day without meat is next to impossible for you, try one meatless meal first. As you realize you won't go hungry or be bored with a vegetarian meal, you'll see how easy it is to go for a whole day, or several days if you like, without meat.

Most people in the Orient eat very little meat. They survive primarily on what is known as "complementary protein," from combinations of legumes, grains, and seeds. This provides the same nutritional benefit as protein from meat. Authorities agree that people who eat a wide variety of foods don't need to concern themselves with making specific combinations of foods to obtain sufficient protein, but in case your diet is limited, or if you are just curious, here's an explanation of complementarity.

Think of mechanical gears meshing: One gear can't turn without at least one other. Likewise with complete proteins, which are made up of "gears" called amino acids. There are twenty-two amino acids we need; our bodies can manufacture fourteen of them. The other eight amino acids must come from the foods we eat.

We need larger amounts of some amino acids than we do of others in order to utilize the protein effectively. You might think of amino acids, then, as *different-sized* gears, all moving together to keep our bodies moving.

Fish, poultry, meat, eggs, and dairy products provide essentially complete, *usable* protein: All the amino acids are present in these foods at levels our bodies can use.

But did you know that soy flour has twice as much protein in it as some meat products? And that legumes, such as dried beans and peas, lentils, and peanuts, have about the same amount of protein as meat? Yet these foods are limited in their protein *usability* because one or more of those eight essential amino acids are missing, or are present in limited amounts.

So we come to the concept of "complementary protein." To complement means "to make complete or perfect." In order for the amino acid "gears" from plant foods to mesh and be completely usable, we must combine two or more different kinds of plant foods.

Here is one simplified example: Wheat flour is low in lysine, while beans are high in lysine. Put them together in a bean burrito and you have complementary protein because the beans supply what the wheat flour lacks.

You can also use small amounts of dairy products and/or meat products to boost the usability of your plant proteins. To make it easy for you to experiment on your own with complementary protein combinations, here are the basic guidelines. Use:

—grains with legumes (for example, rice and beans)
—seeds with legumes (sesame with beans)
—grains with dairy products (macaroni and cheese)
—grains with sesame or sunflower seeds (breads with seeds)
—dairy products with sesame (sprinkle sesame on cheesy casseroles)

—dairy products with some legumes (cheese on chili with beans)

LEGUMES, SPROUTS, GRAINS, NUTS, AND SEEDS

These are the basic non-animal sources for protein and they are valuable sources of other nutrients including dietary fiber. We'd like to provide a few tips for combining and cooking these healthful foods so that you will use them more frequently.

LEGUMES

First, all beans are legumes, but not all legumes are beans. Any plant that has seeds growing in a pod is considered a legume; these include peas, string beans, other beans, and even peanuts, which are usually mistakenly thought of as nuts.

Among the many varieties of legumes in the world are the flavorful black bean, black-eyed peas, garbanzos (chickpeas), kidney beans, navy beans, lentils, pinto beans, split peas, and white beans. Soybeans, highest in protein of all the beans, are the most bland in flavor, but you can use them in any recipe calling for beans.

Beans seem to require more salt to bring out their flavor than many foods, and you will find that our bean recipes contain more salt than our other recipes. However, as always, we combine salt with herbs, stock, and other seasoning agents.

Before cooking, rinse dried beans and discard any small stones that may have gotten mixed in with them.

Different-sized beans require different cooking times, as we illustrate in recipes calling for several varieties of beans. They also expand in size, as do grains, when cooked. On average, 1 cup of dried beans will provide anywhere from 2½ to 3½ cups of cooked beans.

Though we generally use the slow method of bean cookery, which involves soaking them overnight first, there is a quick method if you forget to soak them the night before.

Cover the beans well with water or stock, bring to a boil, and cook for 2 minutes. Remove from heat, cover, and let stand for 1 hour. Add more liquid if necessary. Then cook as you would if you had soaked them overnight.

Canned beans are fine, but not as tasty or pleasant in texture as those made from scratch.

SPROUTS

Sprouts from beans and seeds are high in nutrients and low in calories. You can grow your own fairly easily (there are many books that can tell you how), or look for them "ready-made" in the produce section of your local supermarket. They are especially suitable for use in salads and sandwiches, or as a garnish.

GRAINS

Generally, when cooking grains, you'll need almost twice as much liquid (stock or water) as grain. Some of the larger grains need more water and the smaller ones less.

Stirring is not necessary when cooking grains, and in fact seems to interfere with the even cooking and the final texture of the grain.

The best combination for brown rice seems to be about 1¾ cups of liquid to 1 cup of rice. Bring the liquid to a boil, add the grain, and bring back to a boil. Then cover, reduce heat, and let simmer until tender and fluffy. Long-grain brown rice takes about 40 to 45 minutes. Long-grain brown rice stays separated better and is fluffier than the medium- or short-grain brown rice; experiment until you find the one you like the best. Short-grain brown rice is good for casseroles and stuffings, since it does tend to stick together.

The tiny kernels of millet take less cooking time, while larger grains, such as whole wheat and barley, take about the same time as rice or a few minutes longer.

Millet and brown rice cooked together in vegetable or chicken stock make a delicious combination. Experiment with combining one or more grains: long-, medium-, or short-grain brown rice; wild rice, which isn't a rice at all but the seed of an aquatic grass; barley; millet; oats; wheat; bulgur; buckwheat; wheat berries; rye; triticale, which is a cross between rye and wheat; amaranth; and so on.

Though some purists say that when combining grains for a dish you should cook them separately, Terri often throws them in a pot together, sacrificing perhaps a small amount of delicate consistency in exchange for ease of preparation and shorter clean-up time.

NUTS AND SEEDS

Nuts and seeds are good sources of protein, but unfortunately they contain a high proportion of fat as well. We use them sparingly as a protein booster in meatless cooking and as a garnish (for example, Thai Stir-Fry, page 126, uses sesame seeds in this way).

Toasting your own seeds and nuts means you can control the amount of fat and salt added—you don't really need to add any, especially when the final product will be used in another recipe. You can sometimes find dry-roasted, unsalted nuts and seeds in a supermarket; a better bet for finding raw nuts and seeds is health-food stores.

To toast your own, use one of the following methods:

Oven-Toasting—Spread the nuts or seeds in a single layer on a baking sheet and place in a 375- to 400-degree oven. Let bake, stirring occasionally, until golden brown, which could take anywhere from 3 to 10 minutes depending on the type of nut or seed. A general rule of thumb is the smaller the nut or seed, the shorter the roasting time. Try a small amount first so you can monitor the time and heat.

Pan-Toasting—Place the nuts or seeds in a hot, dry skillet, and toast over medium heat, stirring often, until golden brown.

By the way, toasted pumpkin and squash seeds are delicious. We do them in the oven and they are among our favorite snacks.

Now we are ready to go on to some of our favorite meatless main dish recipes, and we hope to get you started on the road to at least one meatless day each week.

Classic Steamed Veggies and Rice

PREPARATION TIME: 10 MINUTES   COOKING TIME: 40 MINUTES

This is a standard vegetarian recipe, easy to prepare, with complementary protein provided by the brown rice and the cheese. Our favorite vegetable combination for this recipe is broccoli, carrots, onions, yellow squash, and mushrooms. We start cooking the broccoli and carrots first, because they take longer. Then we add the other veggies as we go along.

We also like chunks of red cabbage, zucchini, tomatoes, green beans, cauliflower—well, just put in your favorite vegetables, and enjoy!

1¾ cups water
  or Vegetable Stock (p. 66)
1 cup brown rice
2 cups mixed vegetables of
  choice, cut in chunks

Water for steaming
4 tablespoons grated light
  cheddar cheese
Dash tamari sauce or soy sauce
  (optional)

1. Pour the water or vegetable stock into a saucepan, cover, and bring to a boil. Pour in the brown rice, cover, and reduce heat to simmer. Do not stir.
2. After rice has been cooking for about 20 minutes, start steaming your vegetables (see directions for steaming, p. 263).
3. When all veggies are just tender, ladle them over the cooked rice, and top with the cheese. Let everyone add their own bit of tamari sauce if they desire.

4 servings. Serving size is ½ cup rice, ½ cup veggies, 1 tablespoon cheese.

Per serving: **4 g. fat,** 254 calories, 7 mg. cholesterol, 5 g. dietary fiber, 149 mg. sodium

"Joey says he's not used to cold stuffed zucchini boats." © 1986 *GOURMET* MAGAZINE. REPRINTED BY PERMISSION OF DONALD REILLY.

Eggplant Parmesan ✓

PREPARATION TIME: 35 MINUTES   COOKING TIME: 40 MINUTES

Eggplant is known for its ability to absorb huge quantities of oil. This "no-fry" version of a delectable Italian dish eliminates almost all of the oil, and therefore several hundred calories. Protein in this recipe comes from the egg, milk, and cheese, along with the wheat germ and whole-wheat bread crumbs.

1 medium eggplant (about 1 pound)
1 egg
   OR 2 egg whites
2 tablespoons skim milk
½ cup Whole-Wheat Bread Crumbs (p. 305)
¼ cup wheat germ
1 tablespoon Parmesan cheese
Nonstick vegetable cooking spray
2 cups Real Italian Tomato Sauce (pp. 288–89)
¾ cup part-skim mozzarella

1. Slice the eggplant into 8 slices, ½ inch thick.
2. Beat together the egg and milk in a small, shallow bowl.
3. In another bowl, combine the bread crumbs, wheat germ, and Parmesan cheese.
4. Spray a foil-lined baking sheet with cooking spray. Dip the eggplant slices into the egg mixture, coating well. Then dip them into the bread crumb mixture. Place the slices on the baking sheet, and bake at 350 degrees for 15 minutes. Turn the slices over, and bake for 10 more minutes. Remove from oven.
5. Make a layer of eggplant in a casserole dish, top with tomato sauce, then mozzarella. Repeat the layers until no ingredients remain.
6. Bake covered at 350 degrees for 25 minutes, then uncover and bake 15 minutes more.

4 servings. Serving size is 2 slices each, plus sauce.

Per serving: **8 g. fat**, 244 calories, 60 mg. cholesterol, 7 g. dietary fiber, 581 mg. sodium

Basic Beans ✓

PREPARATION TIME: 15 MINUTES   COOKING TIME: 4½ HOURS
(PLUS SOAKING TIME)

Here's a basic bean recipe that you can use with virtually any dried bean. Serve over grain to provide complementary protein for your main course, or as a side dish. Add the optional crushed red pepper if you like spicy food.

2 cups dried beans
Water
½ bulb garlic (about 4 or 5
    cloves), minced
1 teaspoon salt

1 tablespoon olive oil –opt.
2 medium onions, cut in
    chunks
1 to 1½ teaspoons crushed red
    pepper (optional)

1. Rinse the beans thoroughly in water to remove dirt. Pick over to remove any small stones that may have gotten mixed in with the beans. Soak the beans overnight in a large kettle, in 5 cups of water. (Before cooking the beans, some people will change the water. Since we are more likely to use the following recipe for Basic Better Beans, which calls for soaking beans in stock, we don't discard the liquid.)
2. The next day, bring the beans to a boil. Turn to simmer, and add the remaining ingredients. Let simmer about 4 hours, until most or all of the water is gone, stirring occasionally.

8 servings. Serving size is about ½ cup.

Per serving: **2 g. fat,** 183 calories, no cholesterol, 10 g. dietary fiber, 273 mg. sodium

Basic Better Beans

PREPARATION TIME: 15 MINUTES   COOKING TIME: 4½ HOURS
(PLUS SOAKING TIME)

The use of stock—along with a whole onion stuck with whole cloves—instead of water for soaking and cooking makes beans even more flavorful.

2 cups dried beans	6 whole cloves
4 cups low-sodium stock	1 tablespoon olive oil
2 large onions	Dash of salt and pepper

1. Place the beans in a pot with the stock. Peel the onions, stick the whole cloves in them, and place in the pot with the beans. Soak overnight.
2. Remove the onions and cloves, bring the beans to a boil, then reduce heat and cook, covered, until just tender, about 3 hours.
3. Discard the cloves, chop the onions, and sauté in the oil until translucent.
4. Place all ingredients in a large casserole dish and bake for 1 hour at 325 degrees.

8 servings. Serving size is about ½ cup.

Per serving: 3 g. fat, 203 calories, no cholesterol, 11 g. dietary fiber, 109 mg. sodium

Swiss-Mozzarella Bake

PREPARATION TIME: 10 MINUTES,   COOKING TIME: 1 HOUR
PLUS 30 TO 45 MINUTES STANDING TIME

This is a very good and simple dish that's especially handy if you have some leftover bread that's beginning to get stale. Fresh bread works wonderfully too. This dish is like a soufflé or pudding, and is baked by setting the pan in a larger pan of hot water in the oven, which helps keep the consistency moist and light.

We like to use whole mustard seed and crush it ourselves with a mortar and pestle, but if you prefer, you can substitute ground dry mustard. As always, you can leave out the tamari sauce if you wish to cut back on salt.

1 cup grated Jarlesberg Lite cheese
2 cups grated part-skim mozzarella
5 slices whole-grain bread
1½ cups low-fat milk
2 eggs
½ cup plain nonfat yogurt

¾ teaspoon dried thyme
½ teaspoon crushed mustard seed or ground dry mustard
½ teaspoon fresh-ground black pepper
1 teaspoon dried parsley
½ teaspoon tamari sauce or soy sauce (optional)

1. Combine the two cheeses. Then, in an 8-inch-square baking dish, alternate layers of bread and cheese until used up.
2. Combine the remaining ingredients and pour over the bread and cheese. Let stand for 30 to 45 minutes, until the bread soaks up the liquid.
3. Place the casserole in a larger pan of hot water, and bake at 350 degrees for 1 hour.

6 servings. Serving size is about 1 cup.

Per serving: **11 g. fat,** 268 calories, 95 mg. cholesterol, 2 g. dietary fiber, 473 mg. sodium

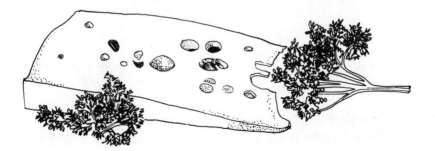

Terrific Tater Toppers

A hot, freshly baked potato can be the foundation for a complete, delicious meal. We hope the following ideas and recipes will tantalize your taste buds, and trigger your imagination to create your own delectable, low-calorie tater-topping alternatives to sour cream and butter. Here are some ideas for toppings; use them singly or in combination. The *majority* of these Tater Topper ideas are meatless, but we include a few that do have meat in order to show you the wide variety that is possible.

(*Note:* Tater Topper cooking times do not include time for baking the potatoes. A "medium" potato is about 5–6 ounces, or 3 per pound.)

Mix-and-Match Tater Topper ideas:

Low-fat cottage cheese
Sapsago cheese
Farmer cheese
Neufchâtel cheese
Imitation bacon bits (made from soy)
Steamed vegetables (mushrooms, broccoli, carrots, spinach, zucchini, tomatoes, or onions)
Meatless tomato sauce
Meatless chili
Beans and legumes
Tofu
Chives
Herbs and spices
Chunks of lean meat or poultry
Boiled shrimp, lobster, crabmeat, or imitation crabmeat

Mexican Tater Topper

PREPARATION TIME: COOKING TIME (USING JUST-BAKED POTATOES):
5 MINUTES   10 TO 15 MINUTES

Here's another "meal-in-one" that's high in protein and has no meat. The protein is provided by the beans, cheese, and potato.

2 cups cooked kidney beans
¼ cup minced onion
½ teaspoon cayenne pepper
1 teaspoon chili powder
1 teaspoon garlic powder
2 tablespoons water

4 medium baked potatoes, hot
Shredded lettuce
½ cup diced tomato
½ cup grated light sharp
   cheddar cheese

1. In a hot skillet, combine the beans, onion, seasonings, and water. Mash with a fork as the mixture heats, for a chunky-smooth texture.
2. Spoon the "refried beans" into the hot, split potatoes. Top with as much shredded lettuce as you like, and 2 tablespoons each of tomatoes and cheese for each potato.

4 servings. Serving size is about ½ cup sauce, 1 potato, plus condiments.

Per serving: **1 g. fat,** 284 calories, 3 mg. cholesterol, 11 g. dietary fiber, 113 mg. sodium

Italian Tater Topper

PREPARATION TIME: COOKING TIME (USING JUST-BAKED POTATOES):
5 MINUTES   5 MINUTES

1 cup Real Italian Tomato
   Sauce (pp. 288–89) or your
   favorite tomato sauce

4 medium baked potatoes, hot
½ cup part-skim mozzarella,
   grated

1. Heat the sauce in a small saucepan.
2. Top each hot, split potato with ¼ cup of sauce and 2 tablespoons of cheese.

4 servings. Serving size is ¼ cup sauce, 1 potato, 2 tablespoons cheese.

Per serving: **3 g. fat,** 198 calories, 8 mg. cholesterol, 4 g. dietary fiber, 237 mg. sodium

Twice-Baked Stuffed Potatoes ✓

PREPARATION TIME: COOKING TIME (USING JUST-BAKED POTATOES):
12 MINUTES   10 MINUTES

4 medium baked potatoes
1 cup 1% low-fat cottage cheese
  OR ½ cup reduced-fat
  shredded cheese, such as
  part-skim mozzarella,
  Monterey Jack, or Swiss
1 egg white

¼ teaspoon salt
2 teaspoons prepared mustard
1 tablespoon minced onion
Dash fresh-ground black
  pepper
Dried parsley or paprika
  (optional)

1. Cut the potatoes in half, lengthwise. Scoop the insides into a mixing bowl, leaving the skins intact.
2. Add the remaining ingredients to the bowl except the parsley or paprika, and beat with a wire whisk or electric mixer until smooth and fluffy.
3. Arrange the potato skins on an ungreased baking sheet. Spoon the potato mixture into the skins. Sprinkle with the dried parsley or paprika if desired.
4. Bake at 375 degrees for about 10 minutes, or until lightly browned.

4 servings.

Per serving: **1 g. fat,** 181 calories, 2 mg. cholesterol, 3 g. dietary fiber, 419 mg. sodium

Broccoli-and-Chicken (or Lean-Beef) Tater Topper

PREPARATION TIME: COOKING TIME (USING JUST-BAKED POTATOES):
5 MINUTES   15 MINUTES

¼ cup chopped onion
1 cup sliced mushrooms
1 tablespoon vegetable oil
2 tablespoons water
¼ cup whole-wheat flour
1½ cups skim or low-fat milk
Herb blend and/or
  fresh-ground black pepper to
  taste

2 cups cooked chicken
  or lean beef, cubed
1 large bunch broccoli, steamed
  and chopped (about 2 cups)
4 medium baked potatoes, hot

1. Sauté the onion and mushrooms in the oil in a large skillet. Stir in the water and flour.
2. Gradually add the milk, stirring until slightly thickened.
3. Add the seasonings, chicken or beef, and the broccoli. Cook uncovered, stirring occasionally, for 2 to 3 minutes.
4. Slice open the baked potatoes, and pour the broccoli mixture on top.

4 servings. Serving size is about 1 1/2 cups over 1 potato.

Per serving: **9 g. fat,** 374 calories, 60 mg. cholesterol, 6 g. dietary fiber, 128 mg. sodium

Zucchini Soufflé

PREPARATION TIME: 20 MINUTES   COOKING TIME: 45 MINUTES

3/4 cups shredded zucchini
3 tablespoons onion, minced
4 ounces fresh mushrooms, sliced
2 teaspoons cornstarch
3/4 cup skim milk
2 eggs

1/2 teaspoon salt
1/4 teaspoon fresh-ground black pepper
1/4 teaspoon nutmeg
1/3 cup part-skim mozzarella, diced

1. In a large bowl, combine the zucchini, onion, and mushrooms.
2. In a medium bowl, mix together the cornstarch and 1 tablespoon of the milk, then stir in the remaining milk. Beat in the eggs and seasonings.
3. Stir the egg mixture into the vegetables, then stir in the cheese.
4. Pour into a 9-inch pie plate, and bake at 350 degrees for 45 minutes.

4 servings. Serving size is about 3/4 cup.

Per serving: **4 g. fat,** 92 calories, 100 mg. cholesterol, 1 g. dietary fiber, 363 mg. sodium

Three-Way Beans and Rice

PREPARATION TIME: 5 MINUTES   COOKING TIME: 4 HOURS AND
15 MINUTES

You may substitute chicken or beef stock for the water if you are not concerned about whether this meal is totally meatless.

1 cup black beans
1 cup white beans
¼ cup lentils
6 cups water
   or low-sodium vegetable
   stock

2 medium onions
½ bulb (about 4 or 5 cloves)
   garlic, minced
1 teaspoon salt
1 tablespoon olive oil
1 cup brown rice

1. Wash and drain the beans and lentils, picking over to be sure there are no stones. Reserve the lentils.
2. Place the black and white beans in a large soup pot with the water or stock, and bring to a boil.
3. Turn the heat down to simmer. Add the onions, garlic, salt, and oil. Let simmer for about 3½ hours, stirring occasionally.
4. Add the lentils and the rice. Bring to a boil again, then reduce heat and let simmer for 40 minutes, until rice and lentils are tender, and the broth is like a thick gravy.

12 servings of about 1 cup each.

Per serving: **2 g. fat,** 201 calories, no cholesterol, 8 g. dietary fiber, 187 mg. sodium

Stir-Fry Vegetables

PREPARATION TIME: 5 MINUTES   COOKING TIME: 15 TO 20 MINUTES

2 cups finely chopped fresh
  vegetables
1 tablespoon peanut oil
1 clove garlic, minced
¼ teaspoon ginger

2 tablespoons grated hard
  cheese (Parmesan, white
  cheddar)
Tamari sauce or soy sauce to
  taste

1. Have your vegetables ready; use any combination you like. In a large skillet or wok, heat the oil. Add the garlic and ginger, then add the vegetables requiring the most cooking, such as carrots, broccoli, green pepper, and so on.
2. Stir constantly, adding the vegetables that require less cooking as you go along. If necessary, add a tablespoon or two of water to prevent sticking. Cook until tender-crisp.
3. Spoon over cooked grain, sprinkle with cheese and tamari sauce if desired, and serve.

Serves 1 as a main course, 4 as a side dish.

Per complete recipe (with 2 cups brown rice and ½ cup each carrots, onions, celery, and broccoli): **18 g. fat,** 271 calories, 10 mg. cholesterol, 6 g. dietary fiber, 486 mg. sodium

Per serving (as a side dish, ½ cup mixed Stir-Fry Vegetables recipe, with ½ cup brown rice): **5 g. fat,** 176 calories, 2 mg. cholesterol, 3 g. dietary fiber, 126 mg. sodium

(*Note:* ½ cup cooked brown rice contains 1 g. fat, 108 calories, no cholesterol, 2 g. dietary fiber, 5 mg. sodium.)

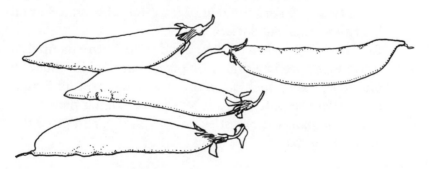

Spinach Pizza

PREPARATION TIME: 50 MINUTES   COOKING TIME: 30 MINUTES

If you like spinach and pizza, you will love this combination! You can use the same crust as in the Summer's Bounty Pizza (pp. 250–51), or you can use this rapid-rise version. The water needs to be a little warmer than usual (but never hot!) for the rapid-rise version, since you are combining the yeast with so many ingredients at once.

Serve with a salad on the side.

The crust:

½ cup whole-wheat flour
⅛ cup all-purpose flour
¼ cup low-fat soy flour
½ teaspoon salt
1 tablespoon rapid-rise yeast

½ cup warm water (120° to 130°F)
Nonstick vegetable cooking spray

The filling:

½ medium onion, minced
4 ounces fresh mushrooms, sliced
1 package (10 ounces) frozen chopped spinach, thawed
1¼ cups shredded part-skim mozzarella

¾ cup nonfat ricotta or dry-curd nonfat cottage cheese
1 egg OR 2 egg whites
1 clove garlic, crushed
1 tablespoon Traditional Italian Herb Blend (p. 333)

1. To prepare the crust, combine the flours, salt, and yeast in a large bowl with the water. Mix well. If necessary, add a little more all-purpose flour to make the dough the right consistency. Knead the dough for 5 minutes on a floured board or other flat surface.
2. Replace the dough in the bowl, and cover with a damp dish towel to let rise in a draft-free place. Let double (about 30 minutes), then punch down. Let the dough rest for 5 minutes, then roll out to fit a 9 × 13-inch baking pan.
3. Spray the pan with nonstick cooking spray, and place the crust in the pan.

4. Steam the onions and mushrooms over a small amount of water until tender. Meanwhile, drain the thawed spinach in a colander, pressing out as much liquid as possible. (You can save the liquid for stock, if you wish.)
5. Combine the cooked onions and mushrooms with the spinach and all remaining ingredients in a large bowl, mixing well. Pour into the crust, and bake at 375 degrees for 30 minutes.

4 servings. Serving size is ¼ pizza.

Per serving: **8 g. fat,** 254 calories, 69 mg. cholesterol, 5 g. dietary fiber, 570 mg. sodium

White-Bean Casserole

PREPARATION TIME: 10 MINUTES   COOKING TIME: 1 HOUR

2 cups dried white beans
1 teaspoon butter
  or margarine
1 tablespoon olive oil
1 can (10 ounces) tomato purée
1 cup shredded light sharp
  cheddar cheese

1 cup shredded part-skim
  mozzarella
3 tablespoons whole-wheat
  flour
2 tablespoons dried oregano

1. Cook the beans according to the Basic Beans recipe (p. 239), cooking off as much liquid as possible.
2. Lightly butter an 8½ × 11-inch casserole dish. Mix the cooked beans with the olive oil and tomato purée, and pour into the dish.
3. Combine the cheeses, flour, and oregano, and spread on top of the beans.
4. Bake uncovered at 275 degrees for 1 hour.

8 servings. Serving size is about 1 cup.

Per serving: **7 g. fat,** 294 calories, 15 mg. cholesterol, 12 g. dietary fiber, 231 mg. sodium

Summer's Bounty Pizza

PREPARATION TIME: 1 HOUR AND 10 MINUTES   COOKING TIME: 30 MINUTES

This is *marvelous!* Tastes like a "real" pizza, even though it has no meat or tomato sauce. Serve it hot or cold as a main dish with a salad on the side, or cut it up in small pieces and serve as an hors d'oeuvre.

The crust:
1 tablespoon active dry yeast
½ cup lukewarm water (105° to 115°F)
⅛ teaspoon sugar
½ cup whole-wheat flour
¼ cup all-purpose flour
¼ cup low-fat soy flour
½ teaspoon salt
2 additional tablespoons all-purpose flour

The filling:
1 tablespoon olive oil
1 medium onion, chopped
1 clove garlic, minced or crushed
2 cups yellow crookneck squash, sliced thin
2 cups zucchini, sliced thin
2 eggs
1½ cups grated part-skim mozzarella
2 tablespoons fresh parsley, chopped
1½ teaspoons Traditional Italian Herb Blend (p. 333)
½ teaspoon fresh-ground black pepper

1. Dissolve the yeast in ¼ cup of the lukewarm water, along with the sugar. In another bowl, combine the whole-wheat flour, the ¼ cup of all-purpose flour, the soy flour, and the salt.

2. Stir the other ¼ cup lukewarm water into the yeast mixture, then stir the mixture into the dry ingredients. Turn out on a lightly floured board or flat surface and knead for about 5 minutes, or until smooth and elastic, adding a little more all-purpose flour as needed. Return the dough to the bowl, cover with a damp dish towel, and set in a warm, draft-free place to rise for 45 minutes.

3. Meanwhile, heat the oil in a large skillet over medium heat, and add the onion and garlic. Cover, and sauté/steam until onions are translucent.
4. Add the yellow squash and zucchini, cover, and reduce heat to low. Cook for 10 minutes, or until squash is tender.
5. Preheat the oven to 375 degrees.
6. Combine the eggs, the cheese, and the seasonings in a large bowl. When the vegetables are cooked, drain them thoroughly, and stir them into the egg mixture.
7. Punch down the dough after it doubles, and let it rest for 5 minutes on the board. Then roll it out to fit a 9 × 13-inch baking dish. Place the dough into the ungreased dish, and press into the sides. (If it cracks in places, pat it with lightly floured fingers to smooth it out.) Pour the vegetable mixture on top and spread evenly.
8. Bake for about 30 minutes, or until a knife or toothpick inserted in the center comes out clean. Let cool for 10 minutes before slicing.

4 servings. Serving size is ¼ pizza.

Per serving: **14 g. fat,** 327 calories, 118 mg. cholesterol, 5 g. dietary fiber, 534 mg. sodium

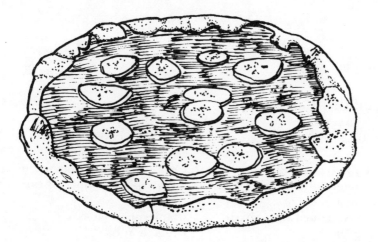

Peas and Rice ✓

PREPARATION TIME: 10 MINUTES   COOKING TIME: 45 TO 50 MINUTES

Here's a special vegetable-and-grain dish that cooks in one pan.

1 tablespoon vegetable oil
1 small onion, chopped
1 clove garlic, crushed
1 teaspoon dried basil
1 cup brown rice
1½ cups low-sodium vegetable (or chicken) stock

1 bay leaf
Salt and fresh-ground black pepper to taste
1 cup fresh or frozen peas

1. Heat the oil in a large saucepan over medium heat. Add the onion, garlic, and basil. Cover and sauté, stirring occasionally, until onions are translucent. Add the rice, and stir.
2. Add the stock, bay leaf, salt, and pepper, and bring to a boil.
3. Cover, and reduce heat to simmer. Let cook about 20 to 25 minutes.
4. Pour the peas on top. Do not stir.
5. Cover and let cook until the peas are just tender and the liquid has boiled away.

4 servings. Serving size is about ¾ cup.

Per serving: **5 g. fat,** 253 calories, no cholesterol, 4 g. dietary fiber, 138 mg. sodium

Zucchini Casserole

PREPARATION TIME: 10 MINUTES   COOKING TIME: 1 HOUR

2½ pounds zucchini
1 teaspoon butter or margarine
¾ cup shredded light sharp cheddar cheese
¾ cup shredded part-skim mozzarella

1 can (10 ounces) tomato purée
4 tablespoons whole-wheat flour
1 tablespoon olive oil
1 teaspoon basil
½ teaspoon salt
½ teaspoon garlic powder

1. Wash the zucchini and chop into chunks.
2. Lightly butter an 8 × 11½-inch casserole dish or similar-sized baking dish. Put the zucchini in. Spread the cheeses over the squash, then the tomato purée. Sprinkle the flour over the top, then the oil, and then the spices, spreading all the ingredients as evenly as possible.
3. Cover and bake at 350 degrees for 1 hour.

6 servings. Serving size is about 1 cup.

Per serving: **7 g. fat,** 150 calories, 13 mg. cholesterol, 4 g. dietary fiber, 447 mg. sodium

Welsh Rarebit

PREPARATION TIME: 7 MINUTES   COOKING TIME: 12 MINUTES

We like real Swiss cheese in this recipe.

1 cup Swiss cheese, diced
1 egg
½ cup skim milk
1 teaspoon dry mustard
¼ teaspoon Tabasco sauce

¼ teaspoon salt
¼ teaspoon fresh-ground black pepper
1 teaspoon cornstarch
4 slices whole-grain toast

1. Melt the cheese in a double boiler. While the cheese is melting, beat together the remaining ingredients except for the cornstarch and toast.
2. When cheese is melted, add the cornstarch, stirring constantly until it is absorbed.
3. Add the egg mixture and stir constantly (a wire whisk is best for this) until the sauce thickens. Serve immediately over whole-grain toast.

4 servings. Serving size is about ⅓ cup each, plus toast.

Per serving: **10 g. fat,** 215 calories, 72 mg. cholesterol, 3 g. dietary fiber, 407 mg. sodium

Tofu

Tofu, soybean curd, soy cheese—these terms all refer to the same thing. At best, they may sound unusual to most of us. At worst, they sound downright unappetizing!

Yet this light, mild-tasting, and versatile meat substitute is extremely high in protein and extremely low in calories, saturated fat, and salt. It has no cholesterol and is a staple in many Oriental countries where meat is not as readily available as it is in the Western world. Plus, it's high in calcium, iron, and other valuable minerals and vitamins.

Due to its delicate flavor, tofu blends well with practically everything. It can be grilled, sautéed, stir-fried, added to soups, or mashed or blended to resemble cottage cheese and then used as a base for desserts, dips, salads, sandwiches, and main courses.

Tofu is available in an array of textures—regular, firm, extra-firm, silken, wine-fermented, and so on. You can use whatever kind you find packaged in the refrigerated section of your supermarket. Be sure to follow any directions in the recipes for draining or pressing the tofu before using it in order to get the right consistency.

Although we had used tofu occasionally before writing this cookbook, we learned a great deal more about this versatile and healthful food as we tested the following recipes, many of which were created especially for us by Margaret Nofziger Dotzler.

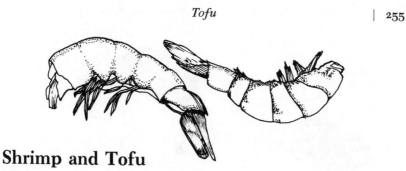

Shrimp and Tofu

PREPARATION TIME: 7 MINUTES   COOKING TIME: 10 MINUTES

Another of Chef Wang Chia Hsin's creations from the Peking Garden restaurant. If you're not already a fan of tofu, this will do the trick.

2 teaspoons vegetable oil
½-inch piece of gingerroot, peeled and chopped
1 scallion, chopped
8 ounces shrimp, shelled and deveined
6 ounces tofu, cut into 1-inch pieces

Dash of salt
Fresh-ground black pepper to taste
Dash of sugar
½ cup low-sodium chicken stock
¼ teaspoon cornstarch, dissolved in a bit of water

1. In a wok or skillet, heat the oil, add the gingerroot and scallion and stir for 10 seconds, then add the shrimp and tofu and cook until the shrimp are almost done (about 3 minutes).
2. Add the salt, pepper, sugar, chicken stock, and dissolved cornstarch. Bring to a boil, stirring frequently. Reduce heat and simmer for about 1 minute more, or until sauce is at desired consistency.

2 servings. Serving size is about 1 cup.

Per serving: **10 g. fat,** 233 calories, 221 mg. cholesterol, 1 g. dietary fiber, 413 mg. sodium

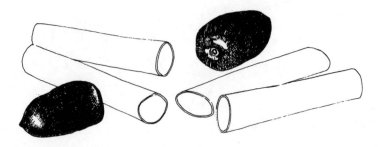

Tofu Manicotti

PREPARATION TIME: 30 MINUTES   COOKING TIME: 1 HOUR AND 5
                                                              MINUTES

If you can't find firm tofu, you can make regular tofu into "firm" tofu by placing the rinsed tofu on a dish towel or several paper towels. Set a foil pan with some water in it, or another light weight such as a plate or two, on top of the cake of tofu, and let stand for about 10 to 20 minutes. Then crumble it as directed below, and proceed with the recipe.

1 pound firm tofu
¼ teaspoon salt
1 cup grated part-skim
   mozzarella
¼ cup fresh parsley, finely
   chopped
1 can (28 ounces) whole
   tomatoes with juice

1 can (6 ounces) tomato paste
1 tablespoon leaf oregano
2 teaspoons basil leaf
¼ teaspoon garlic powder
2 cups water
1 package manicotti noodles (8
   ounces or 6 large noodles)

1. Rinse the tofu, and crumble finely into a mixing bowl. Add the salt, mozzarella, and parsley. Mix well, and set aside.
2. Place the tomatoes with their juice, the tomato paste, oregano, basil, garlic powder, and water in a blender. Blend briefly, for a chunky consistency.
3. Place 2 cups of the tomato sauce in the bottom of a 9 × 12-inch glass or stainless-steel baking pan (*not* aluminum).
4. Fill the uncooked manicotti noodles with the tofu mixture.

Using your hands, pack the noodles firmly. You should have exactly enough filling for all of the noodles in the package.

5. Place the noodles side by side in the baking pan. Pour the remaining sauce over the top. Make sure the noodles are completely covered. Cover the pan with foil.

6. Bake at 400 degrees for 45 minutes. Then remove the foil, being careful not to let the hot steam burn your hands. Turn the manicotti with tongs. Cover again, and bake another 20 minutes. Remove from the oven and let stand for 10 minutes before serving.

6 servings. Serving size is 1 filled noodle each, plus sauce.

Per serving: **8 g. fat,** 299 calories, 11 mg. cholesterol, 5 g. dietary fiber, 539 mg. sodium

"Tonight I plan to have something for dinner you never had before but it is *very* good for you." DRAWING BY MODELL; ©
1985 THE NEW YORKER MAGAZINE, INC.

Oriental Tofu Soup

PREPARATION TIME: 15 MINUTES   COOKING TIME: 30 MINUTES

5 cups low-sodium vegetable or chicken stock (see Onion Stock, pp. 66–67)

1 medium carrot, sliced thinly on the diagonal

1 cup chopped Chinese cabbage

1 small stalk celery, with leaves, sliced thinly (about ¼ cup)

½ can (5-ounce can) sliced bamboo shoots, drained

1 tablespoon tamari sauce or soy sauce

4 large mushrooms, sliced

1 tablespoon cornstarch

¼ cup water

½ pound tofu

¼ teaspoon crushed red pepper

3 slices fresh gingerroot, dime size

1 whole black peppercorn

1. Bring the stock to a boil in a large pot. Add the carrot, cabbage, and celery, and bring back to a boil. Then reduce the heat to medium or medium low, and simmer, covered, for 10 minutes.
2. Add the bamboo shoots, tamari sauce or soy sauce, and the mushrooms.
3. Put the cornstarch in a small bowl, and stir in the water to make a smooth paste. Add this to the soup.
4. Bring the soup back to a gentle boil. Meanwhile, handling the tofu carefully, cut it into julienne strips, and add to the soup. The tofu will become firmer after it simmers for a short time.
5. Put the red pepper, gingerroot, and black pepper into a stainless-steel teaball or a cheesecloth bag. Add to the soup, and let simmer for 10 minutes.
6. Remove the teaball or bag, and serve the soup at once, ladling the tofu carefully.

6 servings. Serving size is about 1½ cups.

Per serving: **3 g. fat,** 87 calories, 0 cholesterol, 2 g. dietary fiber, 217 mg. sodium

Potato-Tofu Salad

PREPARATION TIME: 20 MINUTES   COOKING TIME: ABOUT 45 MINUTES

As a complete lunch, this recipe will serve four. Use the sugar if you like a sweeter-tasting salad. It is also good served on a bed of your favorite lettuce and garnished with sliced hard-boiled eggs.

(*Note:* No cooking time if potatoes have been previously cooked.)

6 medium red potatoes
¼ cup water
2 tablespoons vegetable oil
1 tablespoon lemon juice
2 tablespoons vinegar
2 teaspoons prepared mustard
1 teaspoon sugar (optional)

½ to 1 teaspoon salt
⅛ teaspoon garlic powder
1 pound tofu, crumbled
½ cup celery, sliced thinly
4 radishes, sliced thinly
¼ cup minced onion

1. Steam, microwave, or boil the potatoes until tender. Drain (if boiled) and let cool. (You can set the pan of potatoes over ice cubes to hurry this process, or put the potatoes in the refrigerator or freezer. Don't let them freeze though!) Trim any blemishes.
2. Meanwhile, place the water, oil, lemon juice, vinegar, mustard, sugar if desired, salt, and garlic powder in a blender or food processor and blend briefly to mix. Add the crumbled tofu, and blend until smooth.
3. When the potatoes are cool, dice them. Add the celery, radishes, and onion, tossing gently. Add the tofu mixture, and mix gently. Adjust the salt if necessary.

4 servings. Serving size is about 2 cups.

Per serving: **13 g. fat,** 261 calories, no cholesterol, 4 g. dietary fiber, 329 mg. sodium

Tofu Stir-Fry

PREPARATION TIME: 6 MINUTES   COOKING TIME: 20 MINUTES

Serve this over cooked grain, along with a dark green or yellow vegetable on the side. See the introduction to the recipe for Tofu Manicotti (p. 256) for directions on how to make your tofu firmer, if desired.

½ pound tofu, regular or firm
1 tablespoon peanut oil
  or vegetable oil
1½ teaspoons tamari sauce
  or soy sauce
½ cup celery, sliced thinly
1 cup coarsely shredded white
  cabbage

3 cups fresh bean sprouts
1 can (2½ ounces) water
  chestnuts, drained
1 tablespoon cornstarch
2 tablespoons water
1½ tablespoons tamari sauce
  or soy sauce

1. Cut the tofu into pieces about ½ inch wide by ¼ inch thick by 1 inch long.
2. Heat the oil in a large frying pan or wok. Carefully place the pieces of tofu in the pan, side by side. Sprinkle with the 1½ teaspoons of tamari sauce. Fry over medium heat until the bottom of the tofu starts to brown. Carefully turn over, and cook the other side until it starts to brown. Remove the tofu, and set aside.
3. Add the celery and cabbage, and stir-fry for 3 minutes. Add the bean sprouts and water chestnuts, and stir-fry for 3 more minutes.
4. Mix the cornstarch with the water and the 1½ tablespoons of tamari sauce. Pour the mixture over the vegetables, and stir well. Add the tofu, mix gently, and cover. Steam for a few minutes, until the liquid has thickened and the tofu is hot. Serve immediately.

4 servings. Serving size is about 1½ cups.

Per serving: **6 g. fat,** 124 calories, no cholesterol, 4 g. dietary fiber, 431 mg. sodium

Crêpes with Tofu Filling

PREPARATION TIME: 20 MINUTES   COOKING TIME: 10 MINUTES

1½ quarts water
1 pound tofu
Dash or two of lemon juice
Dash of salt
½ cup whole-wheat flour
½ cup all-purpose flour
1 teaspoon baking powder
1 tablespoon sugar
1 large egg

1¼ cups skim milk
½ teaspoon vanilla extract
1 tablespoon vegetable oil
1 package (10 ounces) frozen
  berries, thawed
½ cup plain nonfat yogurt
  (optional)
½ cup light sour cream
  (optional)

1. In a 2-quart saucepan, bring the water to a boil. Gently crumble the tofu, and add to the boiling water. Reduce heat and let simmer for 1 minute. Drain in a mesh strainer until fairly dry, and stir in the lemon juice and salt. Set aside.
2. Combine the flours, baking powder, and sugar in a medium bowl.
3. In another bowl, beat the egg. Beat in the milk and vanilla, and add to the flour mixture. Stir until smooth.
4. Heat a small (5-inch) nonstick pan on medium heat. Place the oil in a small bowl, and brush the pan with a small amount of oil. Pour in a scant ¼ cup of the batter, tipping the pan around to spread the batter thinly and evenly. Cook over medium-high heat until the top is dry and the bottom is browned. Turn over using a pancake turner and cook for about 10 seconds.
5. Fill the crêpe with 2 tablespoons of tofu, roll up, and set in a warm oven as the others are cooked. When the crêpes are all cooked and assembled, top with about 2 tablespoons of berries. If you are using the yogurt and sour cream, blend them together in a small bowl, and top each serving with 2 tablespoons of the mixture.

8 crêpes. Serving size is 1 crêpe.

Per serving: **7 g. fat,** 193 calories, 33 mg. cholesterol, 3 g. dietary fiber, 89 mg. sodium

Tofu "Cheesecake"

PREPARATION TIME: 20 MINUTES   COOKING TIME: 40 MINUTES

¾ cup graham cracker crumbs
  (about 9 squares)
1 teaspoon brown sugar
1 tablespoon melted butter
  or margarine
1 pound tofu
2 eggs
1 tablespoon vegetable oil
½ cup sugar
¼ teaspoon salt
1 teaspoon vanilla
2 tablespoons all-purpose flour
8 ounces frozen strawberries
  or other berries, thawed, OR 1
  cup of unsweetened
  applesauce

1. Preheat the oven to 350 degrees. Combine the crumbs, the brown sugar, and the melted butter or margarine in a small bowl. Press firmly into the bottom of an 8-inch pie pan. Bake for 10 minutes, then set aside and let cool.
2. Crumble the tofu into a blender or food processor. Add all the other ingredients except the fruit, and blend for about 3 minutes or until very smooth.
3. Pour the mixture into the cooled crust, and bake at 350 degrees for 40 minutes.
4. Turn off the oven, open the oven door, and let the pie stand in the open oven for 20 minutes. Then chill in the refrigerator overnight or for at least 4 hours. Keep chilled until serving time. Just before serving, top with the fruit.

8 servings.

Per serving: **8 g. fat,** 189 calories, 51 mg. cholesterol, 2 g. dietary fiber, 148 mg. sodium

Vegetable Side Dishes

Almost any cooked vegetable tastes fantastic simply steamed over hot water. You can eat them plain, or add a touch of salt and pepper if you wish. The naturally sweet flavor of fresh vegetables needs no other enhancement.

Here's how to steam vegetables: Put about an inch of water in a pot. Place a stainless-steel, bamboo, or ceramic steamer in the water. (The stainless-steel steamers are cheap, conduct heat quickly, and are available in almost any supermarket or cookware store.) Put the vegetables that need the longest cooking time in the steamer. Cover, and bring to a boil. Then reduce the heat to medium low, allowing the steam to cook the vegetables. After about 3 to 5 minutes, add the vegetables that need less cooking time.

Hard vegetables, such as carrots, broccoli, cauliflower, bell peppers, and so on, need about 10 to 20 minutes of cooking time, depending on how thinly you've sliced them, and how tender you like your vegetables to be. The less cooked they are, the more vitamins and minerals are retained, so getting them just barely tender is best. Onions, summer squashes, mushrooms, and similarly textured vegetables take less time, while spinach and other greens take only a minute or two.

Of course, it's also fun to doctor up the taste of fresh vegetables with seasonings and spices. We hope you enjoy the "fancier" recipes we have here. Most of them are really quite simple—fast yet festive. But if you're ever in such a rush that you don't want to bother with a recipe, plain steamed vegetables are the answer.

You can also use a microwave oven to good advantage with vegetables. If you have a microwave, check the instruction manual that came with it. Vegetables cooked in a microwave retain their nutrients better perhaps than through any other way of cooking.

To prepare vegetables for *any* cooking method, leave edible skins on most vegetables and fruits (such as potatoes, carrots, apples, tomatoes); the skins contain healthful fiber and nutrients. If your produce has been waxed for longer shelf life, as is often the case these days with apples, try scraping the wax off with a paring knife, or washing the produce under hot, soapy water with a scrub brush. The wax is *supposed* to be harmless and quite edible (there is some controversy about that), but regardless, it seems to give an off-flavor to the peel.

Frozen vegetables are good to have on hand in case you run out of fresh ones. In terms of time, however, it really doesn't take longer to rinse a couple of squashes, slice them, and toss them in the steamer than it does to unwrap a freezer package, take the vegetables out of the box, and put them in a pot with water.

Canned vegetables are usually overcooked, over-salted, or preserved with other ingredients you may wish to avoid, so check labels carefully.

Nutritionists formerly suggested that we have green or yellow vegetables every other day for their vitamin A content, but many are now changing and increasing that recommendation to a leafy green every day because of the additional calcium contained in greens. Collards, for example, are about as good a source of calcium as milk products—and they contain no fat! For the record, a survey of research in the journal *Contemporary Nutrition* suggests that oxalic acid in spinach does not prevent the absorption of calcium from that green to any appreciable extent. So, go to it, spinach lovers!

"Why, yes . . . we do have two children who won't eat their vegetables." *THE FAR SIDE.* COURTESY CHRONICLE FEATURES, SAN FRANCISCO.

"Spaghetti" Parmesan

PREPARATION TIME: 5 MINUTES   COOKING TIME: 1 TO 1¼ HOURS

1 whole spaghetti squash, about 8 inches long
2 tablespoons butter or margarine

4 tablespoons grated Parmesan cheese
1 teaspoon garlic powder

1. Boil the whole squash in a large pot of water for about 1 hour to 1¼ hours or until tender, turning it every 15 minutes.
2. Cut the squash in half and remove the seeds. Scoop out the squash and toss with the remaining ingredients.

8 servings. Serving size is about ½ cup.

Per serving: **4 g. fat,** 63 calories, 10 mg. cholesterol, 2 g. dietary fiber, 102 mg. sodium

Shades of Green

PREPARATION TIME: 8 MINUTES   COOKING TIME: 15 TO 20 MINUTES

2 stalks celery, sliced
1 green pepper, diced
3 scallions, chopped (separate white parts from green)
1 tablespoon water

3 ounces green beans, cut into 1-inch pieces
1 stalk broccoli, chopped into flowerets
1 large zucchini, sliced

1. In a covered pan, sauté/steam the celery, green pepper, and the white parts of the scallions in the water until tender.
2. Add the green beans and steam until the beans are tender. Then add the broccoli, zucchini, and the green parts of the scallions. Steam until just tender, and serve.

4 servings. Serving size is about 1 ¼ cup.

Per serving: **no fat**, 29 calories, no cholesterol, 3 g. dietary fiber, 25 mg. sodium

Cherry Tomato Bake

PREPARATION TIME: 7 MINUTES   COOKING TIME: 6 MINUTES

Serve hot or cold, as a side dish, an appetizer, or a salad.

1 pint ripe cherry tomatoes
3 tablespoons scallion, diced
¼ cup fresh parsley, minced
1 medium clove garlic, crushed
¼ teaspoon thyme

¼ teaspoon salt
⅛ teaspoon black pepper
2 tablespoons grated Parmesan cheese

1. Remove any stems from the tomatoes, and place the tomatoes in a baking dish. Sprinkle the scallion on top.
2. In a small bowl, combine the remaining ingredients. Sprinkle this mixture over the tomatoes.
3. Bake at 375 degrees for 3 minutes. Stir, turning the

tomatoes, and bake an additional 3 minutes. Mix, and serve.

4 servings. Serving size is about ½ cup.

Per serving: **1 g. fat,** 37 calories, 2 mg. cholesterol, 2 g. dietary fiber, 202 mg. sodium

Cauliflower-Cheese Bake

PREPARATION TIME: 15 MINUTES   COOKING TIME: 10 MINUTES

1 large head cauliflower
2 eggs
2 tablespoons skim milk
1 teaspoon dried dillweed

2 tablespoons grated Jarlesberg Lite or light sharp cheddar cheese

1. Trim the leaves and stem off the cauliflower, and steam the whole head for about 10 to 15 minutes, until just tender. (If you don't have a steamer big enough, cut the cauliflower into chunks.)
2. Meanwhile, beat together the eggs, milk, dillweed, and cheese.
3. Place the cooked cauliflower in a casserole dish, and pour the egg mixture on top. Cover and bake at 375 degrees for about 10 minutes, until the egg has begun to set and the cheese has melted.

8 servings. Serving size is about ½ cup.

Per serving: **2 g. fat,** 39 calories, 48 mg. cholesterol, 1 g. dietary fiber, 30 mg. sodium

Broccoli with Water Chestnuts ✓

PREPARATION TIME: 5 MINUTES   COOKING TIME: 10 TO 15 MINUTES

1 onion, chopped
1 can (2½ ounces) water
  chestnuts, drained and
  chopped
1 tablespoon butter

1 small head fresh broccoli
  OR 1 package (10 ounces)
  frozen chopped broccoli
Salt and fresh-ground black
  pepper to taste

1. Sauté onion and water chestnuts in butter until onion is translucent.
2. Add the broccoli. Cover and cook on low heat until the broccoli is tender. Add a small amount of water during cooking if necessary, to keep the vegetables from sticking to the pan.
3. Add salt and pepper to taste, or leave unseasoned so everyone can add their own at the table.

4 servings. Serving size is about ½ cup.

Per serving: **3 g. fat,** 65 calories, 8 mg. cholesterol, 3 g. dietary fiber, 117 mg. sodium

Yellow Squash with Dill

PREPARATION TIME: 5 MINUTES   COOKING TIME: 15 MINUTES

This attractive and easy dish, created by my wife, Enid, is also delightful with zucchini; or try mixing the two types of squash.

4 to 6 yellow squash
1 medium onion, diced
1 tablespoon butter
  or margarine

¼ teaspoon salt
Fresh-ground black pepper to
  taste
Dried or fresh dillweed to taste

1. Cut the larger summer squashes in halves or quarters; leave the small ones whole. Place the squash in a steamer over hot water, and let cook until tender.

2. Meanwhile, sauté the onion in the butter or margarine until translucent. Add the seasonings.
3. When the squash is done, place it in a serving bowl, top with the seasoned onions, and serve.

4 servings. Serving size is about 1 cup.

Per serving: **3 g. fat,** 72 calories, 8 mg. cholesterol, 3 g. dietary fiber, 165 mg. sodium

Ginger Carrots

PREPARATION TIME: 10 MINUTES   COOKING TIME: 30 MINUTES

This is a mild recipe that goes well with just about any main course. However, if you like your carrots spicier, add more ginger to taste.

8 medium carrots (4 cups, sliced)
1 tablespoon butter or margarine

2 teaspoons lemon juice
1 teaspoon fresh gingerroot, minced

1. Scrub the carrots well and slice into julienne strips. Heat a skillet on medium heat, and add the butter. When the butter is melted, reduce the heat to low, and add the carrots, lemon juice, and ginger.
2. Cover the skillet, and sauté/steam about 25 minutes, stirring occasionally, until the carrots are tender. Add a little bit of water if necessary to prevent sticking.

8 servings. Serving size is about 1/2 cup.

Per serving: **2 g. fat,** 44 calories, 4 mg. cholesterol, 2 g. dietary fiber, 40 mg. sodium

Sautéed Zucchini (Villa Romano)

PREPARATION TIME: 5 MINUTES   COOKING TIME: 8 TO 10 MINUTES

This recipe from the Villa Romano illustrates how a small amount of butter, when mixed with an oil and seasoning (in this case, olive oil and basil), can add flavor.

2 teaspoons butter
2 tablespoons minced shallots
2 teaspoons minced garlic
1 large OR 2 small zucchini, sliced into rounds (about 4 cups raw slices)
1 teaspoon dried basil OR 2 tablespoons fresh, chopped

Coarse fresh-ground black pepper to taste
Pinch of salt
1 teaspoon olive oil (extra-virgin if available)

1. Melt the butter in a skillet over medium heat. Add the shallots, garlic, and zucchini. Sauté for 3 to 4 minutes.
2. Season with the basil, pepper, and salt, and cook 3 to 4 additional minutes, until zucchini is cooked but still firm.
3. Sprinkle the olive oil over all, stir well, and serve.

4 servings. Serving size is about ½ cup.

Per serving: **3 g. fat,** 54 calories, 5 mg. cholesterol, 2 g. dietary fiber, 75 mg. sodium

Sunshine Vegetable Medley

PREPARATION TIME: 8 MINUTES   COOKING TIME: 30 TO 35 MINUTES

1 tablespoon olive oil
1 medium yellow onion, sliced
1 large tomato, chopped
1 pound yellow squash, sliced (about 3 cups raw)
½ pound carrots, sliced (about 1½ cups raw)

2 medium red or yellow bell peppers, cut into chunks
1 teaspoon Traditional Italian Herb Blend (p. 333)

1. Heat the oil in a large skillet over medium heat. Add the onions, and sauté until onions are translucent.
2. Add the tomatoes, and reduce the heat to low. Cover, and sauté/steam for 3 minutes.
3. Add the remaining ingredients, and continue cooking until vegetables are just tender, about 20 to 25 minutes. Add a little water if necessary to prevent sticking.

6 servings. Serving size is about 1 cup.

Per serving: **3 g. fat,** 70 calories, no cholesterol, 3 g. dietary fiber, 33 mg. sodium

Honey-Nut Glazed Carrots

PREPARATION TIME: 5 MINUTES   COOKING TIME: 20 MINUTES

2 cups carrots, sliced into
  rounds ¼ inch thick
Water
2 teaspoons sliced almonds

1 teaspoon butter
2 teaspoons honey
Dash nutmeg

1. Steam the carrots over a small amount of water until just tender.
2. Heat a small skillet over medium heat. Measure the almonds into the skillet and toast, stirring constantly, until golden brown. Remove the pan from the heat and remove the almonds, setting aside.
3. When the carrots are done, melt the butter in the same skillet you used for the almonds. Add 2 to 3 teaspoons of liquid from the steaming carrots, and add the carrots.
4. Stir in the honey and toasted almonds until the carrots are well coated. Sprinkle with nutmeg, and serve.

4 servings. Serving size is ½ cup.

Per serving: **2 g. fat,** 61 calories, 3 mg. cholesterol, 3 g. dietary fiber, 62 mg. sodium

Eggplant Stove-Top Casserole

PREPARATION TIME: 5 MINUTES   COOKING TIME: 20 MINUTES

1 medium eggplant (about 1
  pound)
1 tablespoon vegetable oil
1 teaspoon instant low-sodium
  beef bouillon granules
¼ cup water

2 stalks celery, chopped
1 small onion, diced
⅛ teaspoon cardamom
1 tablespoon unsalted,
  dry-roasted peanuts, chopped

1. Cut eggplant into ¾-inch cubes.
2. Heat the oil in a large skillet, add the eggplant, and toss to
   coat.
3. Mix the bouillon and water, and add to the pan. Cover and
   let cook over medium-low heat for 15 minutes, stirring
   every 5 minutes or so.
4. Stir in the remaining ingredients, cover, and cook an additional 5 minutes.

6 servings. Serving size is about ½ cup.

Per serving: **3 g. fat,** 57 calories, no cholesterol, 2 g. dietary fiber,
185 mg. sodium

Beans with Tomato Sauce

PREPARATION TIME: 10 MINUTES   COOKING TIME: 1 TO 4 HOURS,
                                    DEPENDING ON VARIETY OF BEANS

½ pound dried beans (red, or
  your choice)
Water or low-sodium stock
1 medium onion
6 whole cloves
2 cloves garlic, pressed
½ teaspoon basil
2 tablespoons red wine

1 can (10½ ounces) tomato
  sauce OR 1⅜ cups Real
  Italian Tomato Sauce
  (pp. 288–89)
Meat scraps (optional)
Fresh-ground black pepper to
  taste

1. Soak the beans overnight, covered with water or stock, together with the onion, in which you have stuck the cloves. Remove the cloves from the onion and discard them before cooking the beans; chop the onion.
2. Bring the beans together with the onion to a boil, covered, then reduce heat and simmer until fork-tender (this can take from one to several hours, depending on the variety of beans you have chosen). Add water as needed to keep the beans covered during cooking.
3. Pour off any remaining liquid from the cooked beans, and save it to be used as stock for other dishes. Then add the garlic and the remaining ingredients. Blend, and simmer for about 30 minutes. Depending upon the sauce you use, you may wish to add a dash of salt, and if you like your beans hot, a dash of cayenne pepper.

8 servings. Serving size is about ½ cup.

Per serving (without meat scraps): **no fat**, 119 calories, no cholesterol, 7 g. dietary fiber, 230 mg. sodium

Spinach Bake

PREPARATION TIME: 15 MINUTES   COOKING TIME: 30 MINUTES

This recipe is easy to prepare.

2 pounds fresh spinach
  OR 1 package (10 ounces) frozen spinach, cooked and drained
½ cup part-skim mozzarella, diced

1 cup fresh mushrooms, sliced
½ teaspoon salt
¼ teaspoon fresh-ground black pepper
1 teaspoon basil

Mix all ingredients thoroughly and bake at 350 degrees for 30 minutes.

6 servings. Serving size is about ⅓ cup.

Per serving: **2 g. fat**, 39 calories, 5 mg. cholesterol, 1 g. dietary fiber, 257 mg. sodium

Fresh Beets

Many of us are used to canned beets, and have never bothered to cook fresh beets ourselves. Yet it's as easy as baking a potato. You can also boil beets, a slightly messier but quicker method. Try them either way, plain or with a dollop of plain nonfat yogurt and a dash of salt and pepper. Or use them in another beet recipe. Beware the beet juice, as it is a powerful staining agent!

TO BAKE:

PREPARATION TIME: 5 MINUTES   COOKING TIME: 1½ HOURS

1 pound fresh beets   **Aluminum foil**

1. Preheat the oven to 350 degrees. Wash the fresh beets, trim off the stems, and tightly wrap each beet in aluminum foil. Place them in the oven for about 1½ hours.
2. Remove the beets from the oven and unwrap the foil. Peel the beets with a paring knife as soon as they're cool enough to handle, and enjoy!

TO BOIL:

PREPARATION TIME: 5 MINUTES   COOKING TIME: 35 MINUTES

1 pound fresh beets   **Water to cover**

1. Place the washed, trimmed beets in a kettle and cover with cold water. Bring to a boil and simmer, uncovered, about 35 minutes, or until the beets are tender.
2. Pour the beets in a colander and run cold water over them to stop the cooking process, drain, and peel.

4 servings. Serving size is about ½ cup.

Per serving: **no fat**, 50 calories, no cholesterol, 3 g. dietary fiber, 87 mg. sodium

Sweet Spiced Beets ✓

PREPARATION TIME (USING FRESH BEETS): 10 MINUTES   COOKING TIME:
30 MINUTES

Here's a recipe that calls for boiling fresh beets. You can use canned if you're in a hurry; just skip the first two steps, add the raisins, cloves, and allspice with the ginger, and the beets later. Delicious hot or cold.

1 pound small fresh beets, washed and trimmed	1 slice fresh gingerroot, 1/4 inch thick, minced
Water to cover	1 teaspoon grated orange or lemon rind
3 whole cloves	
1/4 cup raisins	1 teaspoon red wine vinegar
Dash allspice	2 teaspoons honey
2 teaspoons butter or margarine	

1. Place the beets in water to cover in a saucepan. Bring to a boil, add the cloves, and reduce the heat to simmer. Let cook, uncovered, for 20 minutes. Add the raisins and allspice and cook 5 minutes more.
2. Drain, and rinse with cold water until the beets are cool enough to handle. Peel, and cut them into bite-size chunks.
3. Heat a large saucepan over medium heat. Add the butter. When the butter is melted, add the ginger, orange or lemon rind, and vinegar, and cook, covered, about 5 minutes.
4. Add the beets and raisins, and the honey. Stir, and cook until heated through.

4 servings. Serving size is about 1/2 cup.

Per serving: **2 g. fat,** 107 calories, 5 mg. cholesterol, 3 g. dietary fiber, 109 mg. sodium

Poached Vegetables with Shallots (Arthur's)

PREPARATION TIME: 3 MINUTES   COOKING TIME: 5 MINUTES

The chef at Arthur's restaurant suggests trying this with carrots, yellow squash, or zucchini.

¼ cup water   ½ cup vegetable of choice
¼ cup white wine   Dash salt and pepper
1 teaspoon chopped shallots   Herbs to taste

1. Put the water, wine, and shallots in a hot frying pan and simmer for 1 minute on medium heat.
2. Add the ½ cup vegetables, cover, and simmer for 2 minutes. Add the seasonings, and serve at once.

1 serving.

Per serving (with carrots): **no fat,** 20 calories, no cholesterol, 1 g. dietary fiber, 81 mg. sodium (with dash of salt)—if you use squash, the calories will be about 14 per ½ cup

Kohlrabi

PREPARATION TIME: 8 MINUTES   COOKING TIME: 20 MINUTES

Some say kohlrabi tastes like a cross between an artichoke and a mild turnip. Others compare it to cabbages, radishes, and cucumbers (singly or combined). We have decided that kohlrabi tastes like kohlrabi; try expanding your vegetable repertoire to include it. For variety, you might occasionally substitute it in recipes that call for some of the other vegetables listed above. Buy the small knobs of kohlrabi, which are more tender than the larger ones. Here is the basic recipe for cooking them.

16 small kohlrabi   Boiling water

1. Wash the kohlrabi, cut off and reserve the tops, and pare the knobs.

2. Slice and drop the knobs into a small amount of boiling water. Cook, uncovered, about 20 minutes. Drain.
3. Meanwhile, in another pot, boil the tops of the kohlrabi, and drain when tender.
4. Finely chop the tops and add to the cooked knobs.

4 servings. Serving size is 4 kohlrabi.

Per serving: **no fat,** 66 calories, no cholesterol, 3 g. dietary fiber, 47 mg. sodium

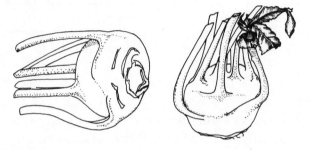

Brussels Sprouts with Wine Sauce

PREPARATION TIME: 7 MINUTES   COOKING TIME: 20 MINUTES

2 cups fresh brussels sprouts
  OR 1 package frozen (10
  ounces), thawed
¼ cup white wine
1 teaspoon lemon juice

8 fresh mushrooms, sliced
¼ teaspoon salt
Fresh-ground black pepper to
  taste
Dash oregano

1. Place the trimmed sprouts, wine, and lemon juice in a saucepan, cover, and heat over medium-low heat for 10 minutes.
2. Add the mushrooms and seasonings. Cover and let simmer for another 10 minutes, or until sprouts and mushrooms are tender.

4 servings. Serving size is ½ cup sprouts, plus sauce.

Per serving: **no fat,** 39 calories, no cholesterol, 3 g. dietary fiber, 146 mg. sodium

Chinese Cabbage Stir-Fry

PREPARATION TIME: 12 MINUTES   COOKING TIME: 10 MINUTES

This vegetable combination is especially good with Oriental Pork Chops (p. 145).

1 small head fresh cauliflower
  OR 1 package (10 ounces)
  frozen cauliflower
¼ cup water
2 teaspoons peanut oil
1 cup Chinese cabbage (or
  other cabbage), chopped
¼ bell pepper, diced
¼ cup chopped mushrooms
½ teaspoon salt
1 teaspoon tamari sauce or soy
  sauce
1 tablespoon dry-roasted,
  unsalted peanuts, chopped

1. Partially cook the cauliflower in the water, about 7 minutes.
2. Brush a wok or skillet with the oil, and heat over medium to medium-high heat. Add the cauliflower and cabbage, and stir. Add the remaining ingredients and cook, stirring often, until tender.

4 servings. Serving size is about ½ cup.

Per serving: **4 g. fat,** 56 calories, no cholesterol, 2 g. dietary fiber, 367 mg. sodium

Carrot Crunch

PREPARATION TIME: 15 MINUTES   COOKING TIME: 20 MINUTES

The carrots in this recipe stay slightly crunchy—very satisfying for those who are cutting back on food intake and feel the urge to do a lot of chewing!

2 teaspoons olive oil
1½ tablespoons onion, diced
1 egg
¼ cup skim milk
½ teaspoon salt
½ teaspoon fresh-ground black
  pepper
1 teaspoon oregano
1 small clove garlic, crushed

1 teaspoon Traditional Italian Herb Blend (p. 333)

2 cups grated carrots

3/4 cup frozen peas (you may use a 10-ounce package and reserve the leftover peas for another recipe)

1. Brush a skillet with oil, heat over medium heat, and add the onions. Sauté, stirring constantly, until onions are translucent.
2. Beat together the egg and milk. Add the seasonings. Blend in the cooked onions and grated carrots. Pour the mixture into a casserole dish, and bake at 350 degrees for 20 minutes.
3. While the casserole is baking, cook the peas according to package directions, but without added salt.
4. Stir the cooked peas into the carrots, mixing well.

6 servings. Serving size is about 1/2 cup.

Per serving: **2 g. fat,** 61 calories, 31 mg. cholesterol, 2 g. dietary fiber, 240 mg. sodium

Zucchini with Olives

PREPARATION TIME: 5 MINUTES   COOKING TIME: 10 MINUTES

This is another recipe that can be served hot or cold.

2 medium zucchini
1 tablespoon olive oil
1 large clove garlic, crushed
6 black olives, diced
1 teaspoon dried parsley

1/4 teaspoon salt
1/4 teaspoon fresh-ground black pepper
1/2 teaspoon marjoram

1. Wash and dice the zucchini.
2. Heat the oil in a saucepan. Stir in all ingredients, and reduce the heat to low. Cook, covered, for about 10 minutes.

4 servings. Serving size is about 2/3 cup.

Per serving: **4 g. fat,** 56 calories, no cholesterol, 2 g. dietary fiber, 169 mg. sodium

Brussels Sprouts in Light Béchamel

PREPARATION TIME: 5 MINUTES   COOKING TIME: 10 MINUTES

Small, baby brussels sprouts have a tender, more delicate flavor than the full-grown ones, although you may use full-grown instead if they are all you can find.

4 cups fresh brussels sprouts
¼ cup water
1 teaspoon basil
Pinch of chervil (optional)
1 tablespoon butter
  or margarine

1 tablespoon all-purpose flour
1 cup low-fat milk
2 to 4 cloves garlic, minced or
  crushed

1. Wash the brussels sprouts, and pull off any yellowing leaves, then trim the ends, and make a small gash in the bottom of each one to help them cook to tenderness. Place them in a saucepan with the water, basil, and chervil, and bring to a boil. Then reduce heat and simmer for about 10 minutes.
2. Melt the butter or margarine in a large skillet over medium-low heat. Add the flour and brown, stirring constantly, to form a roux. Stir in the milk and garlic, and cook until the sauce has thickened slightly. Serve over the cooked brussels sprouts. (This makes about 1 cup sauce.)

8 servings. Serving size is ½ cup sprouts, with 2 tablespoons of sauce.

Per serving: **2 g. fat,** 51 calories, 5 mg. cholesterol, 2 g. dietary fiber, 42 mg. sodium

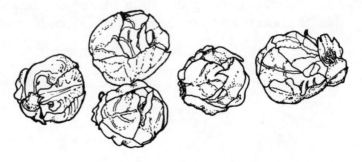

Oven-Fried Potato Sticks

PREPARATION TIME: 8 MINUTES   COOKING TIME: 35 MINUTES

Potatoes are a powerhouse when it comes to nutritional value: They are good to excellent sources of protein, phosphorus, thiamine, niacin, vitamin C, potassium, and a broad array of other vitamins and minerals. You could survive for months, possibly years, on potatoes alone, plus some green vegetables and a small amount of dairy products! We eat a lot of potatoes, usually just baked, but here is a recipe for people (like ourselves) who occasionally just can't do without something that resembles a french fry.

4 medium potatoes	**1½ teaspoons paprika**
1 tablespoon oil	**¼ teaspoon salt**
⅛ teaspoon garlic powder	**¼ teaspoon fresh-ground black**
⅛ teaspoon onion powder	**pepper**

1. Wash the potatoes well, and slice them lengthwise into strips, leaving the skins on.
2. Line a shallow baking pan with foil, and put all the ingredients into the pan, tossing well to coat the potatoes with the oil and seasonings.
3. Bake at 425 degrees for about 35 minutes, stirring often, until the potatoes are tender. Adjust the seasoning if necessary.

4 servings of about 1 cup each.

Per serving: **4 g. fat,** 166 calories, no cholesterol, 3 g. dietary fiber, 143 mg. sodium

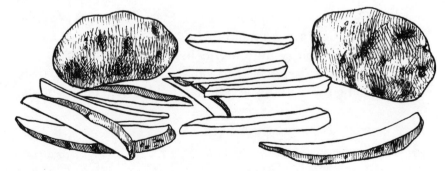

Creamy Potatoes with Herbs

PREPARATION TIME: 25 MINUTES   COOKING TIME: 35 MINUTES

4 medium potatoes, unpeeled,
   boiled or baked until tender
6 ounces Neufchâtel cheese,
   softened
¼ cup skim or low-fat milk
1 egg
½ teaspoon basil

½ teaspoon thyme
½ teaspoon salt
½ teaspoon fresh-ground black
   pepper
1 medium bell pepper, diced
Nonstick vegetable cooking
   spray

1. Mash potatoes in a large bowl. Using an electric mixer, blend potatoes with Neufchâtel, milk, egg, and seasonings.
2. Stir in diced bell pepper.
3. Place mixture in an 8-inch-square baking dish that has been sprayed with cooking spray. Bake uncovered at 350 degrees for 35 minutes.

10 servings. Serving size is about ½ cup.

Per serving: **5 g.** fat, 113 calories, 34 mg. cholesterol, 1 g. dietary fiber, 190 mg. sodium

Sweet Potato Strudel

PREPARATION TIME: 15 MINUTES   COOKING TIME: 50 MINUTES

3 medium sweet potatoes
   or yams
1 tablespoon vegetable oil
4 tablespoons grated Parmesan
   cheese
1 teaspoon dried parsley

1 tablespoon toasted sesame
   seeds
¼ teaspoon fresh-ground black
   pepper
¼ teaspoon salt

1. Peel and slice the raw sweet potatoes as thinly as possible.
2. Measure oil into a small bowl.
3. Combine the dry ingredients in another small bowl.
4. Layer one-quarter of the potatoes in a casserole dish, brushing the tops of the potatoes lightly with oil as you go,

using a pastry brush. Then sprinkle about a tablespoon of the Parmesan cheese mixture on top.

5. Repeat step 4 until potatoes and cheese are used up.
6. Bake, covered, at 425 degrees for 30 minutes. Uncover, and bake about 20 minutes more, until browned on top.

6 servings. Serving size is about ½ cup.

Per serving: **4 g. fat,** 130 calories, 3 mg. cholesterol, 2 g. dietary fiber, 177 mg. sodium

Dill Potatoes

PREPARATION TIME: 5 MINUTES   COOKING TIME: 20 MINUTES

This recipe is simple, tasty, and filling.

4 medium potatoes, cut into chunks
¾ cup low-sodium vegetable or meat stock

1 teaspoon dried dillweed
¼ teaspoon salt (optional)
Fresh-ground black pepper to taste

1. Place all ingredients except salt and pepper in a saucepan and bring to a boil. Then lower the heat to simmer and cook until the potatoes are tender and the broth has reduced somewhat.
2. Mash potatoes just a little with a fork, add the salt (if desired) and the pepper, and serve.

4 servings. Serving size is about 1 cup, plus broth.

Per serving: **no fat,** 141 calories, no cholesterol, 3 g. dietary fiber, 157 mg. sodium

Orange-Glazed Sweet Potatoes ✓

PREPARATION TIME: 5 MINUTES   COOKING TIME: 35 TO 45 MINUTES

Potatoes, sweet potatoes, and winter squashes are considered to be "grains" rather than "vegetables" in the famous Four-Food-Group plan because of their starch content, which makes them somewhat higher in calories. But, in contrast with grains, sweet potatoes (and winter squash) are high in vitamins A and C and potassium. A boiled sweet potato has 30 percent fewer calories than a baked sweet potato because some of the sugars are dissolved in the water.

4 medium sweet potatoes
Boiling water to cover
¼ cup orange juice

¼ teaspoon cinnamon
⅛ teaspoon salt

1. Wash the sweet potatoes, and drop them in enough boiling water to cover them. Cover the pan. When the water comes to a boil again, reduce the heat to low, and cook until tender.
2. Drain the potatoes, let cool for a few minutes, and peel. (Rinsing in tepid water will help make them cool enough to hold.)
3. In a medium saucepan, combine the orange juice, cinnamon, salt, and cooked sweet potatoes. Cook over low heat, stirring occasionally, until most of the juice is gone, about 6 to 7 minutes.

4 servings of 1 potato each.

Per serving: **no fat,** 171 calories, no cholesterol, 5 g. dietary fiber, 87 mg. sodium

Spanish Rice

PREPARATION TIME: 10 MINUTES

COOKING TIME: 1 HOUR

1 tablespoon olive oil
½ cup brown rice, uncooked
½ cup chopped onions
1 medium green bell pepper,
  chopped fine

1¼ cups canned tomatoes
1 clove garlic, minced or
  crushed
¼ teaspoon salt
1 teaspoon paprika

1. Heat the oil in a large skillet on medium heat. Add the rice and cook until browned, stirring constantly. Add the onions, and cook until golden, still stirring constantly. Add a little water if necessary to prevent sticking.
2. Place the rice and onions in the top part of a double boiler, and set it over boiling water. Add the remaining ingredients to the rice, cover, and steam for about 1 hour.

4 servings. Serving size is about ¾ cup.

Per serving: **4 g. fat,** 146 calories, no cholesterol, 3 g. dietary fiber, 258 mg. sodium

Yellow Rice

PREPARATION TIME: 5 MINUTES

COOKING TIME: 15 MINUTES

1 medium onion, diced
1 clove garlic, crushed
4 large mushrooms, diced
¼ teaspoon salt
¼ teaspoon fresh-ground black
  pepper
¼ teaspoon turmeric

1 tablespoon fresh parsley,
  minced
1 tablespoon oil
2 cups cooked brown rice
⅓ cup golden raisins
¼ cup chopped, unsalted,
  dry-roasted nuts

1. Sauté the onion, garlic, mushrooms, and seasonings in the oil in a large skillet until onions are translucent.
2. Stir in the rice, raisins, and nuts. Heat through, and serve.

6 servings. Serving size is about 1 cup.

Per serving: **6 g. fat,** 168 calories, no cholesterol, 3 g. dietary fiber, 95 mg. sodium

Zucchini–Brown Rice Pilaf

PREPARATION TIME: 15 MINUTES   COOKING TIME: 20 MINUTES

This dish has a remarkable taste, similar to a clam sauce. Try making it without the rice sometime. You can pour the sauce over linguine. You may need to thicken it with a tablespoon or more of cornstarch, however.

2 medium zucchini
1 tablespoon olive oil
2 cloves garlic, minced or
  crushed
1 cup brown rice, uncooked

1½ cups low-sodium stock
½ cup dry white wine
1 bay leaf
1 teaspoon dried basil
½ teaspoon salt

1. Wash and dice the zucchini. Sauté it in the oil and garlic, then remove it from the pan.
2. Add the rice to the pan, stirring to coat the grains with whatever oil is remaining. Add the stock, wine, and bay leaf, and bring to a boil. Add the basil and salt, and return the zucchini to the pan. Cover, and let simmer until rice is tender, about 20 minutes.

6 servings. Serving size is about ½ cup.

Per serving: **4 g. fat**, 171 calories, no cholesterol, 2 g. dietary fiber, 201 mg. sodium

Sauces

Looking through the sauce recipes in the average cookbook is almost like watching a contest to see how much butterfat a chef can squeeze into a sauce using, well, nothing but butter. In fact, usually there are recipes for herb butters, garlic butters, and a host of cream sauces with a base of heavy cream and, you guessed it, butter.

We like butter as well as anyone, but find that small amounts mixed with a bit of olive oil, and with herbs and spices, do perfectly well for flavor, and are much easier on the arteries!

You will see that our sauces rely more on seasonings or wine than on butter and cream. As always, we substitute skim or low-fat milk for cream, sometimes in combination with yogurt. We also use yogurt alone, or in a mixture of part sour cream and part yogurt, which is higher in fat but milder in taste than plain yogurt (see especially Mushroom Sauce, pages 292–93).

We also include a low-fat béchamel sauce in our vegetable side dishes section (see Brussels Sprouts in Light Béchamel, page 280), which can be used with other vegetables or on fish.

Barbecue Sauce

PREPARATION TIME: 15 MINUTES   COOKING TIME: 30 MINUTES

This sauce will keep for about a week and a half in the refriger-ator. Liquid smoke is usually available in the condiments sec-tion of supermarkets.

1 can (12 ounces) tomato paste
⅓ cup dry red wine (or
   substitute water)
1½ cups water
   or low-sodium stock
2 tablespoons red wine vinegar
2 teaspoons lemon juice
½ medium onion, chopped fine
½ medium bell pepper,
   chopped fine
1 tablespoon Worcestershire
   sauce

2 tablespoons brown sugar
1 tablespoon honey
2 teaspoons liquid smoke
1 teaspoon garlic powder
1 tablespoon chili powder
1 tablespoon dry mustard
Crushed red pepper to taste
Dash of Tabasco
2 tablespoons fresh parsley,
   minced
¼ teaspoon celery seed
½ teaspoon salt (optional)

1. Combine all ingredients except parsley and celery seed (and salt, if you're using any) in a large kettle or saucepan. Bring to a low boil, then reduce heat and simmer about 20 minutes.
2. Add the parsley, celery seed, and salt if desired, and sim-mer for another 5 minutes or so.

Makes about 1 quart. Serving size is 1 tablespoon.

Per serving (without added salt, and using water): **no fat,** 8 calories, no cholesterol, no dietary fiber, 5 mg. sodium

Real Italian Tomato Sauce

PREPARATION TIME: 10 MINUTES   COOKING TIME: 1 HOUR

The Italians we have met tell us that the only *real* Italian tomato sauce uses basil, garlic, a bit of salt and pepper, and maybe a bay leaf for seasonings. That's all. No oregano!

Here is our favorite basic sauce. This sauce can be used for any recipe calling for tomato sauce, from pasta to eggplant to fish. It's wonderful with our Turkey-Sage Sausage or Meatballs (p. 190). You can leave out the mushrooms if you prefer; we just happen to like mushrooms.

If you don't care if your tomato sauce is authentically Italian, try adding about a teaspoon of crushed, dried red pepper. This gives the sauce a little bite.

Also, look for the no-salt-added variety of canned tomato products if you're trying to cut down on salt.

You can store this in a tightly sealed container in the refrigerator for up to a week, or freeze it indefinitely in freezer containers for later use.

1 tablespoon olive oil
1 medium onion, cut in chunks
8 ounces fresh mushrooms, sliced or quartered
1 to 3 *tablespoons* dried basil (½ cup if you use fresh!)
2 large cloves garlic, crushed or minced

1 large bay leaf
1 can (28 ounces) whole tomatoes
1 can (10¾ ounces) tomato purée
1 can (6 ounces) tomato paste
Fresh-ground black pepper to taste

1. Heat a large kettle on medium heat. Put in the oil, onion, mushrooms, basil, and garlic. Cover, and reduce the heat to medium low. Stir frequently—you may need to add a tablespoon or two of water to keep it from sticking.
2. When the onions are translucent, add the remaining ingredients, except the pepper. Bring to a boil on high heat, then reduce to simmer and let cook for an hour or so, stirring occasionally.
3. Add pepper to taste.

Makes about 6 cups. Serving size is 1 cup.

Per serving: **3 g. fat,** 115 calories, no cholesterol, 6 g. dietary fiber, 645 mg. sodium

"He's on a diet. Tell him he looks thin." DRAWING
BY MODELL; © 1984 THE NEW YORKER
MAGAZINE, INC.

Roux

PREPARATION TIME: 1 MINUTE   COOKING TIME: 5 TO 10 MINUTES

This roux can be used to thicken soups, sauces, or just about
any cooked item that needs thickening. It is also the basis for
gravies.

1 tablespoon vegetable oil   2 tablespoons flour (all-purpose
  or butter   or whole-wheat or
    combination)

Heat the oil in a skillet over medium heat. Slowly add the flour,
stirring constantly. Cook until golden brown, stirring constantly. Stir into the main recipe.

Gravy

PREPARATION TIME: 1 MINUTE   COOKING TIME: 20 TO 30 MINUTES

Add to the above roux 1 cup of stock, and stir over medium-low
to medium heat until thickened. Season your gravy with a dash

of salt and fresh-ground black pepper if desired; we like to add a few pinches of rosemary, sage, marjoram, and/or thyme to our yearly Thanksgiving turkey gravy. Sodium content will vary with the stock you use and the amount of salt. We use ¼ teaspoon salt and a low-sodium, homemade stock.

Makes about 1 cup. Serving size is ⅛ cup.

Per serving: **2 g. fat,** 22 calories, no cholesterol, no dietary fiber, 63 mg. sodium

Nutty Pesto

PREPARATION TIME: 10 MINUTES

Many pesto recipes combine basil, huge amounts of oil, and sometimes pine nuts. The resulting mixture is then tossed with cooked pasta. The recipe below is a lot lighter on the oil, and goes well with cooked vermicelli, baked potatoes, and other cooked vegetables or grains. (If you were to use butter or oil alone on a potato for flavoring instead of this sauce, it would have over twice the fat and calories of this mixture, per tablespoon.)

½ cup unsalted, raw nuts
  (almonds, pecans, whatever
  you like)
¼ cup fresh parsley
2 cloves garlic, chopped

½ cup fresh basil leaves
  OR ¼ cup dried basil
2 tablespoons olive oil
¼ teaspoon salt (optional)

Blend all ingredients in a food processor or blender.

Makes about ¾ cup. Serving size is 1 tablespoon.

Per serving: **5 g. fat,** 55 calories, no cholesterol, 1 g. dietary fiber, 46 mg. sodium

Savory Spoon-Topping ✓

PREPARATION TIME: 5 MINUTES   COOKING TIME: 12 TO 15 MINUTES

Try sprinkling this on baked potatoes, hot cooked vegetables, salads, or cottage cheese. Or mix it into dips or meat loaf for added flavor and fiber.

2 tablespoons Worcestershire
  sauce
1 tablespoon lemon juice

½ teaspoon hot pepper sauce
2 cups All-Bran cereal

1. Mix together the Worcestershire sauce, lemon juice, and hot pepper sauce, blending thoroughly. Pour the cereal into a large bowl, and pour the sauce over it. Immediately toss to moisten evenly.
2. Spread evenly on a lightly greased baking sheet.
3. Bake at 325 degrees until dry and crisp, about 12 to 15 minutes. Cool completely, and store in an airtight container.

Makes about 2 cups. Serving size is 1 tablespoon.

Per serving: **no fat,** 15 calories, no cholesterol, 2 g. dietary fiber, 60 mg. sodium

Mushroom Sauce

PREPARATION TIME: 10 MINUTES   COOKING TIME: 15 TO 20 MINUTES

Though you may prepare this sauce with yogurt alone, the tartness of the yogurt is mellowed by the addition of a small amount of light sour cream. If you are being especially careful about fat in your diet, replace the ½ cup of sour cream with ¼ cup more yogurt and ¼ cup of skim milk. The milk also helps reduce the tart taste.

Serve the sauce over baked or boiled potatoes, cooked grain, or pasta.

1 tablespoon olive oil
12 ounces fresh mushrooms, sliced
2 medium onions, sliced or diced
2 cloves garlic, minced or crushed
6 pimientos, chopped (optional)
2 cups plain nonfat yogurt

1 tablespoon cornstarch
½ cup light sour cream
1 tablespoon tamari sauce or soy sauce
2 teaspoons dried basil
1 teaspoon dried thyme
Fresh-ground black pepper to taste

1. Heat a skillet over medium heat. Add the oil, mushrooms, onion, garlic, and pimentos if desired, and turn the heat to medium low. Cover, and let cook until onions are translucent, stirring occasionally.
2. Meanwhile, mix 1 tablespoon of the yogurt with the cornstarch, then mix in the rest of the yogurt. Stir in the sour cream, and set aside.
3. When the onions are done, remove the pan from heat, and turn heat to low. Add tamari sauce and seasonings to the pan, stir, and add the yogurt–sour cream mixture.
4. Place the skillet back on the burner, and heat through. Do not boil.

Makes about 4 cups, or 4 main course servings over 1 cup of cooked grain or pasta or 1 medium potato per serving. Makes 16 servings as a sauce for a side dish.

Per serving (4): **8 g. fat,** 198 calories, 14 mg. cholesterol, 3 g. dietary fiber, 315 mg. sodium

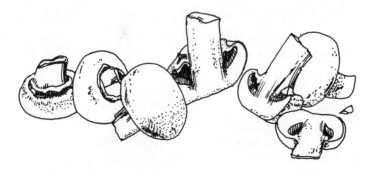

Red Clam Sauce

PREPARATION TIME: 5 MINUTES   COOKING TIME: 10 MINUTES

For a quick, easy dinner, try this sauce over chicken. Simply place 4 skinned chicken breasts, or 8 thighs, in a casserole dish. Spread 1 cup of Red Clam Sauce on top of the chicken, cover, and bake at 350 degrees for about an hour. Delicious!

3 cups Real Italian Tomato Sauce (pp. 288–89)
1 can (6½ ounces) minced clams, drained (reserve juice)
⅓ cup of the reserved clam juice
¼ cup dry red wine (optional)
2 teaspoons dried parsley

Heat the tomato sauce in a large saucepan. Stir in the remaining ingredients, and heat through. Serve over pasta or in any Italian recipe.

Makes 4 cups. Serving size is 1 cup.

Per serving: **3 g. fat,** 134 calories, 16 mg. cholesterol, 5 g. dietary fiber, 559 mg. sodium

Basil-Tomato Sauce

PREPARATION TIME: 5 MINUTES   COOKING TIME: 10 TO 15 MINUTES

Here is a basic, traditional Italian tomato sauce created by Chef Ramovich, at the old Villa Romano. We've reduced the fat content and use it with our version of two of Chef Ramovich's specialties, *Capellini di angelo al filetto di pomodoro* (pp. 228–29) and the incredibly good *Linguine al frutti di mare* (pp. 222–23).

1 tablespoon olive oil (extra-virgin if available)
4 or 5 cloves garlic, minced
1 large shallot, minced
Salt and coarse fresh-ground black pepper to taste
¼ cup fresh basil, chopped

1 medium can (28 ounces)
Italian plum tomatoes,
quartered,

OR 3 large ripe tomatoes,
skinned, seeded, and
chopped

Heat the oil over medium heat. Add the garlic and shallot, and sauté until wilted and golden. Add the tomatoes. Season with salt, pepper, and basil.

Makes about 2 to 3 cups, depending on the size of your tomatoes.

Per recipe: **15 g. fat,** 269 calories, no cholesterol, 8 g. dietary fiber, 587 mg. sodium (assuming ¼ teaspoon of added salt and fresh tomatoes; the recipe will contain about 25 mg. sodium if you add no salt, and about 1200 mg. sodium if you use canned tomatoes; ¼ teaspoon of salt contains about 550 mg. sodium)

Seafood Sauce

PREPARATION TIME: 5 MINUTES

This versatile sauce needs no cooking, and can be used as a dipping sauce for seafood, vegetables, and even meat. Usually served unheated, it can be served hot. Add it to an Oriental-style dish in the final stages of cooking, and heat through.

1 cup ketchup
2 tablespoons prepared mustard
¼ cup water

2 tablespoons tamari sauce or
   soy sauce
⅛ teaspoon Tabasco sauce

Combine all ingredients, blending well. Store in the refrigerator.

Makes about 1½ cups. Serving size is 1 tablespoon.

Per serving: **no fat,** 12 calories, no cholesterol, no dietary fiber, 205 mg. sodium

Dijon Sauce

PREPARATION TIME: 5 MINUTES

For meats, especially lamb, this pungent sauce is fantastic. Try it with Sesame-Ginger Lamb Chops (p. 158). The sauce is at its best when prepared a day ahead of time.

¼ cup Dijon mustard
¼ cup lemon juice
2 teaspoons tamari sauce or soy sauce

1 teaspoon salt
1 teaspoon fresh-ground black pepper
2 large cloves garlic, crushed

Combine all ingredients, and chill. Serve cold.

Makes about ½ cup. Serving size is 1 tablespoon.

Per serving: **no fat,** 11 calories, no cholesterol, no dietary fiber, 450 mg. sodium

Fresh Tomato Sauce with White Wine

PREPARATION TIME: 7 MINUTES   COOKING TIME: 15 MINUTES

This sauce is a good way to dress up leftovers of all kinds, as an accompaniment to simple baked chicken, fish, or other entrées and vegetables. With only 1 teaspoon of oil in the entire recipe, it is very low in fat. The fresh tomatoes add enough liquid to the sauté to keep the ingredients from sticking to the pan.

1 teaspoon vegetable oil or olive oil
1 medium onion, diced
1 tablespoon white wine
2 large tomatoes, diced
¼ green pepper, diced

4 ounces fresh mushrooms, sliced (about 1¼ cups)
¼ teaspoon salt
½ teaspoon fresh-ground pepper

1. Brush a skillet with the oil, and heat over medium heat. Add the onions, stir, and cover. Sauté, stirring often, until onions are translucent.

2. Stir in the remaining ingredients, and let cook, covered, stirring occasionally, until vegetables are tender. Drain if you want a more solid sauce, or leave as is.

Makes about 2½ cups. Serving size is about ½ cup.

Per serving: **1 g. fat,** 41 calories, no cholesterol, 2 g. dietary fiber, 115 mg. sodium

Horseradish Sauce ✓

PREPARATION TIME: 5 MINUTES

Use this versatile low-fat sauce for topping baked potatoes, beets, or other cooked vegetables, as a sauce for meats, a dip for raw vegetables, or as a spread for sandwiches in place of or mixed with a little light mayonnaise.

2 tablespoons pure horseradish
1 cup plain nonfat yogurt
2 tablespoons skim milk
½ teaspoon dried dillweed
Salt and fresh-ground black
    pepper to taste

Combine all ingredients, chill, and serve.

VARIATION: Omit dill and horseradish; use 2 tablespoons of chives instead.

Makes about 1¼ cups. Serving size is 1 tablespoon.

Per serving: **no fat,** 8 calories, no cholesterol, no dietary fiber, 25 mg. sodium

Orange-Cranberry Sauce

PREPARATION TIME: 15 MINUTES   COOKING TIME: 25 TO 30 MINUTES

Fruit juice and rind replace much of the sugar that is normally called for in cranberry sauce recipes.

1 package (12 ounces) fresh
  cranberries
1 cup orange juice

½ cup sugar
Grated rind of 1 small orange

1. Rinse and drain the cranberries. Combine the orange juice, sugar, and orange rind in a saucepan and bring to a boil.
2. Add the cranberries. Bring to a boil again. Reduce the heat and let cook for 10 minutes, stirring occasionally. Remove from the heat, cover, and let cool. Refrigerate after the sauce reaches room temperature.

Makes about 2 cups. Serving size is ¼ cup.

Per serving: **no fat,** 84 calories, no cholesterol, 2 g. dietary fiber, 1 mg. sodium

Pineapple-Cranberry Sauce

PREPARATION TIME: 5 MINUTES   COOKING TIME: 25 TO 30 MINUTES

We like this sauce even better than the tasty orange version. Perhaps we have gone overboard by including two cranberry sauce recipes in this book, but since this is a "lifetime" cookbook, we wanted recipes that would be appropriate all year long. Most people tend to put on a few pounds over the Thanksgiving-Christmas-Hanukkah holiday season, because goodies are so prevalent, but you can avoid gaining weight every year at holiday time by staying active and by preparing lower-calorie treats, such as this one. Once you taste this, you may want to serve cranberry sauce on all sorts of occasions.

1 package (12 ounces) fresh
  cranberries
1 can (16 ounces) crushed
  unsweetened pineapple

Water
½ cup sugar

1. Rinse and drain the cranberries. Press the juice from the pineapple into a measuring cup, and add enough water to make 1 cup.
2. In a saucepan, combine the sugar and pineapple-juice mixture. Bring to a boil. Add the cranberries and bring to a boil again, then reduce the heat and boil, add the crushed pineapple, and cook for 10 minutes. Remove from the heat and let cool. Store refrigerated.

Makes about 4½ cups. Serving size is ¼ cup.

Per serving: **no fat,** 43 calories, no cholesterol, 1 g. dietary fiber, 1 mg. sodium

Apricot Sauce

PREPARATION TIME: 4 MINUTES   COOKING TIME: 20 MINUTES

This pungent, sweet sauce is good with lean pork. A small amount is enough; this is more like a relish than a sauce. You may substitute other nuts for the peanuts.

6 whole dried apricots, diced
Water
1 tablespoon honey
5 tablespoons white wine
1 clove garlic, crushed

¼ teaspoon salt
¼ teaspoon fresh-ground black
  pepper
1 tablespoon chopped, unsalted,
  dry-roasted peanuts

1. Cook the apricots in a small amount of water until tender.
2. In a small saucepan, heat the honey until warm. Add the wine, stirring well to blend. Add the remaining ingredients, along with the cooked apricots, and heat through.

Makes about ½ cup. Serving size is 1 tablespoon.

Per serving: **1 g. fat,** 34 calories, no cholesterol, 1 g. dietary fiber, 68 mg. sodium

Breads and Muffins

BREADS

There is good reason to call bread the staff of life: When made with whole wheat it contains a very broad spectrum of vitamins and minerals. In fact, except for vitamin B_{12}, whole-wheat bread has much the same vitamin and mineral content as beef. When you eat bread with certain foods, such as legumes, nuts, seeds, or a small amount of a dairy product, the combination makes the protein in bread more available to the human body. Thus, peanut butter sandwiches on whole-wheat bread not only taste good to those of us who enjoy them (as we do), they are nourishing, especially when you use natural peanut butter without added sugar. (See our discussion of complementary protein on page 232.)

Calorie for calorie, whole-grain foods are far less expensive to produce and yield far more nutritional value than animal foods. An acre of land devoted to grain production for human consumption can feed many more people than an acre devoted to grain production for livestock, especially cattle. In the future, this may prove to be very important as the world's population increases.

Bread in its earliest forms some eight thousand years ago, before the discovery of leavening, was not very appetizing. Produced in rock-hard slabs, it wore down the teeth of the ancient peoples who gnawed on it for nourishment. Perhaps by accident, as the story goes, an Egyptian baker let his flour-

and-water mixture lie for a time in the sun, and it began to ferment. The bread rose as it baked and this was the beginning of bread in the form that we know it.

If you've never baked bread, you've missed out on one of the most satisfying creations of the kitchen. Many people are afraid to bake bread, thinking it's too difficult. However, many persons who have become wonderful home bread-bakers will tell you that their first loaves were disappointing: hard, flat, and unappetizing, if not inedible.

Please don't be put off by the long instructions included in some of our bread recipes. The steps are simple, and we want to take you through each one of them so you will have a perfect loaf when you're through.

It usually takes a couple of "practice loaves" to get the hang of it. One essential step is to make sure your yeast is mixed with a liquid at the correct temperature. Mix it with lukewarm liquid, usually water, as listed in the recipes, and go on from there. The suggested temperature of the liquid is between 105 and 115 degrees Fahrenheit—that is, lukewarm. (We call it "baby-bottle warm.") You may use a thermometer if you wish; you will probably soon learn to do it by "feel."

Yeast is actually made up of microorganisms that feed on sugar and liquid and release carbon dioxide, which is one part of what makes your dough rise. So remember, yeast is alive—or should be. Proof it (make sure it's alive) by combining it with a small amount of water, sugar, and maybe a pinch of ground ginger. Within 15 minutes, it should be bubbly. If not, throw it out and start a new batch. (If the water is the correct temperature, check the "use-by" date on your yeast package for its expiration date.) Some of our recipes call for the new rapid-rise yeast, which works very well and requires far less rising time. It can also be mixed directly with dry ingredients, eliminating the proofing step, although you may proof it if you so desire. You can always substitute regular active dry yeast for rapid-rise. Remember, however, that rapid-rise yeast can withstand slightly higher temperatures in liquids than can regular yeast.

As yeast feeds on sugars in the bread dough, it gives off

alcohol and carbon dioxide, which are what make the bread rise. When you put the dough in the oven, the high heat kills the yeast, the dough stops rising, the crust forms, and you have your bread.

HOW MUCH FLOUR?

You may need slightly more or less flour, depending on the humidity and temperature of the kitchen and other factors. This is why a bread recipe often calls for extra flour. Always add your flour slowly. You can add more as you go along, but you can't take any out! If you do find you've added too much, you can wet your hands a little while kneading and add moisture that way, but it's best to avoid this.

THE NEED TO KNEAD

Kneading is fun, burns a few calories, doesn't take long, and gets you used to how the dough is supposed to feel. You can use kneading attachments on food processors and the like, but Terri and our bread-baking friends prefer getting in there with their hands.

Kneading, which develops the gluten in the dough, works with the yeast to help the dough to rise. Different flours have different protein contents, and since the gluten is formed when liquids are mixed with the protein in flour, flours with high protein levels produce the best breads. Bread flour and all-purpose flour (a blend of hard and soft wheat flours) have high protein levels (over 10 percent). They absorb more water and, when kneaded, give larger volume and lighter texture than soft flours (less than 10 percent protein). An enriched flour has been fortified with thiamin, riboflavin, niacin, and iron, which were removed in the milling process. Bleaching does what it says it does, and doesn't help the flour (white flour is still often a bit brownish). Some enriched, all-purpose flours contain a small amount of other flours, such as malted barley flour. There are quick yeast breads that require no kneading and are still healthful and delicious, but it seems the best-textured breads are kneaded. The following sequence will familiarize you with the basics of the bread-making process.

Rising: Some doughs need no rising time, including non-yeast and some batter breads. Others require several risings.

DRAWING BY LEVIN; © 1983 THE NEW YORKER MAGAZINE, INC.

Usually, you will place the dough in a bowl, cover it with a damp dish towel, and set it in a warm, draft-free place. We just put it in the oven so it's out of the way. In winter, if the house is cold, warm the oven on its lowest setting for a few minutes, turn it off, and put the dough in. Or use a cupboard next to the oven if the oven is in use—the warmth from the oven will permeate the cupboard and keep the dough happy.

Punch down: This is just what it says. Punch the dough with your fist, and it will collapse so you can allow the dough to rise again.

The floured board: When you knead or roll out dough, do so on a large surface lightly dusted with flour. You can add more flour as you go along, if necessary. If you don't have a board, wipe an area of your kitchen counter or table with a damp cloth, cover it with a large piece of wax paper, and dust the wax paper with flour. The damp underneath keeps the paper from sliding.

How to knead: Press the heels of your hands into the dough, fold the dough over, turn it about one-quarter of the way around, and repeat the process. Dough is ready to rise when it appears smooth, elastic, and bounces back from a poke with a finger.

Greasing and dusting: Usually, baked bread will fall out of the pan easily if you follow this procedure: Spray pans lightly with nonstick cooking spray, or lightly grease with some oil, margarine, or butter smeared on a paper towel. To dust the pans, add about 2 teaspoons of whole-wheat flour or cornmeal to each pan, and tap it while holding it at different angles until flour coats all sides. Then tap out the excess flour. Your completed raw loaf will meet the corners of the pan and will usually fill a loaf pan about two-thirds full.

To test for doneness, tap on the top and *bottom* of the loaf with your knuckles. If it sounds hollow, and if the crust is nicely browned, it's done. If your knock *isn't* hollow, return the loaf to the pan and the oven, but be cautious about how long it stays in the oven.

It's easy to overeat fresh, hot, homemade bread that's just out of the oven. There really is no better food we can imagine. BUT—restrain yourself. Allow yourself one slice, if you must. Tell yourself it doesn't slice as well when it's warm (it doesn't: it tears). Let the bread cool completely before serving, preferably on a wire rack, or your crust may get damp from the steam in the loaf. Joyce Weingartner, who created a number of the breads in this cookbook, never slices hers until it has cooled for 2 hours. How she can resist, we will never know, but we admire her for it.

After the bread cools, slice it with a long serrated knife. You can store the bread in airtight plastic bags and freeze a loaf for later use.

You can vary the type of crust on your breads in the following ways. Brushing the crust with 1 beaten egg mixed with 1 tablespoon of water results in a shiny crust. A soft, glazed crust is obtained by brushing with 1 egg white beaten with 1 tablespoon of water. For a soft crust, brush a smidgen of melted butter or vegetable oil on top just before the last rising of the dough, or while baking. For a crisp crust, brush with cold water, a noncaloric alternative to a soft crust! Sweeteners and / or milk in the dough will make a darker crust.

Whole-Wheat Bread Crumbs

Take any whole-wheat or nonsweet whole-grain bread, and whir in a blender or food processor. (Yes, in a pinch, you may use white bread.)

One average slice of fresh bread makes about ½ cup, while 1 average slice of dry (stale) bread makes about ⅓ cup. Use for casserole toppings, breading meats, etc. Commercial breads vary greatly in their nutritional value, so read the labels to determine fat, calories, cholesterol, dietary fiber, and sodium.

Italian Whole-Wheat Bread

PREPARATION TIME: 3 HOURS   BAKING TIME: 40 MINUTES

2 packages active dry yeast
¼ cup lukewarm water (105° to 115°F)
¼ teaspoon sugar
¼ teaspoon ground ginger
1½ cups lukewarm water
1 tablespoon sugar
¼ cup melted butter
2 teaspoons salt

2 cups whole-wheat flour
3 cups all-purpose flour (approximately)
Nonstick vegetable cooking spray
2½ tablespoons cornmeal
1 egg white
1 tablespoon water

1. Proof the yeast by pouring it into a small bowl with the ¼ cup water, ¼ teaspoon sugar, and the ginger. Wait about 5 to 15 minutes, or until bubbly.
2. In a large bowl, combine the remaining lukewarm water, the sugar, the butter, and the salt. Add the proofed yeast.
3. Add 1 cup of whole-wheat flour and 1 cup of all-purpose flour. Mix 100 strokes. Add another 1 cup each of the flours, mixing well. Then slowly add the remaining cup of all-purpose flour, a little at a time, to make sure the dough is the correct consistency.
4. Knead for 8 to 10 minutes, adding up to ¼ cup more all-purpose flour if necessary. Place in a lightly greased bowl, cover with a damp towel, and set in a draft-free place until doubled in bulk.
5. Punch down the dough with your fist. Knead on a lightly floured surface for about 2 minutes until smooth and elastic. Divide the dough into 2 equal balls. Cover with the damp towel and let stand for 10 minutes.
6. Spray a baking sheet with cooking spray, and dust with cornmeal, pouring off excess cornmeal.
7. Shape each ball of dough into a long loaf—like a French loaf—about 14 inches in length, by holding each end and gently stretching the dough, shaking it gently at the same time. Pat into shape if necessary. Place loaves—not touch-

ing—on the baking sheet, cover with wax paper, and let rise in a warm, draft-free place until doubled in bulk, about 1 hour.

8. Beat the egg white with the 1 tablespoon of water, and brush the tops of the loaves with it. Make five shallow diagonal slashes in the tops of each loaf to let steam escape while baking.

9. Bake at 425 degrees for 40 minutes, or until the loaves are a rich golden color. If they begin getting too dark, you may cover them with a piece of foil; however, don't open the oven during the first 20 minutes, or your bread may collapse. To test for doneness, tap the bread top and bottom; if it does not sound hollow, return it to the oven until it taps hollow. Cool on a wire rack.

Makes 2 loaves of 16 slices each. Serving size is 1 slice.

Per serving: **2 g. fat,** 86 calories, 4 mg. cholesterol, 1. g. dietary fiber, 151 mg. sodium

Croutons

PREPARATION TIME: 5 MINUTES   COOKING TIME: 8 TO 10 MINUTES

4 slices whole-grain bread
1 tablespoon margarine
  or butter
1 teaspoon basil
¼ teaspoon oregano

¼ teaspoon onion powder
⅛ teaspoon thyme
½ teaspoon garlic powder
Other herbs and spices of your
  choice (optional)

1. Cut the bread into ½-inch cubes. In a skillet, melt the margarine, then add the seasonings.
2. Stir in the bread cubes and sauté until crisp.

Makes about 2 cups. Serving size is ¼ cup.

Per serving: **2 g. fat,** 57 calories, 4 mg. cholesterol, 1 g. dietary fiber, 107 mg. sodium

Whole-Wheat French Bread

PREPARATION TIME: 3 HOURS   BAKING TIME: 25 TO 30 MINUTES

If you enjoy French bread, which goes with just about any meal, you may want to invest in a French-bread pan, which is a heavy pan made especially for its long shape. You can find one in most cookware shops. This bread freezes well wrapped in foil and placed in a sealed plastic bag.

2 packages active dry yeast
¼ cup lukewarm water (105° to 115°F)
¼ teaspoon sugar
¼ teaspoon ground ginger
¾ cup plus 2 tablespoons lukewarm water
1 tablespoon sugar
2 tablespoons unsalted melted butter or margarine

2 teaspoons salt
1½ cups all-purpose flour
¾ cup whole-wheat flour
1 to 2 teaspoons vegetable oil
2½ tablespoons cornmeal
1 egg white
1 tablespoon water

1. Proof the yeast by putting it in a small bowl with the ¼ cup lukewarm water, the sugar, and the ginger. In about 5 to 15 minutes, it should be bubbly. If not, throw it out and start over with two more packages of yeast.
2. Meanwhile, in another bowl, combine the ¾ cup plus 2 tablespoons lukewarm water, the tablespoon of sugar, the butter, and the salt.
3. Add the proofed yeast to the water mixture. Mix in 1 cup of all-purpose flour, and the whole-wheat flour. Stir 100 strokes.
4. Mix in another ¼ cup all-purpose flour, then slowly add up to an additional ¼ cup. Knead the dough for 10 minutes.
5. Rub a small amount of vegetable oil over the surface of a bowl, place the dough in it, and cover with a damp towel until doubled, about 1 hour. Punch down the dough, knead 2 minutes more, then let rest with the towel over it for 10 minutes.

6. Divide the dough into 2 pieces. Shape into loaves by holding each end of a piece and gently stretching and shaking the bread into the shape of a long French loaf. Pat into shape if necessary.
7. Brush a baking sheet lightly with vegetable oil, and evenly spread cornmeal over it. Place the loaves on the baking sheet, and cover with a damp cloth. Let double, about 30 to 45 minutes.
8. Brush each loaf with the egg white mixed with the 1 tablespoon of water. Put several diagonal slashes, ¼ inch deep, in the bread to let steam escape while it bakes. Bake the bread at 425 degrees for 25 to 30 minutes, until golden brown. Remove from the oven immediately and let cool on a rack.
9. If you serve the bread the same day you bake it, simply crisp it in the oven for 5 minutes before serving. This is the secret to getting traditional "crusty" French bread. To thaw frozen bread and serve, warm in foil for 15 minutes at 350 degrees. Then remove the foil, and leave in the oven for another 5 minutes.

VARIATION: For a pungent, East Indian-style loaf, add to the above recipe ½ teaspoon Indian Spice Blend (p. 332) or other curry powder, and 3 tablespoons scallion, minced, green part only. Reduce salt to 1½ teaspoons.

Makes 2 loaves of 8 slices each. Serving size is 1 slice.

Per serving: **2 g. fat,** 88 calories, 4 mg. cholesterol, 1 g. dietary fiber, 286 mg. sodium

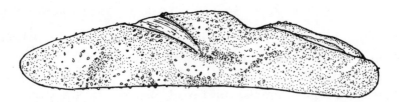

Buttermilk Corn Bread

PREPARATION TIME: 30 MINUTES   BAKING TIME: ¾ TO 1 HOUR

For several weeks, Enid tested revision after revision of this recipe until she triumphed with a light, tasty corn bread that rivals any other we have tasted. You can make this recipe into a loaf or muffins. If you decide to make muffins, lightly coat the muffin tins with a small amount of the butter, and bake for 25 to 30 minutes.

3 tablespoons butter
  or margarine
1½ cups yellow cornmeal,
  sifted
½ cup whole-wheat flour,
  sifted

1½ cups buttermilk
½ teaspoon baking soda
¼ teaspoon salt

1. Use a small amount of the butter to coat a loaf pan. Melt the remaining amount in a small saucepan.
2. Combine all ingredients in a mixing bowl. Let stand for 20 minutes. Pour into the loaf pan, and bake at 350 degrees for 45 minutes to 1 hour, until beginning to lightly brown on top.

Makes 1 loaf of 16 slices, or a dozen muffins. Serving size is 1 slice or 1 muffin.

Per serving (16 slices): **3 g. fat,** 82 calories, 7 mg. cholesterol, 2 g. dietary fiber, 109 mg. sodium (each muffin will contain one-third more of each nutrient)

Back-to-Basics Bread

PREPARATION TIME: ¾ TO 1 HOUR   BAKING TIME: 1 TO 1¼ HOURS

Our longtime friend Denni Llovet says of her bread creation: "Only 1½ hours from bowl to mouth!"

We think she's more efficient than we are, because it usually takes us 2 hours to make this bread. Regardless of how long it takes to make, it is truly plain old, down-home *good* bread.

1 teaspoon or less butter
Whole-wheat flour—a little
½ cup lukewarm water (105° to
 115°F)
3 packages yeast (may use
 rapid-rise)

½ cup vegetable oil
⅔ cup honey
1 teaspoon salt
5 cups hot water from tap
About 10 cups whole-wheat
 flour

1. Lightly grease 3 loaf pans with the butter, and dust with a little bit of whole-wheat flour.
2. Place the ½ cup of lukewarm water in a small bowl, and sprinkle the yeast on top. Do not stir.
3. Measure the oil into a measuring cup, then pour into a small bowl. Measure the honey into the same measuring cup you used for the oil; this will keep the honey from sticking in the cup. Pour the honey into the bowl with the oil, and add the salt.
4. Mix the 5 cups of hot water with 7 cups of the flour in the largest mixing bowl you have—use a soup pot if you want! Keep the flour handy. Add the yeast-and-water mixture, then add the oil-honey-salt mixture, and blend. Keep mixing in flour, a little at a time, to make a pliant dough, firm but not stiff. Turn the dough out onto a floured board and knead for 10 minutes with a folding-over, punching-down motion.
5. Divide the dough into three loaves and place in the loaf pans. Cover with a damp cloth and let rise until half again as big.
6. Bake at 350 degrees until dark brown on top (about 1 hour to 1 hour and fifteen minutes). Let cool on a wire rack 5 to 10 minutes before slicing if you want it to slice cleanly.

3 loaves of 16 slices each. Serving size is 1 slice.

Per serving: 3 g. fat, 121 calories, no cholesterol, 3 g. dietary fiber, 47 mg. sodium

Four-Grain Wheatless Bread

PREPARATION TIME: 35 MINUTES   BAKING TIME: 1¼ HOURS

We asked Joyce Weingartner, who helped us test many recipes, to create a wheatless bread for us. She delighted us with this, a batter bread that has a rich, nutty flavor, great in sandwiches or all by itself. For those who are allergic to wheat, this bread is a suitable substitute, as buckwheat is actually not in the wheat family. This loaf will not rise as high as most kneaded wheat breads, because there is far less gluten in these flours. Store the loaf in the refrigerator, and slice thin to serve.

2 packages active dry yeast
¼ cup lukewarm water (105° to 115°F)
¼ teaspoon sugar
⅛ teaspoon ground ginger
1 cup lukewarm water
¼ cup molasses
2 tablespoons melted butter

2 teaspoons salt
2 cups rye flour
¼ cup buckwheat
¼ cup soy flour
½ cup oat flour
Nonstick vegetable cooking spray

1. Proof the yeast in the ¼ cup water, sugar, and ginger (the mixture should be bubbly after about 5 to 15 minutes).
2. In a large bowl, combine the 1 cup water, molasses, butter, and salt. Add the proofed yeast, and mix well.
3. In another bowl, combine 1½ cups of the rye flour, and the remaining flours. Add the flours to the yeast mixture, and mix 100 strokes. Be sure to get all the flour at the bottom of the bowl mixed in with the dough.
4. Gradually add the remaining ½ cup of rye flour, stirring well.
5. Preheat the oven to 350 degrees.
6. Spray a loaf pan with nonstick cooking spray, and place the dough in the pan, spreading with a knife to meet the corners and smooth out the top of the loaf. Place the loaf pan in a larger pan that has about 1 inch of hot water in it. Cover the loaf pan with foil, and place both pans in the center of your oven.

7. Bake for 30 minutes, then remove the foil *and* the pan of water. Bake the loaf an additional 45 minutes. This loaf will not sound hollow when you tap it, but will have a rich, dark brown crust. Remove it from the pan and place on a rack to cool.

Makes 1 loaf of 20 thin slices. Serving size is 1 slice.

Per serving: **2 g. fat,** 76 calories, 3 mg. cholesterol, 2 g. dietary fiber, 228 mg. sodium

Sesame Poppy-Seed Loaf

PREPARATION TIME: 10 MINUTES   BAKING TIME: 40 MINUTES

¾ **cup whole-wheat flour**
¾ **cup all-purpose flour**
1 **tablespoon baking powder**
½ **teaspoon salt**
2 **tablespoons sesame seeds**
2 **teaspoons poppy seeds**

¾ **cup orange juice**
2 **tablespoons honey**
1 **egg**
2 **tablespoons vegetable oil**
½ **cup All-Bran cereal**

1. In a medium bowl, stir together the whole-wheat flour, all-purpose flour, baking powder, salt, and seeds. Set aside.
2. In a large mixing bowl, beat together the orange juice, honey, egg, oil, and cereal until well combined. Let stand 2 minutes.
3. Add the flour mixture, stirring only until combined. Spread the batter evenly into a lightly greased 9 × 5 × 3-inch loaf pan.
4. Bake at 350 degrees about 40 minutes, or until a toothpick inserted near the center comes out clean. Let cool 10 minutes before removing from the pan. Cool completely before slicing.

Makes 1 loaf of 16 slices. Serving size is 1 slice.

Per serving: **3 g. fat,** 89 calories, 12 mg. cholesterol, 2 g. dietary fiber, 102 mg. sodium

Whole-Wheat Tortillas

PREPARATION TIME: 45 MINUTES   COOKING TIME: 45 MINUTES

Tortillas are the bread of Mexico. You can use them as you would bread, although we still think the traditional Mexican recipes are the best. You can also find whole-wheat tortillas at a health-food store.

As for the use of vegetable *shortening*, which is often processed into a solid form that is similar to saturated fat, there is so little per serving in this recipe that we felt it was acceptable. You can substitute oil if you wish, although the resulting texture is not quite as good. There are some commercial health-food brands, however, that use sesame oil to good effect.

When cooking these, a little bit of cooking spray goes a long way. You can probably cook several tortillas before needing more fat.

These are great with Fajitas (pp. 114–15); or make your own burritos or soft tacos. They can substitute for bread in Cheese Toast (pp. 338–39); you can sprinkle them with grated cheese, chopped tomato, and/or onion, broil them, and top with chopped lettuce, and maybe some Mexican-Style Hot Sauce (p. 58).

You can also freeze these for later use.

2 cups whole-wheat flour
2 cups all-purpose flour
1 teaspoon salt
¼ cup vegetable shortening

1 cup warm water (or slightly more if needed)
Whole-wheat flour as needed
Nonstick cooking spray

1. Combine all ingredients except the cooking spray in a large bowl to make a light-textured dough. Form into 16 egg-sized balls, and place the balls in the bowl. Let stand for about 20 minutes.
2. Roll each ball of dough out on a lightly floured board to form a very thin circle, about ⅛ inch thick.
3. Spray a griddle or large skillet with cooking spray, and fry each tortilla over medium-low heat for a minute on one side, and a minute on the other. NOTE: When one side is

done, the tortilla will begin puffing up. Turn it over, and fry the other side. They will be slightly browned in spots, not all over. Serve warm.

Makes 16 tortillas. Serving size is 1 tortilla.

Per serving: **4 g. fat,** 136 calories, no cholesterol, 2 g. dietary fiber, 267 mg. sodium

Caraway-Onion Loaf

PREPARATION TIME: 20 MINUTES   BAKING TIME: 30 TO 35 MINUTES

3 tablespoons butter
½ cup finely chopped onion
1 cup minus 1 tablespoon skim
  milk
1 tablespoon lemon juice
1 cup All-Bran cereal

1 egg, slightly beaten
1½ cups all-purpose flour
1 teaspoon baking powder
1 teaspoon baking soda
1 teaspoon salt
2 teaspoons caraway seeds

1. In a medium saucepan, melt the butter. Add the onion, and cook over low heat until tender. Remove from the heat.
2. Combine the milk and the lemon juice to make sour milk. Stir the cereal and the milk into the onions. Let stand for 2 minutes, or until most of the liquid is absorbed. Add the egg and blend well.
3. In a large mixing bowl, mix the flour, baking powder, baking soda, salt, and caraway seeds. Add the cereal mixture to the flour. Stir just until moistened.
4. Spread in a lightly greased 9 × 5 × 3-inch loaf pan. Bake at 350 degrees for 30 to 35 minutes, or until a knife inserted in the center comes out clean. Let cool for 10 minutes. Remove from the pan, and let cool completely before slicing.

Makes 1 loaf of 16 slices. Serving size is 1 slice.

Per serving: **3 g. fat,** 87 calories, 18 mg. cholesterol, 2 g. dietary fiber, 278 mg. sodium

Limpa (Swedish Rye Bread)

PREPARATION TIME: 3 HOURS   BAKING TIME: 40 MINUTES

2 packages active dry yeast
¼ cup lukewarm water (105° to 115°F)
¼ teaspoon sugar
⅛ teaspoon ground ginger
1¼ cups lukewarm water
½ cup unsweetened orange juice
2 tablespoons melted butter

⅓ cup molasses
2½ teaspoons salt
2 tablespoons orange peel
1¾ cups whole-wheat flour
1¾ to 2 cups all-purpose flour
1 cup rye flour
1 egg white
1 tablespoon water

1. In a small bowl, proof the yeast by combining it with the ¼ cup water, sugar, and ginger.
2. In a large bowl, combine the 1¼ cups water with the orange juice, butter, molasses, salt, and orange peel.
3. After the yeast has proofed (about 5 to 15 minutes), add to the orange-juice mixture. Stir in 1 cup of each of the flours, and mix 100 strokes. Add another ½ cup of whole-wheat, then ½ cup of all-purpose, stirring well after each addition. Slowly add about ¼ cup more of both whole-wheat and all-purpose flours. The dough will be sticky.
4. Dust your hands, the kneading board, and the dough with flour, and knead for 8 to 10 minutes, adding more all-purpose flour a little at a time, if necessary.
5. Place the dough in a lightly greased mixing bowl and cover with a damp towel. Place in a warm, draft-free area, and let rise until it doubles, about 1 hour.
6. Punch down, and let rest for 10 minutes with the towel over it.
7. Form the dough into 2 round loaves, or use 2 loaf pans, 8 × 4 × 3 inches each. Let rise again until doubled, about 45 minutes.
8. Mix the egg white with the tablespoon of water, and brush each loaf with the mixture. Put several diagonal slashes on the bread to let out steam while baking.

9. Bake at 350 degrees for 40 minutes, or until the loaves sound hollow when tapped on the top and bottom. Cool on a wire rack for 2 hours before slicing.

2 loaves of 16 slices each. Serving size is 1 slice.

Per serving: **1 g. fat,** 78 calories, 2 mg. cholesterol, 2 g. dietary fiber, 178 mg. sodium

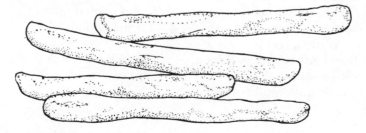

Breadsticks

PREPARATION TIME: 40 MINUTES   BAKING TIME: 15 MINUTES

2 packages active dry yeast
2 teaspoons sugar
Pinch ground ginger
1 cup lukewarm water (105° to 115°F)

2 tablespoons vegetable oil
1 teaspoon salt
3 cups all-purpose flour
   OR half all-purpose, half whole-wheat flour

1. Combine the yeast, sugar, ginger, and water in a large bowl. Let stand for 10 minutes.
2. Mix in the oil and salt, then slowly mix in the flour, adding just enough to get past the sticky stage and allow you to knead the dough.
3. Knead for 5 minutes. Roll into long sticks, about ½ inch thick × 8 inches long. Place the sticks on a lightly oiled baking sheet.
4. Bake at 375 degrees on the high rack of the oven for 15 minutes, or until golden brown. Serve hot.

Makes about 2 dozen sticks. Serving size is 1 stick.

Per serving (with half all-purpose and half whole-wheat flour): **1 g. fat,** 67 calories, no cholesterol, 1 g. dietary fiber, 90 mg. sodium

Quick Whole-Wheat Buttermilk Bread

PREPARATION TIME: 1¼ HOURS   BAKING TIME: 25 MINUTES

This bread has a lovely, even texture.

2 cups whole-wheat flour
2½ cups all-purpose flour
2 packages rapid-rise yeast
½ cup wheat germ
2 teaspoons baking powder
2 teaspoons salt
1¼ cups buttermilk

¾ cup water
¼ cup melted butter
  or margarine
2 tablespoons molasses
Nonstick vegetable cooking
  spray

1. In a large bowl, mix together 1½ cups of the whole-wheat flour, 1½ cups of all-purpose flour, the yeast, wheat germ, baking powder, and salt.
2. In a saucepan, heat the buttermilk and water on medium-low heat until lukewarm, not hot (105 to 115 degrees Fahrenheit). Stir into the flour mixture.
3. Melt the butter or margarine, and blend into the flour mixture. Blend in the molasses, and stir 100 strokes.
4. Slowly stir in the other ½ cup of whole-wheat flour and another ½ cup of all-purpose flour. When the flour is mixed into the batter, add another ¼ cup of all-purpose flour, mix well, and add another ¼ cup of all-purpose flour if necessary. Your dough will be a bit sticky, so dust your kneading board, your hands, and the dough with flour.
5. Knead the dough for 8 to 10 minutes. Place in a lightly greased bowl, and cover with a damp dish towel.
6. Spray 2 loaf pans, 8 × 4 × 3 inches, with nonstick cooking spray, and preheat your oven to 425 degrees.
7. Divide the dough into 2 pieces. Pat each piece into a square about 7 × 8 inches, and about 1 inch thick. Fold the square in thirds. Seal the seam, and place each loaf, seam down, in a loaf pan.
8. Cover the loaves with a damp towel and let rise again until doubled in bulk, about 30 minutes.

9. Place the loaves in the center of the oven, evenly distanced and not touching each other. Bake for 25 minutes, or until the loaves sound hollow when tapped on the top and bottom. They should be nicely browned. Let them cool on a wire rack.

2 loaves of 16 slices each. Serving size is 1 slice.

Per serving: **2 g. fat,** 89 calories, 4 mg. cholesterol, 2 g. dietary fiber, 159 mg. sodium

Cheese Twists

PREPARATION TIME: 35 MINUTES   BAKING TIME: 15 MINUTES

This "snack" bread is good with salads, for example, instead of whole-grain crackers, for a change of pace.

1 cup All-Bran cereal	1 teaspoon baking soda
1⅓ cups skim milk	1 teaspoon salt
1 tablespoon lemon juice	2 tablespoons butter, softened
2 cups all-purpose flour	½ cup grated cheddar cheese
1 tablespoon baking powder	

1. In a small bowl, combine the cereal and the milk, which has been soured with the lemon juice. Set aside.
2. In a large mixing bowl, combine the flour, baking powder, baking soda, and salt. Cut in the butter to make a coarse meal. Add the cereal mixture and blend well. Stir in the cheese.
3. Shape the dough into 20 ropes, about 4½ × 2½ inches each, by rolling the dough between your hands. Fold each rope in half and twist each end. Place on a lightly greased baking sheet.
4. Bake at 425 degrees for 15 minutes or until golden brown.

Makes 20 twists. Serving size is 1 twist.

Per serving: **2 g. fat,** 84 calories, 6 mg. cholesterol, 2 g. dietary fiber, 235 mg. sodium

Applesauce Bread

PREPARATION TIME: 1¼ TO 1½ HOURS   BAKING TIME: 30 MINUTES

¾ cup All-Bran cereal
2 to 2½ cups all-purpose flour
2 tablespoons firmly packed
  brown sugar
½ teaspoon salt
1 package active dry yeast

¾ cup unsweetened
  applesauce
¼ cup skim milk
3 tablespoons butter or
  margarine
1 egg, at room temperature

1. Stir together the cereal, ½ cup of the flour, the sugar, salt, and yeast in a large mixing bowl. Set aside.
2. In a small saucepan, heat the applesauce, milk, and butter until very warm (120 to 130 degrees Fahrenheit; the butter does not need to melt). Gradually add to the cereal mixture, and beat 2 minutes at a medium speed with an electric mixer, occasionally scraping the bowl.
3. Add the egg and another ½ cup of flour. Beat 2 minutes at high speed, scraping the bowl. By hand, stir in enough remaining flour to make a stiff, sticky dough. Cover loosely with a damp towel. Let rise in a warm place until double in volume.
4. Punch down the dough and shape into a loaf. Place in a lightly greased 9 × 5 × 3-inch loaf pan. Cover and let rise in a warm place until double in volume.
5. Bake at 375 degrees about 30 minutes or until done. To prevent over-browning, cover loosely with foil during the last few minutes of baking time. Remove the loaf from the pan, and cool on a wire rack.

Makes 1 loaf of 16 slices. Serving size is 1 slice.

Per serving: **3 g. fat,** 102 calories, 18 mg. cholesterol, 2 g. dietary fiber, 130 mg. sodium

Bran Rolls

PREPARATION TIME: 45 MINUTES   BAKING TIME: 18 TO 20 MINUTES

1 cup All-Bran cereal
2½ to 3 cups all-purpose flour
2 tablespoons sugar
1½ teaspoons salt
1 package rapid-rise yeast

1 cup skim milk
½ cup water
2 tablespoons butter
1 egg, slightly beaten
Poppy seeds (optional)

1. In a large mixing bowl, stir together the cereal, 1 cup of the flour, the sugar, salt, and yeast. Set aside.
2. In a small saucepan, heat the milk, water, and butter until warm (115 to 120 degrees Fahrenheit). Add to the cereal mixture. Reserve 1 tablespoon of the egg. Add the remaining egg to the cereal mixture. Beat for 30 seconds at low speed with an electric mixer, then beat for 3 minutes at high speed.
3. By hand, stir in enough of the remaining flour to make a stiff batter. Cover loosely with a damp towel. Let rise in a warm place until double in volume. Stir down the batter. Portion the batter evenly into 16 lightly greased 2½-inch muffin-pan cups. Brush the tops of the rolls with the reserved egg. Sprinkle with poppy seeds if desired.
4. Bake at 400 degrees for 18 to 20 minutes, or until golden brown. Serve warm.

Makes 16 rolls. Serving size is 1 roll.

Per serving: **2 g. fat,** 117 calories, 16 mg. cholesterol, 3 g. dietary fiber, 287 mg. sodium

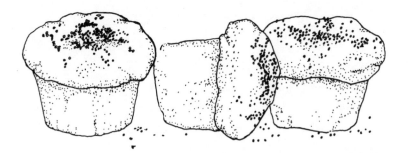

MUFFINS

We are inveterate muffin-makers; nothing seems to give as much pleasure in the making and the eating for so little effort. A muffin is really a "quick bread" made, basically, from a batter that is baked in a muffin pan.

Our muffins blend a high-fiber source, such as a cereal product, with a flour. The batter is produced with the addition of low-fat milk, oil, an egg or two, and the sweetener, which can be sugar, honey, molasses, or a combination of the three. To this you can add an almost limitless combination of various dried fruits and nuts. Because it is so easy to be creative when you make muffins, we usually make two or three different kinds at a time. One might contain raisins, while another has dates and nuts; one might be a blend of oat- or wheat-bran cereal with whole-wheat flour, while another might have small quantities of barley or soy flour blended with the wheat flour.

When it comes to satisfying a desire for something sweet or for something cake-like to go with a good cup of fresh-ground coffee, a muffin is a far healthier alternative than baked goods like pastry, pie, and cake. Also, it is *far* cheaper to bake your own than to buy them in the bakery, and, because you select the ingredients, you know how fresh *and* healthy these muffins are.

Some of the recipes in this section were developed and tested for us in the Kellogg kitchens, so you will note that the recipes in question call for Kellogg products. You can, of course, try these recipes using your own favorite equivalent cereals, for example, any 100% bran for All-Bran (but not 40% bran-content flakes for All-Bran).

Raisin-Bran Muffins

PREPARATION TIME: 10 MINUTES   BAKING TIME: 15 MINUTES

Whole-wheat pastry flour is available in most health-food stores, and gives a slightly finer texture than regular whole-wheat flour. However, you may use regular whole-wheat flour instead.

Nonstick vegetable cooking spray
1¼ cups oat bran
1 cup whole-wheat pastry flour
¼ cup brown sugar
2 teaspoons baking powder
¼ teaspoon salt
½ cup raisins
1 cup 1% milk
1 large egg, beaten
¼ cup molasses
2 tablespoons vegetable oil

1. Heat oven to 425 degrees. Spray bottoms of 12 2½-inch muffin-pan cups with nonstick cooking spray, or line with paper cups.
2. Combine dry ingredients and the raisins in a large mixing bowl.
3. In separate bowl, mix milk, egg, molasses, and oil.
4. Add the liquid mixture to the dry, and mix only until the dry ingredients are moistened (the mixture should be lumpy).
5. Fill muffin cups ¾ full, and bake at 425 degrees for 15 minutes, or until tops are golden brown.

Makes 12 muffins. Serving size is 1 muffin.

Per serving: **4 g. fat,** 140 calories, 16 mg. cholesterol, 3 g. dietary fiber, 65 mg. sodium

Honey Bran Muffins

PREPARATION TIME: 10 MINUTES   BAKING TIME: 25 MINUTES

2 cups All-Bran cereal   1 cup all-purpose flour
⅓ cup honey   1 teaspoon baking soda
1¼ cups skim milk   ½ teaspoon salt
1 egg

1. Combine the cereal, honey, and milk, and let stand for 2 minutes. Add the egg, beating well.
2. Stir together the flour, baking soda, and salt; add to the cereal mixture, stirring *only until combined.* Portion the batter evenly into lightly greased 2½-inch muffin-pan cups.
3. Bake at 400 degrees for 25 minutes or until a toothpick inserted in the center of a muffin comes out clean. Let stand about 5 minutes before removing from the pans. Serve immediately.

Makes 12 muffins. Serving size is 1 muffin.

Per serving: **1 g. fat,** 116 calories, 16 mg. cholesterol, 5 g. dietary fiber, 337 mg. sodium

Apricot Bran Muffins

PREPARATION TIME: 20 MINUTES   BAKING TIME: 25 MINUTES

1½ cups all-purpose flour   1½ cups skim milk
2 tablespoons sugar   1 egg
1 tablespoon baking powder   2 tablespoons vegetable oil
½ teaspoon salt   ½ cup chopped dried apricots
1½ cups All-Bran cereal

1. In a small bowl, stir together the flour, sugar, baking powder, and salt. Set aside.
2. In a large bowl, combine the cereal and the milk; let stand 2 minutes. Add the egg and oil, blending well. Add the

flour mixture, stirring *only until combined.* Stir in the apricots.

3. Portion the batter evenly into lightly greased 2½-inch muffin-pan cups. Bake at 400 degrees for 25 minutes, or until a toothpick inserted in the center of a muffin comes out clean. Serve warm.

Makes 12 muffins. Serving size is 1 muffin.

Per serving: **3 g. fat,** 134 calories, 16 mg. cholesterol, 5 g. dietary fiber, 232 mg. sodium

Bran Muffins

PREPARATION TIME: 20 MINUTES   BAKING TIME: 18 TO 20 MINUTES

1¼ cups all-purpose flour   1½ cups All-Bran cereal
1 tablespoon baking powder   1¼ cups skim milk
¼ teaspoon salt   2 egg whites
2 tablespoons sugar   2 tablespoons vegetable oil

1. Stir together the flour, baking powder, salt, and sugar, and set aside.
2. Measure the cereal and milk into a large mixing bowl. Stir to combine. Let stand 1 to 2 minutes or until cereal is softened.
3. Place the egg whites in a small mixing bowl. Beat until foamy. Add the egg whites and the oil to the cereal mixture, and beat well. Add the flour mixture, stirring *only until combined.* Portion the batter evenly into 12 lightly greased 2½-inch muffin-pan cups.
4. Bake at 400 degrees for 18 to 20 minutes, or until a toothpick inserted in the center of a muffin comes out clean.

Makes 12 muffins. Serving size is 1 muffin.

Per serving: **3 g. fat,** 115 calories, no cholesterol, 4 g. dietary fiber, 189 mg. sodium

Herb Bran Muffins

PREPARATION TIME: 12 TO 15 MINUTES   BAKING TIME: 18 TO 20
                                                        MINUTES

1¼ cups all-purpose flour
1 tablespoon baking powder
¼ teaspoon salt
2 tablespoons sugar
2 tablespoons toasted sesame
  seeds
¼ teaspoon dry mustard
½ teaspoon herb of your
  choice (suggestions: sage,
dillweed, oregano, sweet
basil, chives, parsley,
marjoram, summer savory,
rosemary, coriander, or
cardamom)
1 cup All-Bran cereal
1 cup skim milk
1 egg
2 tablespoons melted butter

1. Stir together the flour, baking powder, salt, sugar, sesame seeds, dry mustard, and herb of choice. Set aside.
2. In a large mixing bowl, combine the cereal and the milk. Let stand 2 minutes. Add the egg and butter, blending well. Add the flour mixture, stirring *only until combined.*
3. Portion the batter evenly into lightly greased 2½-inch muffin-pan cups. Bake at 400 degrees for 18 to 20 minutes, or until a toothpick inserted in the center of a muffin comes out clean.

Makes 12 muffins. Serving size is 1 muffin.

Per serving: **3 g. fat,** 108 calories, 6 mg. cholesterol, 3 g. dietary fiber, 157 mg. sodium

Whole-Wheat Honey Tea Muffins

PREPARATION TIME: 15 MINUTES   BAKING TIME: 18 TO 20 MINUTES

¾ cup whole-wheat flour
1½ teaspoons baking powder
1 cup All-Bran cereal
¾ cup skim milk
1 egg
¼ cup honey
2 tablespoons vegetable oil

1. Stir together the flour and the baking powder. Set aside.
2. Combine the cereal and the milk in a large mixing bowl. Let stand for 2 minutes, or until the cereal is softened. Add the egg, honey, and oil. Beat well.
3. Add the flour mixture, stirring *only until combined.*
4. Portion the batter evenly into lightly greased 2½-inch muffin-pan cups. Bake at 400 degrees for 18 to 20 minutes, or until a toothpick inserted in the center of a muffin comes out clean.

Makes 12 muffins. Serving size is 1 muffin.

Per serving: **3 g. fat,** 96 calories, 16 mg. cholesterol, 3 g. dietary fiber, 94 mg. sodium

Seasonings

Human sensitivity to taste has certain peculiarities. It adapts to the use of salt and sugar, so that the more we use, the less sensitive to the flavor we become. This adaptation does not occur in our perception of bitter and sour.

Some people are "salt sensitive": Their blood pressure rises when they consume salt. The effect is due, in actuality, to the sodium in salt. Table salt is 40 percent sodium and 60 percent chloride.

Although sodium is an essential nutrient, we Americans consume 8 to 10 times more than our bodies need to stay alive and healthy. About 25 to 35 percent of us are "salt sensitive" and can develop high blood pressure if we consume too much salt. For this reason, most health professionals encourage us to cut back on salt. We can do this by cutting back on added salt in our own cooking, and by reducing the consumption of certain processed foods, such as processed meats, soups, and snack foods.

We agree with the suggestion to cut back on salt and have done it ourselves over the past few years. But we don't think you need to cut it out entirely from your cooking unless you are on a severely salt-restricted diet. The reason we include salt or other seasonings that contain some sodium in many of our recipes is that salt seems to bring out the flavors in other ingredients, especially herbs and spices. Try it yourself: Mix up a batch of herbs, taste them, and then add about one part salt to a mixture of six or seven parts other herbs. You will agree, we're quite sure, that the flavor of the other herbs fairly explodes to the taste with a bit of salt.

For this reason, our Herb Salt (pages 332–33) is usually made with one part salt to six or seven parts other herbs, yielding a mixture that has perhaps 285 milligrams of sodium per teaspoon, compared with 2200 milligrams in a teaspoon of salt.

We keep a wide assortment of herbs and spices on our shelves, including just about everything we itemized on pages 34 to 36. We also keep a variety of our own blends, such as the recipes included here. In addition, we keep some commercial preparations on hand for the times we are in a hurry, or seek other variety. These include Mrs. Dash, which is strong on garlic and rather hot; Old Bay, which, although quite high in sodium, is good when lightly sprinkled on fish and poultry; and Perc, which is a salt-free herb blend, somewhat strong on onion, but acceptable in most recipes to which you might ordinarily sprinkle blended dried herbs. Both Mrs. Dash and Perc, for example, will add interest to cottage cheese or cheese toast, and can be sprinkled lightly on just about any meat or vegetable when you are not feeling particularly creative.

We also occasionally use the original Worcestershire in small quantities, over steaks or in a meat loaf. Recently we discovered White Wine Worcestershire, which is an excellent seasoning for fish and chicken and gets our highest recommendation. We almost always use soy sauce in place of salt whenever possible, since a teaspoon of soy sauce, in the usual commercial preparation, has about 1/7 the sodium content of salt.

And here's a hint for seasoning meat, chicken, and turkey before roasting: Place your selection of seasonings (a total of 4 to 6 teaspoons of crushed herbs and spices) in a small bowl, and add 1 tablespoon of oil and 1 tablespoon of soy sauce. Mix it until it forms a paste, and then, before roasting, rub it well into the meat or poultry with your fingers. Each year at either Thanksgiving or Christmas we use Indian Spice Blend (page 332) in this way before smoking a turkey Tandoori style, and it gets rave reviews from our dinner guests. (We think that smoked foods should be used with extreme moderation, since smoking may increase the activity of certain carcinogenic substances. We will smoke a turkey or roast two or three times each year; we avoid smoked foods at other times.)

After they are emptied, save several of the spice jars you obtain when you purchase commercial spices. Wash and dry them well and use them to store your own blends. You can also use them to store any herbs and spices that you buy in bulk. The flavor of herbs and spices is preserved best when they are stored in airtight containers.

When you cannot use the fresh form of an herb, substitute a powder. Garlic and onion powders (and celery seed) are far lower in sodium content than their salt equivalents. The sodium content of the blend is far higher than necessary. If you find that your recipe needs additional salt, add it yourself. You will end up using far less.

Finally, whenever we say "dash" of salt, we mean about 1/16 of a teaspoon, which is what some cooks refer to as a "pinch." When we say "salt to taste," go lightly and let people add a bit more at the table if they wish. We discovered that the instruction was the source of tremendous variation among the "army" of chefs who helped design and taste our recipes. Until we made ourselves understood, this misunderstanding sometimes resulted in food that was so salty we could not believe they had ever tasted it before emptying the salt shaker!

Since nutrients in herbs and spices are so minimal in the quantities sold, we haven't provided nutritional analyses for our herb blends.

Garam Masala

PREPARATION TIME: 3 MINUTES

A traditional Indian "masala" is simply a mixture of spices. A "garam masala" is typically added to a dish just before serving. The preferences of the cook often determine which spices are included in the mixture, and in what quantities. This one is a little sweeter than our Indian Spice Blend (which follows). If you like it, you may want to double or triple this recipe in order to have plenty on hand.

1 tablespoon ground cardamom
1 teaspoon cinnamon
1 teaspoon cumin
½ teaspoon ground cloves

½ teaspoon fresh-ground black
  pepper
¼ teaspoon nutmeg

Combine all ingredients and store in an airtight jar.

Makes a little over 2 tablespoons.

"Is that all it says about eye of newt—add to taste?" DRAWING BY MODELL; © 1983 THE NEW YORKER MAGAZINE, INC.

Indian Spice Blend

PREPARATION TIME: 3 MINUTES

Curry powder is actually a combination of several of various spices, including ginger, coriander, cardamom, cayenne pepper, cinnamon, chiles, mustard seed, turmeric, cumin, black pepper, poppy seeds, fenugreek, fennel, mace, and cloves. There are many different versions of the blend, depending on the type of dish and the cook. You can create your own special curry using some of these spices. Or mix the blend below to have on hand "in a pinch," and use it any time curry powder is called for.

8 teaspoons cumin
4 teaspoons ground ginger
2 teaspoons ground coriander
2 teaspoons cayenne pepper

4 teaspoons turmeric
2 teaspoons fresh-ground black pepper

Combine all ingredients and store in an airtight spice jar.

Makes about 7 tablespoons.

Herb Salt

PREPARATION TIME: 3 MINUTES

Though the following combination of herbs is one of our favorites, you can experiment with your own combination of herbs. You will soon find that an herb salt is an excellent substitute for plain salt, and instead of about 2200 milligrams of sodium per teaspoon, it has only 285 milligrams. Thus a sprinkle (about ⅛ teaspoon) of Herb Salt will give you perhaps 30 or 40 milligrams of sodium, instead of the almost sevenfold amount (200 to 300 milligrams) plain salt would provide.

½ teaspoon basil
¼ teaspoon thyme
¼ teaspoon dillweed

¼ teaspoon celery seed
¼ teaspoon salt
¼ teaspoon dried parsley

Combine all ingredients and grind with a mortar and pestle. Store in a small herb jar.

Makes about 1¾ teaspoons.

Traditional Italian Herb Blend

PREPARATION TIME: 3 MINUTES

Use this blend whenever Italian seasoning is called for but you don't want to take the time to mince or crush garlic, and so on. Add a bay leaf to your recipe along with this blend for the perfect Italian flavor. This mixture will contain 96 milligrams of sodium per teaspoon (less than ½₀ the sodium content of a teaspoon of salt itself, which contains 2200 milligrams of sodium, so it can be considered a low-sodium seasoning).

6 tablespoons dried basil leaves
1 tablespoon garlic powder
1 teaspoon salt

2 teaspoons fresh-ground black pepper

Combine all ingredients and store in a tightly sealed jar in a cool, dry place.

Makes 8 tablespoons.

Sandwiches, Sandwich Spreads, and the Working-World Lunch

My typical quick lunch consists of two slices of whole-grain bread wrapped around an ounce or two of turkey breast with plenty of Dijon mustard, and some fruit for dessert. Unlike the English Lord Sandwich, who wouldn't leave his card games long enough to eat a "proper" lunch, and requested two slices of bread with meat between them, thus inventing the "sandwich," Terri and I are more likely to be glued to our word processors, with our sandwiches on the side. Lord Sandwich probably had no idea he was starting a trend that would still be the last word in lunches right up through the twentieth century.

For starters, you don't have to limit yourself to whole-grain bread as your sandwich foundation. Try whole-grain English muffins, bagels, or pita (Middle Eastern pocket) bread. Even a whole-wheat or corn tortilla can function as sandwich bread.

We prefer cooked chicken or turkey, and low-fat tuna salads and spreads such as we show in our recipes, to processed meats such as bologna or salami, which contain salt, sugar, and other additives. In addition, processed meats are usually higher in fat than in any other nutrient. Because a high consumption of the saturated fats found in meat appears to be related to a high blood cholesterol level, which in turn is a risk factor for cardiovascular disease, many food processors have taken to producing reduced-fat processed meats, including extra-lean ham containing only 1 gram of fat per ounce. But be sure to read the labels: Many of the so-called reduced-fat processed meats from one food packager can be higher than the regular meats of another.

Read about the Combination Sandwich (page 338) for basic preparation tips for sandwiches.

And now, a brief word about lunch in general. What do you do if you're an office worker whose usual lunch consists of either a fast-food burger, fries, and a soft drink or a quick candy bar and a soft drink from a vending machine? Many of us are hampered by lack of time for lunch and less than adequate kitchen facilities in our workplaces.

Of course, more and more restaurants are becoming health-

"Sandwiches!" *THE FAR SIDE.*
COURTESY CHRONICLE FEATURES,
SAN FRANCISCO.

conscious, and offer low-fat selections that go way beyond the boring old "dieter's special" of a bland hamburger patty, cottage cheese, and a limp lettuce leaf. If you are lucky enough to have a good restaurant near you that caters to health, you're ahead of the game. And remember that many restaurants will be happy to prepare a special low-fat meal for you, even if they may not list it on the menu. All you have to do is ask.

Bringing your own lunch is one of the best alternatives. Then you really have control of what you're eating. Sandwiches, fruit, and salads in insulated containers last until lunch-time without refrigeration, and don't require heating up.

In some workplaces, workers band together to fund a "kitchen," with everyone contributing money to buy appli-ances like a hot plate, a toaster oven, a small camper-sized refrigerator, or even a small microwave. Having these kinds of appliances expands the lunch possibilities tremendously. Soups, stir-fries, leftovers—indeed, whole meals—can be stored in the refrigerator and prepared later for a quick, low-cost lunch.

A refrigerator is especially handy for those who like to bring yogurt for lunch or for a snack. And do bring a snack! Mid-afternoon "blahs" are conducive to raids on the candy ma-chines. Fruit and homemade muffins are tops on our list for snacks, or high-fiber cereal and milk.

So, although we present sandwiches in the following section, many of our recipes, especially soups, stews, stir-fries, and left-overs, can do double duty as all or part of a nutritious lunch.

Meat Spread

PREPARATION TIME: 8 TO 10 MINUTES

½ pound cooked meat
   or poultry
1 small onion, diced
¼ cup wheat germ
   or cooked red beans

2 tablespoons low-fat soy flour
Herb Salt (pp. 332–33)
   or other herb blend to taste
Fresh-ground black pepper to
   taste

Blend all ingredients in a food processor. Moisten as needed with ketchup, mustard, or low-fat salad dressing.

Makes about 1¼ cups. Serving size is about 2 ounces, or ¼ cup.

Per serving: **2 g. fat,** 110 calories, 39 mg. cholesterol, 1 g. dietary fiber, 50 mg. sodium (with ¼ cup cooked red beans: **2 g. fat,** 97 calories, 39 mg. cholesterol, 1 g. dietary fiber, 50 mg. sodium)

Turkey Melt

PREPARATION TIME: 10 MINUTES   COOKING TIME: 20 MINUTES

The original recipe called for ham. You can, of course, use extra-lean ham, but try it with turkey, as suggested below, or chicken, for less sodium and fat content. Serve over whole-grain toast or English muffins.

1 teaspoon vegetable oil
4 ounces fresh mushrooms,
  sliced
1 tablespoon butter
  or margarine
1 tablespoon all-purpose flour
1 cup skim
  or low-fat milk

¼ cup white wine
¼ teaspoon nutmeg
¼ teaspoon tarragon
⅓ cup grated Gruyère cheese
2 cups diced cooked turkey
  breast

1. Brush a skillet with the oil, and heat over medium heat. Add the mushrooms, cover, and reduce heat slightly. Let cook for several minutes, until mushrooms are tender, stirring occasionally.
2. Meanwhile, melt the butter or margarine in a large skillet. Stir in the flour and let cook, stirring constantly, until golden brown. Stir in the milk, wine, nutmeg, and tarragon.
3. Combine the cheese and turkey, and stir into the milk mixture. Add the mushrooms, and heat the mixture through without boiling.

4 servings. Serving size is about 1 cup.

Per serving: **8 g. fat**, 217 calories, 79 mg. cholesterol, 1 g. dietary fiber, 132 mg. sodium

Combination Sandwich

The label "combination sandwich" refers to any combination of ingredients between 2 slices of whole-grain bread, such as any slice of meat and cheese, or spreads with vegetables or cheese.

The way to prepare sandwiches with limited fat and calories is to use extra-lean cuts of meat or poultry, and only limited amounts of light mayonnaise or ketchup. You may use as much mustard as you like since it contains no fat and is very low in calories. Then you add lettuce, tomato, or other cut-up fresh vegetables as desired.

Two slices of whole-grain bread, with 1 ounce each of extra-lean meat and light or reduced-fat cheese, will contain approximately 5 grams of fat and 250 calories. Light mayonnaise contains 1 to 2 grams of fat and about 15 calories a teaspoonful, ketchup no fat and 16 calories a tablespoon, and mustard is negligible. Along with fresh vegetables or a piece of fresh fruit, a combination sandwich gives you a satisfying lunch for 5 or 6 grams of fat and about 300 calories. (Compare this lunch with the 30 grams of fat and 550 or so calories you obtain in the typical fast-food hamburger sandwich. The fast-food hamburger, *all by itself,* will have about 6 times the fat content of your lean slice of meat, and 3 to 6 times more mayonnaise or salad dressing will be used to enhance the flavor.)

For variety, try one of the following spreads. They make especially attractive open-faced sandwiches. Serve with sprouts, or a slice of tomato or reduced-fat cheese; broil in the oven for a hot sandwich.

Cheese Toast

PREPARATION TIME: 3 MINUTES   COOKING TIME: 3 TO 5 MINUTES

2 slices whole-grain bread
1 ounce reduced-fat cheese,
   sliced thin, to cover 2 slices
   of bread

2 slices tomato (optional)

Place the bread on a foil-lined baking sheet. Arrange the cheese, and tomato slices if desired, on top of the bread, and place under the broiler for a few minutes, until the cheese is melted.

VARIATIONS: Before broiling, sprinkle the cheese toast with basil, chili powder, cumin, or other herbs and spices.

Serves 1.

Per serving: **7 g. fat,** 259 calories, 15 mg. cholesterol, 5 g. dietary fiber, 471 mg. sodium

Shrimp Spread

PREPARATION TIME: 15 MINUTES

1 pound cooked, peeled shrimp
1 cup 1% low-fat cottage cheese
2 ounces Neufchâtel cheese
½ cup plain nonfat yogurt
1 clove garlic, crushed

1 teaspoon dried tarragon
Dash of Worcestershire sauce
  (optional)
Salt and fresh-ground black
  pepper to taste

1. Mince the shrimp (or use baby shrimp).
2. Put the cottage cheese and the Neufchâtel in a blender or food processor, and blend until smooth. Pour into mixing bowl.
3. Add the remaining ingredients, mixing well. Chill and serve.

Makes about 4 cups. Serving size is ¼ cup.

Per serving: **1 g. fat,** 53 calories, 59 mg. cholesterol, no dietary fiber, 159 mg. sodium

Tuna Salad

PREPARATION TIME: 8 TO 10 MINUTES

This is our basic tuna salad. As a halfway measure for reducing mayonnaise in our diet, we mix a little light mayonnaise (for flavor) with yogurt and mustard. This same dressing goes equally well with cooked chicken, turkey, salmon, crab, lobster, or shrimp. You can vary it by adding a dash of tarragon, dillweed, or other herbs and spices. Use about a pound of cooked seafood, or 2 medium cans, 9¼ ounces each.

On a day when you feel like splurging, add a tablespoon or two of chopped nuts or olives.

2 medium cans (9¼ ounces each) water-packed tuna
½ cup plain nonfat yogurt
2 tablespoons light mayonnaise
2 teaspoons Dijon mustard
1 hard-boiled egg, chopped

1½ stalks celery, chopped
1 tablespoon fresh parsley, chopped
Fresh-ground black pepper to taste

Combine all ingredients in large bowl. Serve chilled on lettuce leaves or in half a melon or tomato.

4 servings. Serving size is about 1 cup.

Per serving: **5 g. fat,** 196 calories, 92 mg. cholesterol, no dietary fiber, 525 mg. sodium

Tuna Salad with Fruit Vinaigrette Dressing

PREPARATION TIME: 5 MINUTES

We suggest a raspberry vinegar for this salad, although you may use any fruit vinegar; substitute regular wine vinegar if that's all you have on hand or if you don't like fruit vinegars.

1 medium can (9¼ ounces)
 water-packed tuna, drained
¼ cup chopped apples,
 unpeeled
¼ cup raisins

¼ cup fruit vinegar
 or red wine vinegar
½ teaspoon Dijon mustard
½ teaspoon dillweed
½ teaspoon celery seed

Combine all ingredients. Serve on lettuce leaves or mixed greens, if desired.

2 servings. Serving size is about 1 cup.

Per serving: **3 g. fat,** 210 calories, 43 mg. cholesterol, 1 g. dietary fiber, 423 g. sodium

Mexican Bean Spread

PREPARATION TIME: 8 TO 10 MINUTES

This can substitute for a Mexican bean dip, and it's great broiled in the oven covered with a slice of reduced-fat cheese or tomato, and sprinkled with oregano.

2 cups cooked OR 1 can (16
 ounces) dark red kidney
 beans, drained
1 small onion

3 tablespoons ketchup
⅛ teaspoon cayenne pepper
Herb Salt (pp. 332–33) to taste
Fresh-ground black pepper

Blend the above ingredients in a food processor or blender, adding more ketchup if needed for desired consistency.

Makes about 1½ cups. Serving size is about 2 ounces, or ¼ cup.

Per serving: **no fat,** 88 calories, no cholesterol, 5 g. dietary fiber, 143 mg. sodium

Curried Turkey Salad

PREPARATION TIME: 10 TO 15 MINUTES

2 cups cooked turkey breast, diced
½ cup plain nonfat yogurt
2 tablespoons light mayonnaise
¼ cup raisins
¼ cup finely chopped nuts or seeds (walnuts, peanuts, sunflower seeds, etc.)

1½ stalks celery, chopped
½ teaspoon Indian Spice Blend (p. 332) or other curry powder
Fresh-ground black pepper to taste

Combine all ingredients in large bowl. Serve chilled on lettuce leaves, in half a melon or tomato, or surrounded by other fresh fruit in season.

4 servings. Serving size is about 1 cup.

Per serving: **7 g. fat,** 211 calories, 62 mg. cholesterol, 1 g. dietary fiber, 116 mg. sodium

Crabmeat Spread

PREPARATION TIME: 8 TO 10 MINUTES

1 cup crabmeat
½ cup celery, diced
1 small onion, diced
Herb Salt (pp. 332–33) to taste

½ green pepper, diced
1 cup sprouts (your choice)
1 cup 1% low-fat cottage cheese

Blend all the ingredients with enough low-fat salad dressing to moisten. (We use about 2 tablespoons of light mayonnaise.)

Makes about 3 cups. Serving size is about 2 ounces, or ¼ cup.

Per serving: **no fat,** 28 calories, 11 mg. cholesterol, no dietary fiber, 134 mg. sodium (with the 2 tablespoons light mayonnaise: **1 g. fat,** 34 calories, 11 mg. cholesterol, no dietary fiber, 147 mg. sodium)

Beverages

We must start by talking about plain, fresh WATER!

Although it may not have occurred to you, water is our most essential nutrient. No beverage (including those in this chapter) should replace plain, fresh water as the primary beverage in your diet. Aim for eight 8-ounce glasses per day.

For many people this is very hard advice to follow. Water doesn't taste very good anymore when it comes out of the tap in many parts of the country. In fact, the consumption of soda pop is greater than that of water in the United States.

Won't diet drinks do? In my opinion, no. Perhaps in moderation they don't do any harm, but using intensely sweetened drinks of any kind seems to dull our sensitivity to sweetness and to keep alive a sweet tooth in those who may find it hard to manage their weight.

But plain water won't do for all occasions and we are constantly asked, "What am I supposed to drink?" Well, coffee or tea may do no harm provided you limit yourself to 2 or 3 cups per day, and many nutritionists believe it's okay to count them among the recommended daily total of 64 fluid ounces of water. But what about treats and special occasions? Isn't there anything you can drink that's really tasty and not bad for you?

This chapter contains some suggestions for making flavored teas and coffees and for other beverages that are satisfying and good for you, such as some tasty blended fruit drinks. Notice the use of vanilla flavoring: It makes beverages taste sweeter without adding any calories and it reduces the need for sugar. Other extracts can do the same. If you live in a part of the country where you can enjoy a real winter, you will find that Herb Rum Tea (page 346) is even more satisfying on snowy nights than it is on rainy nights. It's a favorite of mine after a long walk or run in chilly weather. All of our recommendations are good for entertaining.

An important consideration for making beverages is the taste of the water you're using. If your tap water doesn't taste particularly good, it may be adding an off-flavor to other beverages that you make with it. That may be why you prefer sweetened bottled drinks over water or the drinks that you blend yourself using tap water. Try some bottled spring water for tea, coffee, and the other beverage suggestions in this chapter. If you notice a pleasant improvement, you might consider using bottled water for drinking and cooking. Or you might want to purchase an activated-charcoal filter for your kitchen faucet to remove chlorine and other objectionable organic matter. Be sure to get one that's bacteriostatic, to prevent bacteria from multiplying in water from which chlorine has been removed. You will find it easier to replace sweet-flavored beverages in your diet if your water tastes fresh and clean. You can also try seltzer water.

Two warnings: I do not recommend that you use distilled water as your primary source of fluids. Tap water and spring water contain a number of essential minerals that are removed in the distillation process, and appliances that soften water may add a considerable amount of sodium. Be sure that your water requires softening before you buy this type of water conditioner. The activated-charcoal filters that I advise for making tap water more palatable do not remove essential minerals, nor do they add unnecessary sodium.

Fruit and vegetable juices are good, and for variety, there are many blended juices available in supermarkets and health-food stores if you don't want to combine your own. Fruit juice blended with herb tea also makes a satisfying punch, and the possibilities for combining are practically endless. If you are interested in limiting your calorie intake, however, we recommend you turn to whole fresh fruit rather than juice. Most people end up consuming fewer calories when they eat fresh fruit, which contains considerable fiber, than they do when they drink juice, which is almost devoid of fiber.

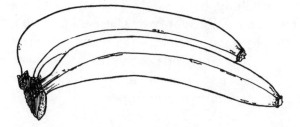

Banana-Strawberry Frozen Delight

PREPARATION TIME: 7 TO 8 MINUTES   FREEZING TIME: 2 HOURS

2 medium bananas, peeled
½ cup evaporated skim milk
½ teaspoon vanilla extract
Strawberry, banana,
  or almond extract (optional)

1 package (10 ounces) frozen
  whole unsweetened
  strawberries

1. Wrap the peeled bananas in plastic wrap and place in the freezer for at least 2 hours, until frozen.
2. Cut the frozen bananas into chunks. Place the chunks in a blender or food processor.
3. Combine the milk and the extract(s) and pour over the bananas. Blend until smooth.
4. Reserve a couple of strawberries to slice for a garnish, if desired. Gradually add the remaining strawberries to the blender or food processor, blending briefly after each addition. Serve immediately.

4 servings. Serving size is about ¾ cup.

Per serving: **no fat,** 103 calories, 1 mg. cholesterol, 3 g. dietary fiber, 39 mg. sodium

Herb Rum Tea

PREPARATION TIME: 8 TO 10 MINUTES

Also known as "Chilly, Rainy Night Tea." We combine a favorite black tea, such as Earl Grey or Darjeeling, with a favorite herb tea (usually mint, lemon, or almond). Then we put a teaspoon of rum in a mug, and pour in the hot, brewed tea. Try adding a whole clove, a piece of cinnamon stick, or an orange or lemon slice. A great warmer-upper.

Coffee Suggestions

For those who are used to drinking coffee with sugar and/or cream, here are a few hints that may help you reduce or completely omit those high-calorie additions. When brewing coffee, add to the grounds one or more of the following:

A dash or two of ground cinnamon, cardamom, or other sweet spices
A piece of vanilla bean (about ⅛ inch per cup)
A bit of orange peel
Ground almonds (about ¼ teaspoon per cup)

We also suggest that you use dairy products rather than the non-dairy substitutes if you don't take coffee black. The substitute may contain even more saturated fat than the dairy product; for example, half-and-half has about the same calories as non-dairy creamers, and, in our opinion, the substitute can't compare in flavor. (Both half-and-half and non-dairy liquids contain 20 calories per tablespoon. The powders contain about 10 per teaspoon. Whole milk is only 10 calories per tablespoon.)

Cool Coffee Special

PREPARATION TIME: 15 TO 20 MINUTES

For a refreshing dessert drink, try this with either regular or decaffeinated coffee, or a blend of the two, which is how we drink it. You can substitute instant coffee if you prefer.

2 cups hot brewed coffee	2 eggs, separated
2 cups cold skim milk	4 teaspoons sugar
2 cups cold water	1 teaspoon vanilla extract

1. Put the hot coffee in a large saucepan.
2. Add the cold milk and cold water and stir. Beat the egg yolks and add to the coffee mixture. Stir in the sugar and vanilla.
3. Beat the egg whites until stiff. Gently fold them into the coffee mixture. Serve over ice.

6 servings. Serving size is about 1 cup.

Per serving: **2 g. fat,** 65 calories, 64 mg. cholesterol, no dietary fiber, 62 mg. sodium

Great Shakes

PREPARATION TIME: 8 TO 10 MINUTES

Here is the basic recipe for a satisfying, sweet substitute for the common, sugar-loaded milkshake. Vary this recipe by using any combination of fruit. Our favorites are orange-banana, as shown below, strawberry-banana, and strawberry-peach. Try different flavorings as well, such as almond extract, cinnamon, cloves, or cardamom. This makes a complete breakfast or lunch for one person, or a dessert drink for one or two people.

1 cup plain nonfat yogurt   **½ teaspoon vanilla extract**
1 small banana   **Dash nutmeg**
1 medium orange

Place yogurt in blender or food processor. Cut the fruit into chunks and add to the yogurt. Blend for 30 seconds. Add vanilla and nutmeg, and blend until smooth. Serve immediately.

1 serving. Serving size is 2 cups.

Per recipe: 1 g. fat, 309 calories, 4 mg. cholesterol, 5 g. dietary fiber, 188 mg. sodium

Fruit 'n' Juice Shake

PREPARATION TIME: 5 TO 10 MINUTES

This recipe combines whole fruit with fruit juice for a refreshing, low-calorie "shake." You can use your imagination with this one; for starters, try banana, orange, apple, and/or berries; mix and match your favorite fruit flavors.

10 ounces fruit juice   **1 medium piece of fruit, sliced**

Combine the ingredients in a blender, and blend for about 30 seconds.

2 servings. Serving size is about 1 cup.

Per serving (using orange juice and pineapple): **no fat,** 82 calories, no cholesterol, 1 g. dietary fiber, 2 mg. sodium

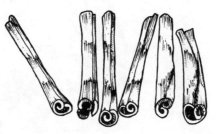

Spiced Tea

PREPARATION TIME: 10 MINUTES

Many spiced teas call for pre-mixed instant teas and lemonades, which are often high in sugar, as well as other additives. Here is our refreshing alternative that lets you control the amount of sugar. Serve hot or cold.

4 cups brewed black tea
2 cinnamon sticks
1 cup unsweetened orange juice

1 to 2 teaspoons sugar
1 teaspoon ground cloves
1 to 2 teaspoons lemon juice OR 4 slices fresh lemon

1. When brewing the tea, place the cinnamon sticks in the same pan or teapot. When the tea is ready, discard the cinnamon sticks.
2. Add the remaining ingredients and serve, or chill first and serve over ice cubes if you want iced tea.

4 servings. Serving size is about 1 1/4 cups.

Per serving: **no fat,** 38 calories, no cholesterol, no dietary fiber, 9 mg. sodium

"That settles it Carl! . . . From now on, you're getting only decaffeinated coffee!" *THE FAR SIDE.* COURTESY CHRONICLE FEATURES, SAN FRANCISCO.

Irish Spiced Coffee

PREPARATION TIME: 10 MINUTES   COOKING TIME: 10 MINUTES

This is a dessert drink, which is satisfying served alone, or with a barely sweet dessert such as Sweet Pineapple Squares (p. 372) or Carrot-Nut Tea Bread (p. 365). You may use "store-bought" bottled lemon and orange peel in this recipe. Though they tend to have small amounts of sugar added, the total sugar in this recipe is minimal for a dessert.

2 cups strong black coffee
  (regular or decaffeinated)
2 teaspoons sugar
2 whole cloves
1 stick cinnamon

1 teaspoon finely grated lemon
  peel
1 teaspoon finely grated orange
  peel
¼ cup Irish whiskey

1. Bring the coffee, sugar, cloves, cinnamon, and lemon and orange rind to a boil in a saucepan. Let boil for a couple of minutes, then remove from heat. Remove the cloves and cinnamon stick and discard.
2. Add the whiskey, and serve. Or chill—it is delicious cold, for a summer dessert drink.

VARIATION: For an exotic chilled dessert, add to the recipe 1 envelope of unflavored gelatin, as follows:

1. Follow step 1.
2. Soften the gelatin in the Irish whiskey. Then add the hot coffee mixture, and stir until the gelatin dissolves.
3. Pour into 2 small serving dishes or parfait glasses, and chill overnight. Garnish with a curl of lemon or orange peel, if desired.

The taste and texture will surprise you!

2 servings. Serving size is about 1 cup.

Per serving: **no fat,** 87 calories, no cholesterol, no dietary fiber, 6 mg. sodium

Desserts

WARNING! It is dangerous to read this chapter without also reading the next chapter!

If you put the recipes of this chapter "into practice," and if you are a sedentary person, you must "go all the way": You must develop the active life-style that will permit you to enjoy them without gaining weight!

We have made a special effort to include desserts that are relatively low in fat and sugar, and high in more valuable nutrients, so that you will see that a treat need not necessarily be a "cheat." Our goal is to reduce fat, sugar, and salt in basic dessert recipes by significant amounts, often by as much as 50 percent in comparison with other recipes of a similar nature.

Sometimes we combine more healthful ingredients with the less healthful processed ingredients that have worked their way into our style of food preparation because they are easier to use, "fluffier," or in other ways more satisfying to the human preference for fat and sugar. We blend whole-grain flour with all-purpose flour, or use only whole-grain flour when appropriate, and we use honey and molasses when they enhance flavor, rather than relying on just granulated white sugar. (If you find that 100 percent whole-wheat flour makes a cookie or cake too heavy for you, try using whole-wheat pastry flour or blending it with unbleached white flour. Whole-wheat pastry flour has had a small part of the fibrous portion removed to make it lighter than 100 percent whole-wheat and we frequently use it.) We also suggest skim or low-fat milk in place of whole milk, and nonfat yogurt, half-and-half, or light sour cream in place of heavy cream, whenever these will do the job both satisfactorily and tastily.

Some of our recipes, such as the Oatmeal Pecan Cookies (page 366), use vegetable oil instead of a solid shortening such as butter or margarine. You can often make this kind of substitution with perfectly acceptable results. Although the calorie content in all fats is about the same, the amounts and types of fats you use, especially in desserts, which tend to be relatively high in fat, can make a difference in your health.

Fats are present in foods in three forms: saturated, monounsaturated, and polyunsaturated. *Saturated fats* have a chemical structure that tends to make them harden at room temperature; lard, butter, some margarines, and some vegetable oils are saturated fats.

Research has shown that there is a link between high intake of fat in the diet and the risk of certain forms of cancer. *Saturated fats* raise the blood level of cholesterol, which is a primary risk factor for heart disease. On the other hand, monounsaturated and polyunsaturated fats either reduce or have no effect on blood cholesterol.

The typical American diet contains 40 to 50 percent calories from fat, yet health authorities recommend 30 percent or, better yet, 25 percent. Saturated fats should equal less than 10 percent of total calories for the day, which is about half of what the average American consumes each day (about 17 percent).

Various foods contain various combinations of the different types of fats, but in any given food, there is usually more of one type. Animal fats, for instance, are primarily saturated. Even some vegetable fats are highly saturated, such as coconut oil, palm oil, and cocoa butter.

Polyunsaturated fats, which tend to lower blood cholesterol, are usually liquid at room temperature. They are corn oil, safflower oil, sunflower oil, soybean oil, or margarines made from these oils. However, hydrogenation, the process which "saturates" or hardens vegetable fats, gives these fats some of the same characteristics as animal fats. Too much can be just as dangerous to your health. Check labels for hydrogenated margarines that have been chemically saturated. The softer the margarine, the better. You can buy margarines in a tub, for example, that are more polyunsaturated than stick margarine.

Monounsaturated fats, which also tend to have a cholesterol-lowering effect, are olive oil and peanut oil. Avocados, too, mainly have monounsaturated fat, but they are high in total fat and calories compared with other fruits and vegetables, so eat them in moderation.

When vegetable oil is called for in a dessert recipe, I usually use corn or canola oil. I normally use olive oil or peanut oil for sautéing, and I sometimes use a little butter with these oils, since nothing can quite equal the flavor that butter imparts to many foods. If you like popcorn, try avocado oil for popping. It adds a faint, but delicious nutty flavor. We don't care much for air-blown popcorn, and corn popped with avocado oil will contain only about 1 to 2 grams of fat and 35 calories per cup, popped. (Our recipe is 1 tablespoon oil with ⅔ cup Reddenbacher's popcorn, which fills our 12-cup popper.) We add no additional fat to the popcorn after popping, and use one of various seasonings, such as nutritional yeast, garlic or onion powder, or chili powder. I like just a light sprinkle of salt on mine.

Although our desserts are relatively low in fat, sugar, and salt, we make no effort to have every recipe come in at, say, just 25 percent of total calories from fat. THAT IS THE AVERAGE, TOTAL TARGET FOR A DAY, NOT EVERY SINGLE MEAL OR DISH. If you eat a well-balanced diet throughout the day, with plenty of fresh fruit and vegetables, low-fat meats and milk products, and if you avoid fried foods, your basic diet, before dessert, may contain as little as 20 to 25 percent fat. Thus, there is no need to fear an occasional dessert of 300 calories, in which 50 percent of the calories come from fat: Your total fat for the day will still fall within the guidelines of a nutritious diet.

Because most people still prefer to use whole eggs rather than egg whites or egg substitutes in baking, we decided to list the nutritional values of almost all recipes using eggs, but Egg Beaters works fine in all recipes except where the egg whites must be beaten stiff separately. If Egg Beaters is listed first, it is used in the nutritional analysis.

Finally, a word of advice when you decide to "go all the way" at your favorite restaurant and indulge in the super-rich

"Let's just go in and see what happens."
DRAWING BY BOOTH; © 1986 THE NEW YORKER MAGAZINE, INC.

New York–style cheesecake or the seven-layer cake in which the layers of frosting are thicker than the layers of cake. If you are an active person in good health, we don't think an occasional indulgence of this sort is harmful. We sometimes do it ourselves, and, having relatively low cholesterol levels and no hypertension, we don't feel guilty about it. You don't need to kick yourself, either. But we *don't* go overboard on a regular basis, and you won't want to either, especially in your own cooking, once you see how you can reduce the fat in your own recipes.

Take a look at Kahlua Chocolate Cheesecake (pages 360–61), for example. There is simply no need to use cream cheese and heavy cream in your own baking once you learn how to use lower-fat ingredients for desserts in the appropriate propor-tions. I challenge anyone to make a better cheesecake, no matter how much fat you use! And do write to me if you can devise a better cheesecake! I love cheesecake and promise to find a way to share your expertise with others who share your (and my) predilections.

Apricot-Banana Bread

PREPARATION TIME: 15 MINUTES   BAKING TIME: 35 TO 40 MINUTES

This makes a lightly sweet, wholesome dessert bread.

2 medium bananas, mashed
4 whole dried apricots, chopped (8 halves)
1½ cups whole-wheat flour
2 teaspoons baking powder
½ teaspoon salt
Dash nutmeg
⅓ cup vegetable oil
⅓ cup honey
1 egg

1. Combine the bananas and apricots in a small bowl.
2. In another bowl, combine the dry ingredients. Add the oil and the honey, then beat in the egg. Add the banana-apricot mixture, blending well.
3. Spray a 9×5×3-inch loaf pan with nonstick vegetable cooking spray, or oil very lightly by rubbing a bit of oil on the pan with a paper towel. Pour the batter into the pan, which will be about ⅓ full.
4. Bake at 350 degrees for 35 to 40 minutes or until slightly browned, and a toothpick inserted in the middle comes out clean.

Makes 10 slices about ⅞ inch thick each. Serving size is 1 slice.

Per serving: **8 g. fat,** 193 calories, 19 mg. cholesterol, 3 g. dietary fiber, 115 mg. sodium

Chocolate-Chip Cookies

PREPARATION TIME: 15 MINUTES   BAKING TIME: 8 TO 10 MINUTES

It would be hard to imagine a dessert chapter that didn't include an example of a recipe for one of America's favorites, chocolate-chip cookies. We think our version of this traditional recipe came out just fine; we cut the fat and the sugar by half, and used Egg Beaters in place of whole eggs.

½ cup butter, softened
½ cup brown sugar, firmly
  packed
½ cup granulated white sugar
1 teaspoon vanilla extract
1 teaspoon water
½ cup Egg Beaters OR 2 eggs

1 cup whole-wheat flour
1 cup all-purpose flour
1 teaspoon baking soda
1 teaspoon salt
6 ounces semisweet chocolate
  chips
½ cup chopped nuts

1. Preheat the oven to 375 degrees.
2. In a large bowl, combine the margarine, sugars, vanilla, and water. Beat in the eggs.
3. In another bowl, combine the flours, baking soda, and salt. Gradually add this to the wet ingredients, blending well. Stir in the chocolate chips and the nuts.
4. Drop by rounded teaspoonful onto Teflon or ungreased baking sheets. Bake until golden brown, about 8 to 10 minutes.

VARIATION: Add a couple of teaspoons of grated orange rind to the batter before baking, for Orange Chocolate-Chip Cookies.

Makes 3 dozen cookies, about 2 inches in diameter.

Per cookie: **5 g. fat,** 99 calories, 7 mg. cholesterol, 1 g. dietary fiber, 114 mg. sodium

Chocolate-Drop Peanut Butter Cookies

PREPARATION TIME: 30 MINUTES   BAKING TIME: 10 MINUTES

What a combination: chocolate chips AND peanut butter! Kids of all ages like the way these cookies look, with the four chocolate chips in the middle.

¼ cup butter
⅓ cup brown sugar, firmly packed
⅓ cup granulated white sugar
¼ cup Egg Beaters OR 1 egg, beaten
⅓ cup peanut butter
1 tablespoon skim milk
1 tablespoon water
1 teaspoon vanilla extract
1 cup all-purpose flour
¾ cup whole-wheat flour
1 teaspoon baking soda
½ teaspoon salt
3 ounces chocolate chips (about ½ cup)

1. Preheat the oven to 375 degrees.
2. Cream the butter and sugars in a large bowl. Beat in the egg, peanut butter, milk, water, and vanilla.
3. In another bowl, combine the flours, baking soda, and salt. Add gradually to the wet ingredients, mixing well.
4. Form the dough into small balls, about 1 inch in diameter. Place the balls on an ungreased baking sheet, and make a depression in each ball by pressing your thumb in the center. Drop 4 chocolate chips into each ball.
5. Bake for about 10 minutes, until the cookies begin to brown on the bottom.

Makes about 3 dozen cookies, about 1½ inches in diameter.

Per cookie: **4 g. fat**, 79 calories, 8 mg. cholesterol, 1 g. dietary fiber, 76 mg. sodium

German Apple Cake

PREPARATION TIME: 45 MINUTES   BAKING TIME: 50 MINUTES

Many recipes call for a little salt to bring out the flavors of the other ingredients. However, this recipe is delicious with no added salt.

4 medium apples, unpeeled
Juice of 2½ lemons (about 6
  tablespoons)
3 tablespoons butter
  or margarine, softened
¾ cup granulated white sugar
2 eggs, separated
Grated peel of ½ lemon
½ cup whole-wheat flour

1 cup all-purpose flour
1 teaspoon baking powder
¾ cup skim milk
1 tablespoon rum
Nonstick vegetable cooking
  spray
1 teaspoon vegetable oil
2 teaspoons powdered sugar

1. Slice the apples in thin wedges, remove the cores, and place in a bowl. Sprinkle with two-thirds of the lemon juice, and set aside.
2. Cream the butter and sugar together. Then gradually beat in the egg yolks, the remaining lemon juice, and the lemon peel.
3. Sift together the flours and the baking powder in one bowl, and combine the milk and rum in another. Gradually add the dry ingredients to the butter-sugar-egg mixture, alternating with the milk-and-rum mixture.
4. Beat the egg whites until they form stiff peaks. Fold into the batter.
5. Spray a springform pan with cooking spray, or lightly oil it with vegetable oil. Pour in the batter and decorate the top with the sliced apples. Lightly brush the apples with the teaspoon of vegetable oil. Bake at 350 degrees in the center of your oven for about 40 minutes, then move to a higher rack in the oven and bake 10 minutes more to finish cooking the apples.
6. Let cool for a few minutes, then remove from the pan, and sprinkle with powdered sugar. (You can use a sifter to evenly distribute the sugar over the top.)

12 servings.

Per serving: **4 g. fat,** 178 calories, 39 mg. cholesterol, 2 g. dietary fiber, 40 mg. sodium

Peach Cobbler

PREPARATION TIME: 15 MINUTES   BAKING TIME: 30 MINUTES

4 cups sliced peaches, fresh or
  canned, unsweetened,
  drained
2 tablespoons lemon juice
½ cup whole-wheat flour
⅓ cup brown sugar

1 teaspoon cinnamon
2 tablespoons butter
  or margarine
6 tablespoons plain nonfat
  yogurt (optional)
Dash cinnamon (optional)

1. Preheat oven to 375 degrees.
2. Place the peaches in a 9-inch pie pan or shallow casserole
   dish and sprinkle with the lemon juice.
3. In a bowl, blend the dry ingredients. Cut in the butter with
   two knives or a pastry blender, to make a coarse, crumbly
   texture. Spread over the peaches.
4. Bake about 30 minutes.
5. If desired, top each serving with a tablespoon of yogurt and
   a dash of cinnamon.

6 servings. Serving size is about ¾ cup.

Per serving: **4 g.** fat, 173 calories, 11 mg. cholesterol, 4 g. dietary
fiber, 56 mg. sodium

Kahlua Chocolate Cheesecake

PREPARATION TIME: 30 MINUTES   BAKING TIME: 1¼ HOURS

This cheesecake tastes as good as it sounds . . . maybe even
better! And it contains only 9 grams of fat per serving, compared with 24 grams in the regular version.

¾ cup graham cracker crumbs
  (about 9 squares)
1 teaspoon brown sugar
1½ tablespoons melted butter
  or margarine

15 ounces part-skim ricotta
  cheese
16 ounces 1% low-fat cottage
  cheese
¾ cup Egg Beaters OR 3 eggs

⅔ cup cocoa
1 cup white sugar
½ cup firmly packed brown
  sugar
2 tablespoons cornstarch

1 cup light sour cream
1 teaspoon vanilla extract
¼ cup Kahlua or other coffee
  liqueur
Fresh strawberries (optional)

1. Preheat the oven to 350 degrees. Combine the crumbs, the 1 teaspoon of brown sugar, and the melted butter or margarine in a small bowl. Press firmly into the bottom of a 10-inch springform pan. Bake for 10 minutes, then set aside and let cool. Turn oven down to 325 degrees.
2. Whir the ricotta and cottage cheese in a blender or food processor, adding small amounts at a time, until smooth.
3. In a large, separate bowl, blend Egg Beaters with cocoa, both sugars, and cornstarch. Add the cheese mixture to the egg/cocoa mixture, together with the sour cream, vanilla, and Kahlua. Blend well.
4. Pour over the baked crust.
5. Bake for 1 hour and 15 minutes, or until cake sets in the middle. Let cake cool in oven with door slightly ajar for about 2 hours.
6. Chill for at least 4 hours. Release sides of pan and garnish with fresh sliced strawberries if desired.

12 servings.

Per serving (including 12 medium strawberries): **9 g. fat,** 287 calories, 24 mg. cholesterol, 2 g. dietary fiber, 277 mg. sodium

Crêpes with Fresh Strawberries (Julian's)

PREPARATION TIME: 30 MINUTES   COOKING TIME: 15 MINUTES

This recipe uses barley-malt sweetener in place of sugar. You may be able to find it in a well-stocked supermarket; if not, use sugar instead. Try serving this dessert with the Grilled Duck Breast (p. 181).

The crêpes:

1 egg
2 egg whites
1¼ cups skim milk

¼ cup unbleached white flour
1½ teaspoons vanilla extract

The filling:

About 1 to 1¼ cups strawberries to yield ¾ cup fresh strawberry purée (see step 3)

1½ cups 1% low-fat cottage cheese
24 fresh strawberries, sliced in halves

The sauce:

1 cup plain nonfat yogurt
2 tablespoons fresh orange juice
1 teaspoon orange rind
1 teaspoon lemon rind

4 teaspoons honey
A pinch or two of barley-malt sweetener
Fresh mint, if available, for garnish

1. Combine all the crêpe ingredients in a blender and blend for 2 minutes. Set aside, and let the mixture rest for 2 hours.
2. Cook the crêpes in a 5-inch nonstick crêpe pan for 30 seconds each. (The batter yields about 12 crêpes.) Set aside and let cool.
3. Meanwhile, whir enough fresh strawberries in a blender to make ¾ cup of purée. Set aside. Prepare the sauce by combining all ingredients except the mint in a small bowl and mixing well.
4. Spread 2 tablespoons of cottage cheese over half of each cooled crêpe. Add 1 tablespoon of strawberry purée, and

4 strawberry halves. Fold the crêpe in half. Spread about 2 tablespoons of the sauce over and around each crêpe. (When we asked how much sauce the chefs used, the answer was, "About 2 tablespoons—whatever looks good!") Garnish with a sprig of fresh mint.

12 servings. Serving size is 1 crêpe.

Per serving: **1 g. fat,** 91 calories, 18 mg. cholesterol, 2 g. dietary fiber, 158 mg. sodium

Honey-Orange Bran Bread

PREPARATION TIME: 15 MINUTES   BAKING TIME: 50 MINUTES

2 cups all-purpose flour	1 cup All-Bran cereal
1 teaspoon baking powder	½ cup honey
½ teaspoon baking soda	¾ cup orange juice
¾ teaspoon salt	1 egg
¾ teaspoon ground cinnamon	2 tablespoons vegetable oil
¼ teaspoon ground cloves	1 teaspoon grated orange peel

1. In a small mixing bowl, combine the flour, baking powder, baking soda, salt, cinnamon, and cloves. Set aside.
2. In a large mixing bowl, combine the cereal, honey, and orange juice. Let stand for 2 minutes. Beat in the egg, vegetable oil, and orange peel. Add the flour mixture. Stir only until moistened. Spread the batter evenly into a lightly greased 9 × 5 × 3-inch loaf pan.
3. Bake at 350 degrees for 50 minutes, or until a knife inserted in the center comes out clean.

Makes 1 loaf of 16 slices. Serving size is 1 slice.

Per serving: **2 g. fat,** 127 calories, 12 mg. cholesterol, 2 g. dietary fiber, 191 mg. sodium

Almond Drops

PREPARATION TIME: 25 MINUTES   BAKING TIME: 15 MINUTES

Here is an example of a cookie in which we revise the original recipe by blending flours and reducing salt by half and sugar and fat by a third. Try this approach in your own cookie recipes. These cookies are great with a cup of fresh coffee.

1 cup whole-wheat flour
1½ cups all-purpose flour
½ teaspoon baking soda
½ teaspoon salt
⅔ cup granulated white sugar
⅔ cup butter

1 egg
¼ cup skim milk
1 teaspoon almond extract
⅓ cup almonds, chopped or
   slivered

1. Preheat oven to 325 degrees.
2. In a large bowl, sift flours, baking soda, salt, and sugar together. Cut in the butter with a pastry blender or two knives until the mixture looks like fine cornmeal.
3. Lightly beat together the egg and the milk, and add to the above mixture, along with the almond extract and almonds. Mix well, and shape into small balls, about ¾ inch in diameter. Place them on an ungreased baking sheet, and press them down with your hand to flatten them slightly.
4. Bake for about 15 minutes, or until golden brown on the bottom. Cool on a wire rack.

Makes about 4 dozen cookies, about 1 to 1½ inches in diameter.

Per cookie: **3 g. fat,** 63 calories, 11 mg. cholesterol, 1 g. dietary fiber, 59 mg. sodium

Carrot-Nut Tea Bread

PREPARATION TIME: 15 MINUTES   BAKING TIME: 45 TO 55 MINUTES

This is a mildly sweet quick bread.

Nonstick vegetable cooking
  spray
2 eggs
3/4 cup granulated white sugar
1/4 cup vegetable oil
1/3 cup water
1 cup whole-wheat flour
1/2 cup all-purpose flour

1 teaspoon baking soda
1 teaspoon baking powder
1 teaspoon salt
1 teaspoon cinnamon
1 cup grated carrots (about 3
  medium)
1/4 cup chopped nuts

1. Preheat the oven to 375 degrees. Spray a 9 × 5 × 3-inch loaf pan with cooking spray and set aside.
2. Beat together the eggs, sugar, oil, and water.
3. In another bowl, combine the flours, baking soda, baking powder, salt, and cinnamon. Add the dry ingredients to the liquid ingredients.
4. Stir in the grated carrots and the chopped nuts. Pour the batter into the pan.
5. Bake for 45 to 55 minutes, testing for doneness by inserting a knife or toothpick into the center of the loaf to see if it comes out clean. The top should be evenly browned when done.

12 servings. Serving size is 1 slice about 3/4 inch thick.

Per serving: **7 g. fat,** 173 calories, 31 mg. cholesterol, 2 g. dietary fiber, 260 mg. sodium

Oatmeal Pecan Cookies

PREPARATION TIME: 10 MINUTES   BAKING TIME: 12 TO 15 MINUTES

We mixed this dough in a matter of minutes one night. A slightly crumbly and crisp cookie.

½ cup vegetable oil
½ cup brown sugar, firmly
   packed
¾ cup granulated white sugar
1 egg
¼ cup water
1 teaspoon vanilla extract

1 teaspoon rum (optional)
3 cups rolled oats
¾ cup whole-wheat flour
½ teaspoon baking soda
¼ cup chopped pecans
   or other nuts

1. Combine oil, sugars, egg, water, vanilla, and rum in a large bowl, blending well. (A fork works fine for this.)
2. Stir in the remaining ingredients.
3. Drop by rounded teaspoonfuls onto an ungreased baking sheet, and bake at 350 degrees for about 12 to 15 minutes.

Makes approximately 3 dozen cookies, about 2 inches in diameter.

Per cookie: **4 g. fat,** 92 calories, 5 mg. cholesterol, 1 g. dietary fiber, 14 mg. sodium

Lemon-Lime Coconut Pie

PREPARATION TIME: 40 MINUTES   REFRIGERATION TIME: 1 HOUR

1 tablespoon butter
   or margarine
1¼ cups flaked coconut
1 tablespoon fresh lemon juice
5 tablespoons fresh lime juice
Water
1 envelope unflavored gelatin

⅓ cup granulated white sugar
½ teaspoon vanilla extract
1 tablespoon grated lime rind
   (about 2 limes)
2 cups plain nonfat yogurt
1 teaspoon grated lemon rind

1. Preheat the oven to 325 degrees. Put the butter or margarine in a 9-inch pie plate, place the plate in the oven, and melt the butter.

2. Remove the plate from the oven, add the coconut, and mix with the butter to coat. Press the coconut onto the bottom of the plate (it will not stick to the sides), return to the oven, and bake for 15 minutes, or until slightly brown. Let cool.

3. Meanwhile, combine the lemon and lime juices in a measuring cup. Add enough water to make ¾ cup, then pour the liquid into a saucepan. Pour in the gelatin, and let stand for a few minutes to soften. Add the sugar, and cook the mixture over low heat until the gelatin and sugar are dissolved, stirring constantly.

4. Remove the pan from the heat, stir in the vanilla and the lime rind, and let cool for about 10 minutes. Then place in the refrigerator or freezer until partially set, about 10 more minutes. It will reach the consistency of raw, unbeaten egg whites.

5. Beat the gelatin mixture with an eggbeater or electric mixer, until fluffy. Fold in the yogurt, and beat the mixture again until smooth. Pour into the cooled crust, sprinkle with the lemon rind, and chill the pie in the refrigerator for at least 1 hour, until firm.

8 servings.

Per serving: **6 g. fat**, 130 calories, 5 mg. cholesterol, 1 g. dietary fiber, 66 mg. sodium

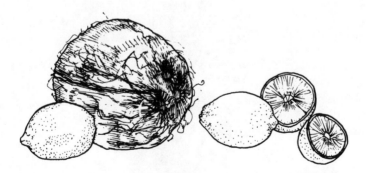

Pineapple Ice

PREPARATION TIME: 10 MINUTES   FREEZING TIME: 3 HOURS

This recipe is "easier than pie"—and has a lot fewer calories. It's also refreshing when frozen into ice cubes and served in beverages.

1 large, ripe pineapple, cut up   2 to 4 tablespoons honey
2 teaspoons lemon juice   (optional)

1. Place the pineapple chunks and the lemon juice (and the honey, if the pineapple doesn't seem very sweet) in a blender or food processor. Purée until smooth.
2. Pour into a plastic container or ice-cube trays, and freeze for about 1 hour.
3. When mixture is slushy-frozen, purée again in the blender until creamy. Pour it back into your freezer containers, and freeze at least 2 hours more.

6 to 8 servings, depending on the size of the pineapple. Serving size is about ½ cup.

Per serving (8): **no fat,** 54 calories, no cholesterol, 1 g. dietary fiber, 1 mg. sodium

Mandelbrot (Almond Bread)

PREPARATION TIME: 25 MINUTES   BAKING TIME: 35 TO 45 MINUTES

Actually, this is not a bread, but cookies that are first baked in a loaf form, and then cut into slices or bars, and baked again. A traditional Jewish recipe, modified for lower fat and sugar content, this is another winner with a good cup of fresh-ground coffee.

3/4 **cup butter, softened to room temperature**
3/4 **cup granulated white sugar**
4 **eggs**
1 **teaspoon vanilla extract**

1 1/2 **teaspoons ground cinnamon**
2 **cups whole-wheat flour**
2 **cups all-purpose flour**
1 **teaspoon baking powder**
1/2 **cup chopped almonds**

1. In a large bowl, cream together the butter and the sugar. Beat in the eggs, vanilla, and cinnamon.
2. In another bowl, combine the flours and baking powder. Add to the wet ingredients, mixing well. Stir in the almonds.
3. Form the dough into a long loaf about 1 inch high and 4 inches wide.
4. Place on an ungreased baking sheet, and bake at 375 degrees until browned on the bottom, about 25 minutes.
5. Remove the bread from the oven, place it on a cutting board, and cut it into 26 1/2-inch-thick slices. Arrange the slices on the baking sheet, and bake until toasted on one side. Turn them over, and toast the other side. Cool on a wire rack.

Makes about 26 cookies, about 3 × 1 1/2 inches.

Per cookie: **8 g. fat,** 161 calories, 43 mg. cholesterol, 2 g. dietary fiber, 64 mg. sodium

Old-Fashioned Blueberry Betty

PREPARATION TIME: 12 TO 15 MINUTES   BAKING TIME: 30 MINUTES

One of our taste-testers' favorites! Use a metal pan for this recipe, as the blueberries may stain white porcelain or stoneware casserole dishes.

2 cups blueberries, fresh or
  frozen (thawed)
¼ cup granulated white sugar
Juice of 1 lemon
4 cups whole-wheat bread
  cubes, about ½ inch square

⅓ cup firmly packed brown
  sugar
1 teaspoon ground cinnamon

1. In a large bowl, combine the blueberries, white sugar, and lemon juice. In another bowl, combine the bread cubes, brown sugar, and cinnamon.
2. Fill an 8- or 9-inch-square metal baking pan by alternating the two mixtures, starting with half the blueberries, then half the bread cubes, and so on.
3. Bake at 350 degrees for about 30 minutes.

8 servings. Serving size is about ¾ cup.

Per serving: **1 g. fat**, 144 calories, no cholesterol, 3 g. dietary fiber, 166 mg. sodium

Cookie-Crust Fruit "Pizza"

PREPARATION TIME: 35 MINUTES   BAKING TIME: 10 MINUTES

A thick cookie crust is made attractive with a creamy topping and a stunning arrangement of colorful fresh fruit. You can prepare the crust ahead of time, since it needs to be refrigerated for several hours. Once the fruit is cut up, it tends to begin turning brown, so the "pizza" is at its best served the same day, although the cut-up fruit will keep in a bowl of water mixed with about a tablespoon of lemon juice. Then put the fruit on the crust just before serving.

This is a great recipe for kids because it looks so good and it's fun to eat.

The crust:

3/4 cup confectioners' sugar
1/2 cup soft margarine (light variety)
3 tablespoons skim milk
1 teaspoon vanilla extract

1/2 teaspoon almond extract
1 cup whole-wheat flour
3/4 cup all-purpose flour
1/2 teaspoon cream of tartar
1/2 teaspoon baking soda

The topping:

6 ounces Neufchâtel cheese, softened
1/2 teaspoon vanilla extract
2 tablespoons sugar or honey

Mixed fresh fruit of choice (e.g., 1 cup pineapple chunks, 2 kiwi fruit, 1 sliced banana, 1/2 cup fresh strawberries, 4 ounces Mandarin oranges)

1. For the crust, cream the sugar and margarine together until fluffy. Add the milk and extracts.
2. In another bowl, sift the dry ingredients and add to the creamed mixture until well blended. Cover and refrigerate for 4 to 6 hours.
3. Press the dough into a 12- or 13-inch pizza pan, or use a similar-sized square pan if necessary. Press the edges of the dough slightly upward to resemble a pizza crust.
4. Bake at 375 degrees for about 10 minutes, or until golden.
5. Meanwhile, prepare the topping by creaming together the Neufchâtel, vanilla, and sugar or honey.
6. Let the crust cool, and spread the topping over it.
7. Slice your favorite fruits into bite-sized pieces, and decorate the pizza with fruit in any pattern you like. Use your imagination! Besides our favorite combination given above, we've also used grapes, peaches, or other berries in season.

12 servings. Serving size is 1/12 pizza.

Per serving (using the selection of fruits suggested above): **8 g. fat,** 204 calories, 13 mg. cholesterol, 2 g. dietary fiber, 130 mg. sodium

Sweet Pineapple Squares

PREPARATION TIME: 20 MINUTES | BAKING TIME: 40 MINUTES

¾ cup whole-wheat flour
¼ cup low-fat soy flour
¾ cup all-purpose flour
2 teaspoons baking powder
½ teaspoon salt
2 tablespoons brown sugar
1 egg

⅓ cup honey
3 tablespoons vegetable oil
1 can (16 ounces) crushed
   unsweetened pineapple, plus
   juice
Nonstick vegetable cooking
   spray

1. In a large bowl, sift together the dry ingredients.
2. In another bowl, beat the egg, then beat in the honey and the oil.
3. Drain the pineapple carefully to get ⅔ cup of juice. Add the juice to the egg-honey-oil mixture. Blend mixture into the dry ingredients.
4. Spray an 8-inch-square baking pan with nonstick vegetable cooking spray. Spread the batter in the pan, and top with the pineapple. Bake at 350 degrees for about 40 minutes.

12 servings of about 2 × 2⅔ inches.

Per serving: **4 g. fat**, 153 calories, 16 mg. cholesterol, 1 g. dietary fiber, 96 mg. sodium

Curried Fruit Compote

PREPARATION TIME: 10 MINUTES | COOKING TIME: 1 HOUR AND 20 MINUTES

This is a "day-before" recipe. It's best after it has been baked, chilled overnight in the refrigerator, and reheated, as directed. It's also good cold, so you may find it mysteriously disappearing from your refrigerator before you have a chance to reheat it.

You may use 2 teaspoons of a commercially prepared curry

powder, of course, but we highly recommend making the investment in the various spices and mixing your own. Try the special blend we've selected, and see how you like it. Once you discover the difference between this and the commercial blends, you may end up always preparing your own, as we do.

1 can (16 ounces) unsweetened peach slices

1 can (16 ounces) unsweetened pear halves

1 can (17 ounces) unsweetened apricot halves

1 can (16 ounces) unsweetened pitted dark cherries

1 can (15½ ounces) unsweetened pineapple chunks

½ cup sliced almonds

½ cup firmly packed brown sugar

½ teaspoon ground cinnamon

½ teaspoon ground coriander

¼ teaspoon ground cardamom

¼ teaspoon ground ginger

¼ teaspoon cumin

⅛ teaspoon turmeric

⅛ teaspoon cayenne pepper

¼ cup melted butter or margarine

1. Drain all liquid from each can of fruit. Pour the fruit into a 9 × 13-inch baking dish, and stir. Top with the almonds.
2. In a small bowl, combine the brown sugar, spices, and melted butter. Sprinkle this mixture over the fruit.
3. Bake at 350 degrees for 1 hour. Let cool at room temperature, then refrigerate overnight. Twenty minutes before serving, reheat at 350 degrees, until bubbly.

16 servings. Serving size is about ½ cup.

Per serving: **4 g. fat,** 133 calories, 8 mg. cholesterol, 3 g. dietary fiber, 36 mg. sodium

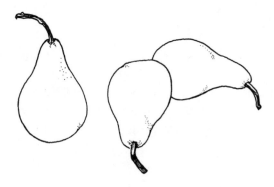

Lemon Pudding

PREPARATION TIME: 20 MINUTES   COOKING TIME: 25 TO 30 MINUTES

1 cup granulated white sugar
2 tablespoons butter
  or margarine, softened
Grated rind of 2 lemons
4 tablespoons lemon juice

4 tablespoons whole-wheat
  flour
4 medium eggs, separated
Nonstick vegetable cooking
  spray

1. Cream together the sugar and butter. Add the lemon rind, lemon juice, flour, and egg yolks, blending well.
2. Beat the egg whites until stiff, and fold into the batter.
3. Spray an 8 × 8-inch baking dish or 8 pudding dishes with nonstick cooking spray, and pour the batter in. Place in a larger ovenproof baking dish that has about 1 inch of hot water in it.
4. Bake at 350 degrees for 25 to 30 minutes (15 to 20 minutes if the individual serving dishes are used), or until set and slightly browned on top.

VARIATION: Substitute the grated rind of one orange for the lemon rind, and 4 tablespoons of orange juice for the lemon juice.

8 servings. Serving size is about ½ cup.

Per serving: **5 g. fat,** 170 calories, 101 mg. cholesterol, 1 g. dietary fiber, 58 mg. sodium

Bread Pudding

PREPARATION TIME: 20 MINUTES   BAKING TIME: 40 MINUTES

Bread pudding has always been a favorite in the Katahn family, along with noodle pudding. As a child, when I was really yearning for a sweet topping, I added a bit of New York State or Vermont maple syrup. I occasionally still do this. And, to be honest, nothing quite compares with maple syrup on bread or noodle pudding, perhaps because of the childhood memories it conjures.

You can top this version in a satisfying and healthful way with fresh fruit, unsweetened applesauce, or a dollop of nonfat plain yogurt mixed with a dash of cinnamon. This is a truly lean bread pudding (Grandma's had PLENTY of butter in it), so if it tastes a bit austere with skim milk, don't abandon the basic recipe, but use low-fat milk on the second go-round. Also, notice that this is, in reality, a combination bread-and-fruit pudding. As usual, we use whole-wheat bread, which adds both a nutty flavor and a form of dietary fiber with a different nutritional effect from the fiber in the fruit.

3 cups skim milk	½ teaspoon salt
3 eggs	Dash of ground ginger
3 tablespoons honey	Dash of mace
2 tablespoons brown sugar	4 cups coarsely crumbled stale
Juice of ½ lemon	whole-grain bread (8–9 slices)
2 teaspoons vanilla extract	1½ cups chopped apple
1 teaspoon cinnamon	¼ cup raisins

1. Beat together the milk, eggs, honey, brown sugar, lemon juice, vanilla, cinnamon, salt, ginger, and mace.
2. In a 9 × 13-inch baking pan, combine the bread crumbs, apple, and raisins. Pour the milk mixture over the crumb mixture, stirring well.
3. Bake at 350 degrees for 40 minutes. Serve hot or cold.

12 servings. Serving size is about ¾ cup.

Per serving (without topping): **2 g. fat,** 140 calories, 48 mg. cholesterol, 3 g. dietary fiber, 264 mg. sodium

Cocoa Zucchini Cake

PREPARATION TIME: 20 TO 25 MINUTES   BAKING TIME: ¾ TO 1 HOUR

This cake is moist, lightly sweet, with a satisfying, rich texture.

1¼ cups granulated white
   sugar
⅓ cup vegetable oil
1 teaspoon vanilla extract
1 egg
2 egg whites
⅔ cup low-fat milk
1 teaspoon baking soda
1 cup all-purpose flour

1½ cups whole-wheat flour
¼ cup cocoa powder
½ teaspoon cinnamon
½ teaspoon salt
2 cups grated zucchini,
   unpeeled (about 1½
   squashes)
Nonstick vegetable cooking
   spray or oil

1. Combine first 6 ingredients in a large bowl.
2. In another bowl, sift together the dry ingredients, and add alternately with the zucchini to the first mixture.
3. Bake at 350 degrees for 1 hour in a lightly oiled bundt pan, or bake 45 minutes in a 9 × 13-inch pan. Remove from oven when a toothpick inserted in the center of the cake comes out clean. Let stand 5 to 10 minutes before removing from pan.

24 servings.

Per serving: **4 g. fat,** 122 calories, 8 mg. cholesterol, 2 g. dietary fiber, 90 mg. sodium

Orange-Almond Ambrosia

PREPARATION TIME: 25 TO 30 MINUTES

4 tablespoons crushed almonds,
   toasted
2 fresh navel oranges
¼ cup honey

6 tablespoons favorite cold
   cereal, crushed (e.g., bran
   flakes, Mueslix)

1. To toast the almonds: Spread them on a baking sheet and place in a 350-degree oven for 5 to 6 minutes.
2. Peel and section the oranges.
3. Place the honey in a small bowl. In another small bowl, combine the cereal and toasted almonds.
4. Brush each orange section with honey, using a pastry brush, then lightly roll each section in the cereal-nut mixture. Arrange on a serving dish or individual plates.

4 servings. Serving size is ½ orange.

Per serving: **3 g. fat,** 142 calories, no cholesterol, 3 g. dietary fiber, 30 mg. sodium

Date Bars

PREPARATION TIME: 15 MINUTES   BAKING TIME: 30 MINUTES

1 cup all-purpose flour
1½ teaspoons baking powder
¾ cup chopped dates
½ cup boiling water
¼ cup butter, softened

1 teaspoon vanilla extract
1 egg, slightly beaten
⅓ cup orange juice
1½ cups All-Bran cereal
¼ cup chopped nuts

1. In a small mixing bowl, stir together the flour and baking powder. Set aside.
2. Stir together the dates and the boiling water. Set aside.
3. In a large mixing bowl, combine the butter, vanilla, and egg. Beat well. Alternately add the flour mixture and the orange juice. Mix well. Fold in the dates, cereal, and nuts. Spread the mixture evenly in a lightly greased 8 × 8 × 2-inch baking pan.
4. Bake at 350 degrees for about 30 minutes or until a wooden toothpick inserted in the center comes out clean. Cool in the pan; cut into 24 bars.

24 servings of about 1⅓ × 2 inches.

Per serving: **3 g. fat,** 78 calories, 13 mg. cholesterol, 3 g. dietary fiber, 83 mg. sodium

Chewy Raisin Bars

PREPARATION TIME: 15 MINUTES   STANDING TIME: ABOUT 1 HOUR

2 cups All-Bran cereal   ½ cup honey
⅔ cup raisins   ¼ cup peanut butter
½ cup chopped nuts   1 teaspoon vanilla extract
1 tablespoon butter   ½ teaspoon ground cinnamon

1. Stir together the cereal, raisins, and nuts. Set aside.
2. In a large saucepan, combine the butter, honey, and peanut butter. Stir over medium heat until the mixture is well blended. Remove from heat. Stir in the remaining ingredients.
3. Press the mixture into a lightly greased 9 × 9 × 2-inch pan. Let cool. Cut into 20 bars when cooled. Store covered in the refrigerator.

MICROWAVE INSTRUCTIONS: In a large glass mixing bowl, combine the butter, honey, and peanut butter. Cover loosely with wax paper or microwave-safe plastic wrap. Microwave on full power for about 2 minutes until the mixture is well blended. Stir in the remaining ingredients. Press the mixture into a lightly greased 9 × 9 × 2-inch pan. Cut into bars when cooled. Store in the refrigerator.

20 servings of about 2¼ × 2 inches.

Per serving: **4 g. fat,** 106 calories, 2 mg. cholesterol, 4 g. dietary fiber, 119 mg. sodium

Orange-Chocolate Pudding

PREPARATION TIME: 25 MINUTES   REFRIGERATION TIME: 2 HOURS

4 ounces semisweet chocolate   1¾ cups skim milk
  (squares or chips)   3 tablespoons cornstarch
3 tablespoons brown sugar,   ¼ cup orange juice
  packed

1. Combine the chocolate, sugar, and milk in a large sauce-pan. Heat slowly over medium heat, stirring constantly (preferably with a wire whisk, if you have one; otherwise use a spoon), until chocolate is melted and milk is just beginning to scald, not boil.
2. Measure the cornstarch into a bowl, and pour in about ⅓ of the hot chocolate mixture. Whisk vigorously until the cornstarch is dissolved, then whisk back into remaining hot chocolate mixture in the saucepan.
3. Cook over very low heat for about 8 more minutes, stirring constantly. As the pudding thickens, you may need to switch to stirring with a spoon (if you've been using a whisk).
4. When the pudding is thick, remove from heat and stir in the orange juice. Pour into a serving bowl or individual pudding cups. Chill for at least 2 hours, and serve.

VARIATIONS: Use 2 cups of skim milk and add ½ teaspoon of almond extract in place of the orange juice for Chocolate-Almond Pudding. Garnish each serving with a teaspoon of toasted almonds if desired. For Mocha Pudding, use vanilla extract instead of almond, and add a couple teaspoons of strongly brewed coffee.

4 servings. Serving size is about ½ cup.

Per serving: **9 g. fat,** 228 calories, 2 mg. cholesterol, 2 g. dietary fiber, 62 mg. sodium

Poppy-Seed Cake

PREPARATION TIME: 20 MINUTES   BAKING TIME: 45 MINUTES

Believe it or not, we often come up with a recipe that works perfectly the first time we try it! This confection had all our taste-testers smiling (mouths full) right away.

Nonstick vegetable cooking
  spray
Whole-wheat flour
¼ cup vegetable oil
¾ cup granulated white sugar
2 eggs, separated

1 teaspoon vanilla extract
1 cup whole-wheat flour
½ teaspoon salt
½ teaspoon baking soda
¾ cup plain nonfat yogurt
⅓ cup poppy seeds

1. Spray an 8-inch tube pan with nonstick vegetable cooking spray, and dust lightly with whole-wheat flour.
2. Blend the oil and sugar in a large bowl. Add the egg yolks one at a time, beating well. Add the vanilla.
3. In another bowl, sift together the flour, salt, and baking soda. Alternately fold the flour mixture and the yogurt into the oil-and-sugar mixture. Set aside.
4. Beat the egg whites until stiff. Fold into the batter. Fold in the poppy seeds. Pour the batter into the pan.
5. Bake at 350 degrees for about 45 minutes, until top is nicely brown, and a toothpick inserted in the center comes out clean.

20 servings. Serving size is 1 slice about ⅜ inch thick.

Per serving: **4 g. fat,** 98 calories, 19 mg. cholesterol, 1 g. dietary fiber, 87 mg. sodium

Gingersnaps

PREPARATION TIME: 20 MINUTES   BAKING TIME: 10 TO 12 MINUTES

Compared with chocolate-chip cookies, gingersnaps generally run a poor second in popularity. Not these! They disappeared first, even in this low-fat version, in all our tasting sessions.

¼ cup vegetable oil
½ cup granulated white sugar
¼ cup brown sugar, firmly packed
¼ cup light molasses
½ cup Egg Beaters OR 2 eggs, well beaten

1½ cups all-purpose flour
½ cup whole-wheat flour
¼ teaspoon salt
2 teaspoons baking soda
1 teaspoon cinnamon
1 teaspoon ground cloves
1 teaspoon ground ginger

1. Preheat the oven to 350 degrees.
2. In a large mixing bowl, combine the oil, sugars, and molasses. Beat in the eggs.
3. In another bowl, combine the flours, salt, baking soda, and spices. Stir into the wet ingredients, mixing well.
4. Drop by the rounded teaspoonful about 2 inches apart on ungreased baking sheets. Bake for about 10 to 12 minutes.

Makes 3 dozen cookies, about 2 inches in diameter.

Per cookie: **2 g. fat,** 63 calories, no cholesterol, no dietary fiber, 67 mg. sodium

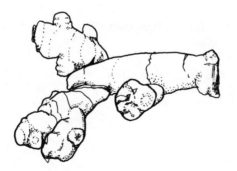

Whole-Grain Goody

PREPARATION TIME: 20 MINUTES   BAKING TIME: 25 TO 30 MINUTES

This has a nutty flavor and a chewy texture because of the rolled oats. It goes almost too well with a glass of milk.

3 eggs OR ¾ cup Egg Beaters
¼ cup firmly packed brown sugar
¼ cup molasses
1 cup rolled oats
1 cup whole-wheat flour
½ teaspoon baking powder
Grated rind of 1 orange
Juice of ½ orange

1 teaspoon vanilla extract
1 teaspoon rum
½ cup buttermilk
2 tablespoons melted butter or margarine
½ cup raisins
Nonstick vegetable cooking spray

1. Beat the eggs with the sugar and molasses until smooth.
2. In another bowl, combine the oats, flour, and baking powder.
3. Add the orange rind and orange juice, the vanilla and the rum, and mix well. Stir in the buttermilk, butter, and raisins. Add to the egg-sugar mixture, blending well.
4. Pour into a 9-inch pie tin that has been sprayed with nonstick vegetable cooking spray, or greased very lightly with oil.
5. Bake at 375 degrees for 25 to 30 minutes, until set.

12 servings.

Per serving: **4 g. fat**, 149 calories, 52 mg. cholesterol, 2 g. dietary fiber, 50 mg. sodium

Per serving (with Egg Beaters): **3 g. fat**, 141 calories, 6 mg. cholesterol, 2 g. dietary fiber, 63 mg. sodium

Using the Low-Fat Good Food Cookbook for Weight Loss

In two of my earlier books, *The T-Factor Diet* and *One Meal at a Time*, I presented the scientific background that explains why the primary culprit in obesity is almost always **too much fat in the diet** and that the primary nutritional factor in heart disease and some forms of cancer is, once again, **too much fat in the diet.**

Since publishing these books, several more scientific studies have appeared showing that almost all overweight persons will lose body fat simply by cutting the fat in their diets. Except in very resistant cases with a metabolic basis, or for those persons who insist on outeating their energy needs continually on carbohydrate foods, there is really no need to count calories. First, find out where the fat is in your favorite recipes and learn to cut what you can, as I show in this cookbook. Second, when it comes to processed foods, find acceptable substitutes (for example, frozen yogurt for ice cream, bagels for croissants).

The average daily target for fat intake for women who want to lose weight is 20 to 40 grams; for men, 30 to 60 grams. When you reach maintenance, women can increase to about 50 grams of fat, but men don't really need more than 60 grams for good health. Whatever extra calories you need to maintain your weight come best from carbohydrate foods: fruits, vegetables, and whole grains. (Do not get so enthusiastic with the results that you go below 20 grams of fat a day. You need fat in your diet, and too little will interfere with the metabolism of other nutrients and result in such symptoms as dry skin, cracked lips, and poor hair texture.)

So, learn where the fat is in your foods. If you don't know, use *The T-Factor Fat Gram Counter* (published by W. W. Norton and Co., and available at your local bookstore) to find out. Then, replace high-fat cuts of meat with lean cuts, choose low-fat or nonfat dairy products, and replace your high-fat desserts and snacks with similar low-fat foods.

One of the nicest things about this approach is that once you learn where the fat is in your diet, discover low-fat substitutes, and use these substitutes about 80 to 90 percent of the time, you can stop counting everything, including fat grams as well as calories, once and for all. Low-fat choices will become automatic and your diet will become second nature.

Another nice thing about this approach is that *you don't have to be absolutely perfect!* This is especially true if you follow the advice on physical activity in the next chapter. You can indulge on occasion, but remember, you must eat a low-fat diet at least 80 to 90 percent of the time.

And I must give you *another word of warning.* **You cannot go overboard on carbohydrate foods.** I have several letters from people saying that they followed my recommendations with respect to fat, but didn't lose weight. They sent eating records and asked me why. I looked at these records, and you won't believe what I found. One man had added over two loaves of bread a day to his low-fat diet to replace the pastries he used to eat; a woman was eating two family-size bags of pretzels in place of potato chips; another woman was eating six bags of jelly beans in place of chocolate candy. Yes, these are great low-fat substitutions for high-fat foods, but you cannot outeat your energy needs like this and expect to lose weight. The man, who was almost 100 pounds overweight, had added over 2500 extra calories in bread to his diet, and each of the women had added about 1200 extra calories in carbohydrates. This great amount of excess calories added to their otherwise sound low-fat diets was way beyond what they could burn off with their modest levels of physical activity.

As my grandmother told me when I was a little boy, "Moderation in all things is the key to the good life." Even good things can become harmful if you overdo them.

An Activity Program to Let You Have Your Cake and Eat It, Too

I simply could not imagine writing a book that had anything to do with health and weight management and failing to discuss the importance of physical activity. So, here you have it: a cookbook that has recipes for physical activity as well as for the dinner table!

You may wonder why I include such a chapter after claiming in my preface that too much fat in the diet is the primary nutritional culprit in obesity. So, let me give you some background.

YES! If you are an overweight person you are likely to lose at least some body fat automatically when you adopt the approach to preparing food that we have shown you in this cookbook, and cut the fat in your diet. This occurs for two reasons.

First, dietary fat is much more easily converted to body fat than is carbohydrate. The body has to work harder (burn more calories) to metabolize carbohydrate, so, if you cut the fat and eat more carbohydrate foods, not as many carbohydrate calories end up being available for fat storage. For example, about 97 out of 100 fat calories can end up in your fat cells, but only about 75 out of 100 carbohydrate calories can end up there, the rest being wasted (burned off) in the metabolic processes that convert the carbohydrate to fat.

Second, most people cannot eat as many calories in carbohydrate foods (fruits, vegetables, and grains) as they can in fatty foods (pastries, candy, fatty snacks such as potato chips). For example, a regular-size croissant contains 15 grams of fat and around 225 calories, while a bagel *weighing three times as much* contains only 1 gram of fat and 165 calories.

BUT—if you are a *sedentary* overweight person, I don't believe it will be possible for you to *sustain* a significant weight loss and maintain desirable weight unless you are willing to change your ways and become active.

Without additional physical activity, no matter what style of cooking you choose, you will have to deprive yourself forever and ever of most of the really good-tasting things you can put on your table.

The human body was *not* designed for sedentary living! From the beginning of our existence on this planet up until the invention of the automobile and the availability of electricity in our homes, the average person had to move the energy equivalent of seven to eight miles of walking every day, *just to get the job of living done.* Today we can get by with a mile or two, and, compared with life just 100 years ago, that's an energy expenditure difference of several hundred calories each day!

Our appetites for fat and sugar, however, have not diminished to compensate for our decrease in physical activity! Quite the contrary: For many of us, when there is little physical work to do, appetites seem to increase. If anything, high-calorie foods are more available to more people in the United States now than have ever been available to large numbers of persons in the history of humankind.

Thus, we have an epidemic of *overnutrition*—OBESITY—as *the* major nutrition problem in this country. Fortunately, the problem has a solution.

In order to match appetite and energy expenditure, to put them in sync, the average sedentary person needs to add *at least* 45 minutes of some sort of brisk physical activity to his or her daily routine. In about 45 minutes of brisk walking, a person who weighs about 150 pounds will burn about 200 calories over and above the calories required to just sit still; if you weigh more than 150 pounds, you burn more in physical activity; if you weigh less, you burn less.

THAT 200 CALORIES IS VERY IMPORTANT FOR WEIGHT MAINTENANCE. That's because it takes about 200 calories a day to keep around 40 to 50 pounds of fat alive in the human body. Fat is relatively inactive tissue and only about 200 calories of your total daily food intake will be used to keep 40 to 50 pounds alive, on the average. I cannot be more exact in this average estimation because there is a great deal of metabolic variability. At the extremes, some people may need only 100 calories a day to maintain 40 to 50 pounds of excess fat, while others may need 300; metabolic needs really do vary by that amount.

Let's assume you have lost extra pounds. The key to weight maintenance, without deprivation at the dinner table, is to exercise enough EACH DAY to burn up the same number of calories it used to take to keep you fat! It's simple arithmetic: If you were 40 to 50 pounds overweight and are now at desirable weight and want to stay that way, exercise 200 calories' worth every day. IF YOU DON'T, THE FAT WILL CREEP RIGHT BACK ON AGAIN, ON THE AVERAGE OF 200 CALORIES' WORTH EVERY DAY. That's an average of about 2 pounds a month. It means that sometime within the next year or two, all the weight you struggled to lose will be right back on again, unless you restrict yourself to an extremely low food intake for the rest of your life—and who can do that? And who would *want* to?

Physically active people can eat like normal human beings.* Yes, there is room for dessert every day, especially if you make it one of the healthier, less fatty desserts included in that chapter of the book. I know I am being repetitious, but if it helps just one person who has lost a significant amount of weight to stay motivated, it's worth warning you once again: If you do not become active and stay active, YOU ARE GOING TO GET FAT ALL OVER AGAIN.

---

*Women of about 128 pounds who follow my recommendations for physical activity will require an average of about 1800–2000 calories per day to maintain their weight. Men at about 154 pounds will require an average of around 2400 calories. Heavier people will need more, lighter people less.

End of lecture. Time now for a few words of encouragement and a little practical advice.

The best activities for weight management, as well as for cardiovascular health, are those in which you continuously move your whole body through space, or those which move the large muscle groups in your thighs and buttocks. Walking, bicycling, swimming, and rowing (in a boat, or with a machine using your legs as well as your arms) are at the top of the list. I don't recommend jogging for overweight persons because of the risk of injury. Bouncing on a minitrampoline is fine, but be careful not to become too vigorous until your legs become accustomed to this type of exercise. The same goes for stair climbers and step aerobics.

You get the best effects, while assuring cardiovascular and pulmonary conditioning as well as safety, when you exercise within what is called your **target** or **training range**. This range is determined to be between 60 and 85 percent of your maximum heart rate. For most persons, maximum heart rate will be about 220 minus their age. For example, the average maximum speed that the heart is capable of beating is about 180 beats per minute at maximum exertion for persons 40 years old.

To determine your own target heart rate for physical activity, subtract your age from 220. Then multiply that figure first by .60 to get the bottom of the range, and then by .85 to get the top. Thus, for a person of 40 years, the range will be .60 × 180, or 108 beats per minute, to .85 × 180, or 153 beats per minute at the maximum. When that person goes for a *brisk* walk, swim, or other aerobic activity, he or she should strive to keep the heartbeat between 108 and 153 beats per minute.*

To find your pulse and determine your heart rate (pulse and heart rate are almost invariably the same), place the first two fingers of one hand on the inside of the other wrist, along a vein leading back from the thumb. Only light pressure is required

---

*These calculations lead to rough estimates only. We suggest you go to a reputable fitness center, such as your local YMCA or YWCA, for accurate testing. The Y's will also offer you professional supervision in your fitness program.

to detect the pulse. Count the beats for 10 seconds, and then multiply by six to get the rate in beats per minute.

Most experts feel that you can improve cardiovascular endurance by exercising within your target range a minimum of three times a week, for 20 minutes at a time. You should warm up for at least 5 minutes before working up into that range, and cool down afterwards for about 5 minutes before stopping, by walking or doing some other exercises less vigorously. A few minutes of gentle stretching exercises in addition may help to prevent injury, especially if you tend to be tight in the joints.

However, weight management requires more than cardiovascular conditioning in terms of time and frequency, as I have said. While it is important for cardiovascular health that you exercise within the target range at least three times a week, it is quite acceptable for weight control that you exercise on other days as well, at the bottom of that range or even below, for comfort.

THE FIRST RULE OF PHYSICAL ACTIVITY IS TO GO AS VIGOROUSLY AS YOU CAN *WITHOUT HURTING YOURSELF.*

We advise people who are sedentary to start slowly and increase gradually. Aim for 15 minutes a day during your first week, increase gradually toward a goal of 30 minutes a day the second week, and end up at 45 minutes a day by the third week. Taking a day off is, of course, in order, if you don't feel well or have overexerted on a previous day!

It may seem strange to you that we suggest you check with your doctor before doing something so simple as going out for a walk, BUT WE DO! We do because we want you to get as vigorous as you can *without hurting yourself.* Sedentary, overweight persons should check with their doctors before going on any diet or starting any activity program. Obesity is related to a number of physical illnesses, some of which may be undetected unless you have had a recent physical. These include heart disease and hypertension, as well as diabetes. Although physical activity can be helpful in dealing with these illnesses, their presence, as well as the presence of a number of other physical problems (arthritis, kidney disease, other circulatory problems), will require a physician's supervision as you become more active.

It seems best from both a physical and a psychological standpoint to exercise for at least 30 minutes at a time. That amount of activity may stimulate your metabolism to burn a few more calories around the clock, and it seems to be the amount of time required in order to feel truly relaxed and refreshed.

However, don't be concerned: You can break up your activity to fit your schedule and still get at least 98 percent of all its benefits. Just get up out of your chair 5 minutes on the hour each hour during the workday and climb a flight of stairs or two and walk the hallways as vigorously as you can without causing chaos! You will end up burning close to the extra 200 calories a day that helps guarantee weight maintenance. Plus, the break will refresh you and you will probably be more productive during the rest of the hour.

Time of day for physical activity has little practical meaning, although some research suggests you may burn a few more calories exercising between four and eight o'clock when the metabolic rate tends to be a bit higher for most people. If you exercise in the morning, you will be more alert and ready for productive work; if you exercise late in the afternoon, you will be relaxed and refreshed at night, and you'll probably sleep better, *unless* you have overexerted. Indeed, just about everyone who completes the workday feeling tired, and perhaps irritable, reports feeling incredibly better after some exercise. (And their spouses and friends report that they are much easier to live with, too!)

Physical activity may not feel good at first if you are overweight or out of shape. Terri and I have both been overweight and inactive. So we both know from experience that once you've gotten used to daily physical activity, it will become one of the high points of your day.

Here are a few facts to help you stay motivated for physical activity until the pleasure of doing it takes over.

When you go for a walk at just 3 miles per hour, you burn

about three times the calories that you burn sitting still. If you walk briskly at 4 miles per hour, you burn almost five times the calories burned when you sit still.

The average person can count on burning a total of around 100 calories for every fifteen minutes of brisk activity, that is, while doing things that are equivalent to walking at 4 miles per hour. A good game of singles tennis, played at a strong intermediate level, is about equivalent. Racquetball and squash are even more vigorous. Doubles tennis, on the other hand, may be good for your social life, but, unless played very vigorously, doesn't burn nearly as many calories as continuous walking.

Perhaps the reason that jogging is so effective in weight management (and remember, we DO NOT recommend jogging for overweight persons; get down to desirable weight first) is that even at a 6-mile-per-hour pace, which is quite gentle once you get into it, you burn from nine to ten times the calories of sitting still. Jogging at that pace will burn 100 calories, or more, every ten minutes. It adds up to a total of 600 to 800 calories an hour. And, for many people, this level of activity, at this intensity, does leave a residual metabolic elevation that burns up 50 to 100 more calories than normal, as the body recovers from activity over the next several hours.*

A time for activity always goes down first on my daily calendar, and on Terri's. It means more to us than just improving our physical condition and increasing our flexibility. As the years go by and I have grown busier and busier, the time I take for a jog or a walk has become more and more important. It's the most creative and refreshing part of my day. Although we encourage people to get active together when they first start and to form "buddy systems" to support and motivate each other, physical activity may well become a time for you to be

*In the examples we have just given, we are referring to total calories burned in activity. This *includes* the amount it would have taken if you had just sat still. Earlier, when we spoke of the need to exercise for at least 45 minutes a day, we spoke of 200 calories being burned in that period of time *in addition* to the sitting requirements. For simplicity's sake, and in view of the great metabolic variability, we are rounding figures to the nearest 100 in these last examples.

alone, to relax, and to completely separate yourself from the rest of the day's activities.

So, we hope you will use and enjoy our recipes for good healthy cooking AND for physical activity. It's the only way you can have your cake and eat it, too!

Index